TRAVELING
THROUGH
EGYPT

TRAVELING
THROUGH
EGYPT

From 450 B.C. to the Twentieth Century

Edited by

DEBORAH MANLEY

and SAHAR ABDEL-HAKIM

With illustrations by W.H. BARTLETT

The American University in Cairo Press

Cairo   New York

The illustrations and their captions are taken from W.H.Bartlett, *The Nile Boat or Glimpses of the Land of Egypt*. London: Arthur Hall, 1849

The editors and publisher are grateful to the followng for permission to use material in this book: Allen and Unwin and HarperCollins for exerpts from *'Abd al-Latif: The Eastern Key*, translated by Kamal Hauth Zand and John A. and Ivy E. Videan; Aris and Phillips Ltd. and Reverend John Wilkinson for excerpts from *Egeria's Travels*; the author and Watkins/Loomis Agency Inc. for excerpts from *A View of the Nile* by Elizabeth Warnock Fernea; Garnet Publishing Ltd. for exerpts from *The Best Divisions of Knowledge of the Regions* by al-Muqaddasi, translated by Basil Anthony Collins with the Centre for Muslim Contributions to Civilization; Libri Publications Ltd. for excerpts from *Nefertiti Lived Here* by Mary Chubb; Methuen Publishing Ltd. for excerpts from H.V. Morton's *Through Lands of the Bible*; Penguin Books for exerpts from *Herodotus: The Histories*, translated by Aubrey de Selincourt, and Penguin Books and Granta for exerpts from *In an Antique Land* by Amitav Ghosh; Pentland Press for excerpts from *Exiles of Empire*, edited by Mona Macmillan and Catriona Miller; Random Century Ltd. for excerpts from *The Travels of Ibn Jubayr*, translated by R.J.C. Broadhurst and published by Jonathan Cape; State University of New York Press for excerpts from Naser-e Khosraw's *Book of Travels*, translated for the Persian Heritage Foundation. Every reasonable effort has been made to contact copyright holders. We apologize and thank any authors or copyright holders who we have not been able to properly acknowledge. If a work in copyright has been inadvertently included, the copyright holder should contact the publisher.

Dar el Kutub No. 3253/3
ISBN 977 424 801 5

Designed by AUC Press Design Center
Printed in Egypt

Contents

Introduction

The long history of travel in Egypt is far from monolithic. As motives for travel, individual preferences, cultural backgrounds, and the cultural and political scenes in the country change, so the points of interest and perceptions in the resultant writing change. In this book, travelers from different countries, different times, and different cultural backgrounds are brought together through an experience they all shared—the experience of having journeyed in Egypt and written their impressions of the land, the people, the culture, and the history. The encounters tell as much of the place visited as of the travelers' personal inclinations, interests, and time. These varied voices give a comprehensive account of the history and geography of Egypt, its archaeology, and social life as perceived by non-Egyptians.

The written map of Egypt presented by this book is also a historic 'road map,' charted over the centuries by both foreign travelers and Egyptians. Over the centuries, new roads were constructed and trodden—and old ones abandoned—in a way that largely reflects the interests of the travelers and their motives for travel. Alterations in roads and itineraries often came about because of changes in means of transport and en route stops: some cities disappeared, while others, meeting the ever-changing needs of the local population and travelers, were established. The construction of the Mahmudiya Canal in the nineteenth century not only allowed the irrigation of new land and easier transport of people and goods but also created a different route between Alexandria and Cairo. It allowed travelers to sail across the Delta and report about the new towns and villages that were developing on the banks of the canal. The once 'beaten track' from the Nile Valley across the Eastern Desert to the Red Sea ports of Aizab and Qolzum, which launched Muslim pilgrims toward Mecca and other destinations, was abandoned as means of transport altered over time. What remains of this route and of those transit cities are only the travelers' narratives of them. The construction of the Suez Canal also created a new itinerary for those who formerly took the overland route to India. New stations and destinations brought places into being in a way that made both travelers and residents charters of the country. This history of adaptation and continuity is what informs this book. By bringing together a patchwork of travelers' voices and testimonies that tell of the palimpsest that is Egypt, this book reflects today's Egypt just as it probes into its history. It reveals not only what is present but also how it came into being and how it was perceived and encountered. It speaks of both what has been and what is.

Egypt has had a generous share of travelers. In 450 B.C. Herodotus wrote about the country, giving a traveler's account that narrates not only what was there but also what he considered worth looking at and recording. A few centuries later, Strabo followed in his footsteps. By the turn of the tenth century A.D, Arab geographers such as Ebn Haukal and al-Muqaddasi were traveling the country recording their own observations. In medieval times, a concert of Muslim travelers, mainly pilgrims heading for Mecca, stopped in Egypt. In the eleventh and twelfth centuries, the Persian Naser-e Khosraw and the Valencian Ibn Jubayr, two pilgrims who arrived in Egypt from the east and the west respectively, kept journals in which they recorded their impressions of the prosperous Fatimid state. Scientists such as 'Abd al-Latif al-Baghdadi visited Egypt in pursuit of learning in the thirteenth century, while in the fourteenth century, Ibn Battuta, one of the world's best-known medieval travelers, was driven largely by curiosity. At the same time, western merchants and pilgrims heading for Jerusalem, such as Friar Felix of Germany, stopped in Egypt and recorded their impressions.

The eighteenth century brought explorers and merchants such as the Dane Frederick Norden and the Englishman W.G. Browne, and officials serving in the East India Company, such as James Capper or their wives, like Eliza Fay, all of whom left vivid accounts of their experiences in Egypt. Yet it was Napoleon's Expedition (1798) that brought French scholars, such as Vivant Denon, to study Egypt and lead Egypt to the full attention of Europe. It also caused a shift of interest from the biblical and historical associations of the country to its pharaonic monuments. Nevertheless, the attention of the scholars who visited and resided in Egypt in the nineteenth century was by no means confined to archaeology. Along with Egyptologists like J.G. Wilkinson of Britain and Richard Lepsius of Germany,

visitors like Edward W. Lane were interested in modern Egyptians and their way
of life. Adventurers and explorers like Frederick Henniker and Richard Burton
continued to travel throughout the country. The rise of Muhammad 'Ali to power
and his projects for the modernization of Egypt were other factors attracting
European travelers. Giovanni Belzoni was one of the important antiquities collectors in Egypt in the early 1800s. Although his wife Sarah traveled with him and
wrote an account of her trip, it was not until the 1840s, with the introduction of
steam navigation and the construction of the overland route, that female travelers
truly started to flock to Egypt—Harriet Martineau was one such tourist. The year
1869 witnessed the opening of the Suez Canal and the beginning of Thomas
Cook's organized tours, making travel in Egypt more a pleasure than an adventure.

Travel in Egypt continued to flourish in the twentieth century, attracting
more scholars and tourists from all over the world. In recent years the Indian
writer Amitav Ghosh wrote of his experience in Egypt and what the encounter
meant to him. Moving between the country's history and its present, he reveals
the continuity and change of Egyptian cultural life, while Elizabeth Fernea narrates her experience as an expatriate housewife in Cairo. Published within the
span of a decade, these three accounts of Egypt further reveal the different perceptions that personal interests and inclinations can produce: the different ways in
which a place can be experienced.

The different cultures, places, and histories that the travelers recorded continue
to coexist with the modern country. One need only cross the Nile to step from
the plateau of the pyramids to Coptic Cairo, and a few strides takes one from the
European-style city center to Islamic Cairo. The deserts and their oases maintain
their character just as they tell of the changes brought about by the diverse ways
they were inhabited, traveled through, and perceived across the centuries. Readers
of this anthology tour Egypt in a way that no travel agent can offer: not only do
they see its present and learn of its history, but they also meet previous travelers.
Time overlaps in this account, bringing different moments together and hence
forming a new narrative of Egypt. In this book Herodotus rubs shoulders with
Ebn Haukal, and Rudyard Kipling speaks to al-Muqaddasi, narrating their experiences and impressions. The chapters are organized according to place, the way
current travelers may experience the country. Following in the footsteps of most
travelers' accounts presented in the book, readers disembark in Alexandria where
Herodotus, Ibn Jubayr, and Edward Lane first set foot, then make the tour up the
Nile and into the deserts. Deborah Manley and Sahar Abdel-Hakim, an
Englishwoman and an Egyptian woman, were brought together through their
shared interest in travelers to Egypt. They first met in 1997 with the establishment
of ASTENE (the Association for the Study of Travel in Egypt and the Near East),
a UK-based association of which they are both founding members. Both had
worked on travel literature about Egypt prior to that, but through ASTENE their
shared interest found a new form of expression. Manley, herself a traveler in Egypt
and an authority on British travelers to that country, became engaged in this area
through her extensive readings of travel accounts of Egypt. Abdel-Hakim started

off as an academic whose interest in travel writing about Egypt stems from a desire to learn about representations of her country in various cultures. Though each came from a different direction, their shared interest in travel accounts of Egypt, of how it felt to be there and to experience Egyptian culture, and how it was that the country seems to change its face in the different narratives, brought them together in a way that probably could not have been anticipated a few decades ago. This book offers one of the shapes in which their work together took expression and reveals their diverse interests and perceptions. It is a book that brings together experiences of Egypt and its always welcome visitors.

1
Egypt
An Overview

Egypt, as Herodotus tells us, is the gift of the Nile, and the Nile once dominated the country even more than it does today, as these first writers show. The rising of the Nile was as significant as the changing of the seasons in other parts of the world—in fact, it created its own seasons for Egypt as its waters provided for both the land and its people. This chapter concludes with a brief look at some of the people of Egypt and their dress and Rudyard Kipling's view of the travelers and foreigners drawn to the country.

The Geography of Egypt, C. 450 B.C.
Herodotus

What they said of their country seemed to me very reasonable. For anyone who sees Egypt, without having heard a word about it before, must perceive, if he has only common powers of observation, that the Egypt to which the Greeks go in their ships is an acquired country—the gift of the river. . . .

The following is a general description of the physical features of Egypt. If you take a cast of the lead a day's sail off-shore, you will get eleven fathoms, muddy bottom—which shows how far out the silt from the river extends. The length of

the Egyptian coastline (defining Egypt, as we usually do, from the gulf of Plinthine
to Lake Serbonis which lies along the base of Mount Casius) is sixty *schoeni*—the
schoenus being an Egyptian measure equivalent to sixty *stades*. The people there
who own very little land measure it by fathoms; those not so poor, by *stades*, or
furlongs; those with much land in *parasangs*; and those with vast estates in *schoeni*.
The *parasang* is equal to thirty *stades*, the *schoenus*, as I have said, to sixty. Thus the
coastline of Egypt is 3600 *stades* in length—(about 420 miles).[1]

From the coast inland as far as Heliopolis—just about the same distance as
along the road from the altar of the Twelve Gods in Athens to the temple of
Olympian Zeus at Pisa—the country is broad and flat, with much swamp and
mud. In point of fact these two distances—from Heliopolis to the sea, and from
Athens to Pisa—are not exactly the same, but very nearly; careful reckoning
would show that they differ by only fifteen *stades*.

Southward of Heliopolis the country narrows. It is confined on the one side
by the range of the Arabian mountains which run north and south and then continue without a break in the direction of the Arabian Gulf. In these mountains are
the quarries where the stone was cut for the pyramids of Memphis. This is the
point where the range changes its direction and bends away towards the Arabian
Gulf. I learnt that its greatest length from east to west is two months' journey, and
that towards the eastern limit frankincense is produced.

On the Libyan side of Egypt there is another range of hills where the pyramids stand; these hills are rocky and covered with sand, and run in a southerly
direction like the Arabian range before it bends eastward. Above Heliopolis, then,
for a distance of four day's journey up the river, Egypt is narrow, and the extent
of the territory, for an important country, is meagre enough. Between the two
mountain ranges—the Libyan and the Arabian—it is a level plain, in its narrowest
part, as far as I could judge, not more than about two hundred furlongs across
South of this the country broadens again.

From Heliopolis to Thebes is nine days' voyage up the Nile, a distance of 81
schoeni or 4860 *stades* (552 miles). Putting together the various measurements I
have given, one finds that the Egyptian coastline is, as I have said, about 420 miles
in length, and on the distance from the sea inland to Thebes about 714 miles. It
is another 210 miles from Thebes to Elephantine.

The Boundaries of the Country, c. 960
Ebn Haukal

One of the boundaries of Egypt begins from the Sea of Roum, between Iskanderiah
and Barkah, at the desert behind Wahh; proceeding to the land of the Nubians, and
to the land of Bajeh, and back from Asouon to the Sea of Roum; and from Bajeh to
the Sea of Kolzum [the Red Sea], till it comes to the Tour Sina [Mount Sinai] . . . .

---

1. A *stade* is about seven miles. A *furlong* is about an eigth of a mile. The *schoenus* is about
50 miles. The parasang is thirty *stades* or about 10 miles.

There are great quantities of dates, and many corn fields, along the banks of the Nile, from that [town of Kirouan] to near Asouon, and to the borders of Iskanderiah. When the weather becomes very warm, the water increases; and when it sinks, they sow their grain; after that, there is no necessity for water. In the land of Egypt there falls not either rain nor snow; nor in the whole country is there any running stream besides the river Nile.

The Rising of the Water, 25 B.C.
Strabo
. . . but at the rising of the Nile the whole country is under water and becomes a lake, except the settlements; and these are situated on natural hills or on artificial mounds, and contain cities of considerable size and villages, which, when viewed from afar, resemble islands. The water stays more than forty days in summer and then goes down gradually just as it rose; and in sixty days the plain is completely bared and begins to dry out; and the sooner the drying takes place, the sooner the ploughing and the sowing; and the drying takes place soonest in those parts where the heat is greater. The parts above the Delta are also watered in the same way, except that the river flows in a straight course about four thousand stadia through only one channel, except where some island intervenes, of which the most note-worthy is that which comprises the Heracleiotic Nome, or except where the river is diverted to a greater extent than usual by a canal into a large lake or a territory which it can water, as, for instance, in the case of the canal which waters the Arsinoite Nome and Lake Moeris and of those which spread over Lake Mareotis. In short, Egypt consists of only the river-land, I mean the last stretch of river-land on either side of the Nile, which beginning at the boundaries of Ethiopia and extending to the vertex of the Delta, scarcely anywhere occupies a continuous habitable space as broad as three hundred stadia. Accordingly, when it is dried, it resembles lengthwise, the greater diversions of the river being excepted. This shape of the river-land of which I am speaking, as also of the country, is caused by the mountains on either side, which extend from the region of Syene [Aswan] down to the Egyptian Sea; for in proportion as these mountains lie near together or at a distance from one another, in that proportion the river is contracted or widened, and gives to the lands that are habitable their different shapes. But the country beyond the mountains is for a great distance uninhabited.

How the Nile Changes the Country, c. 1050
Naser-e Khosraw
When the sun enters Cancer, the Nile begins its increase and gradually rises day by day to twenty cubits above its winter level. In the city of old Cairo measuring devices have been constructed, and there is an agent who receives a salary of one thousand dinars to watch and see how much the level rises. From the day it begins to increase, criers are sent through the city to proclaim how many 'fingers' God

has increased the Nile that day. When it has risen one ell, the good news is heralded and public rejoicing proclaimed until it reaches eighteen cubits, the normal increase. Less than this is considered a deficiency, and alms are distributed, holy intentions vowed, and general sorrow ensues. More is a cause for celebration and rejoicing. Unless the level goes above eighteen cubits, the sultan's land tax is not levied on the peasantry.

Water channels with smaller channels branching off have been dug from the Nile in all directions, and the villages of the countryside are situated along them. There are so many waterwheels that it would be difficult to count them. All country villages in Egypt are built on high places because when the Nile floods the whole land is inundated. . . . People normally travel from village to village by boat, and from one end of the realm to the other they have constructed earthen dikes, along the top of which you can walk beside the river. That structure is repaired yearly by an expert, at a cost of ten thousand dinars from the sultan's treasury. The people of the countryside make all necessary preparations for the four months their land is beneath the water, and everyone bakes and dries enough bread to last these four months without spoiling.

The water usually rises for forty days until it has risen eighteen cubits. Then it remains at that level for another forty days, neither increasing nor decreasing. Thereupon it gradually decreases for another forty days until it reaches the winter level. When the water begins to recede, the people follow it down, planting as the land is left dry. All their agriculture, winter and summer, follows this pattern. They need no other source of water.

Two Seasons, 1767
Charles Thompson

It has been justly observed indeed, by the Ancients as well as the Moderns, that nothing can be a finer Sight than *Egypt* at two Seasons of the Year; for if a Man ascend some Mountain in the Month of *August* or *September,* he beholds a wide Sea, in which appear almost innumerable Towns and Villages, intermixe'd with Groves and Fruit-trees, whose Tops are only visible, and here and there a Causeway for Communication between one Place and another; which all together form a Prospect as agreeable as it is uncommon. On the other hand, in the Spring Months . . . the whole Country is like one continued Meadow, whose Verdure, enamell'd with Flowers, charms the Spectator, who likewise sees Flocks and Herds dispersed over all the Plains, and the Peasants busied in their rural Employments. In a word, Nature, which is then dead as it were in other Climates, seems here to be in Bloom and Gaiety.

The Climate of Egypt, 1882
Samuel Cox

Its climate is balm itself. It is dry. The mud thus survives all its changes. In winter its mildness is a salutary luxury. These features of the climate result from the position of Egypt. It is in the north-east corner of Africa; yet it is not African in its ordinary meaning. It is a small corner of Africa physically; but neither are its people nor its position African. Egypt is the Nile. The Nile made it the cradle of human thought and progress, and the Nile plays for it even yet an important part in civilization. The Nile has created its limits and gifted it with opulence. The Delta, whose apex is near old Memphis and modern Cairo, is the creature of the river. The northern side of the Delta country made by the river is 160 miles along the Mediterranean. From its southern boundary on Nubia, where the templed isles of Philae and Elephantine divide the waters of the foaming river, you have a sweeping stream 550 miles in length; but the fruitfulness it engenders is straitened within a valley, seldom more than seven to ten miles wide. Mountains or hills of sandstone or rock, shut in this strip from the invading sands of the desert.

The Delights of Nile Water, 1826
John Carne
Fatigued with heat and thirst we came to a few cottages in a palm-wood, and stopped to drink of a fountain of delicious water. In this northern climate no idea can be formed of the exquisite luxury of drinking in Egypt: little appetite for food is felt, but when, after crossing the burning sands, you reach the rich line of woods on the brink of the Nile, and pluck the fresh limes, and, mixing their juice with Egyptian sugar and the soft river-water, drink repeated bowls of lemonade, you feel that every other pleasure of the sense must yield to this. One then perceives the beauty and force of those similes in Scriptures, where the sweetest emotions of the heart are compared to the assuaging of thirst in a sultry land.

Nile Water, 1825
Dr. R.R. Madden
In its wholesome properties I believe the water of the Nile exceeds that of any other river in the world. Even when turbid, as at its rise, and depositing a sediment in a tumbler, in thickness of an eighth of an inch at least, and alive with animal-culae, visible to the naked eye, even then it loses none of its salubrious qualities, but, on the contrary, by its gentle action as an aperient, it benefits health.

Notes along the Nile, 1910
Pierre Loti
A monotonous chant on three notes, which must date from the first Pharaohs, may still be heard in our days on the banks of the Nile, from the Delta as far as Nubia. At different places along the river, half-nude men, with torsos of bronze and voices all alike, intone it in the morning when they commence their endless labours and continue it throughout the day, until the evening brings repose.

The shadoof

Whoever has journeyed in a dahabiya up the old river will remember this song of the water-drawers, with its accompaniment, in slow cadence, of creakings of wet wood.

It is the song of the 'shadûf', and the 'shadûf' is a primitive rigging which has remained unchanged since times beyond all reckoning. It is composed of a long antenna, . . . which is supported in a seesaw fashion, on an upright beam, and carries at its extremity a wooden bucket. A man, with movements of singular beauty, works it while he sings, lowers the antenna, draws the water from the river, and raises the filled bucket, which another man catches in its ascent and empties into a basin made out of the mud of the river bank. When the river is low there are three such basins, placed one above the other, as if they were stages by which the precious water mounts to the fields of corn and lucerne. And then three shadûfs, one above the other, creak together, lowering and raising their great scarabaeus' horns to the rhythm of the same song.

All along the banks of the Nile this movement of the antennae of the shadûfs is to be seen. It had its beginning in the earliest ages and is still the characteristic manifestation of human life along the river banks. It ceases only in the summer, when the river, swollen by the rains of equatorial Africa, overflows this land of Egypt, which it itself has made in the middle of the Saharan sands. But, in the winter, which is here a time of luminous drought and changeless blue skies, it is in full swing. Then every day, from dawn until the evening prayer, the men are busy at their water-drawing, transformed for the time into tireless machines, with muscles that work like metal bands. The action never changes, any more than the song, and often their thoughts must wander from their automatic toil, and lose themselves in some dream, akin to that of their ancestors who were yoked to the same rigging four or five thousand years ago. Their torsos, deluged at each rising of the overflowing bucket, stream constantly with cold water; and sometimes the wind is icy, even while the sun burns; but these perpetual workers are, as we have said, of bronze, and their bodies take no harm.

Characteristics of the Soil, c. 1200
'Abd al-Latif al-Baghdadi

There is another characteristic: the soil of Egypt is sandy, which by itself is not good for cultivation, but the waters of the Nile lay out with them, at the time of the rising of the river, a black mud or silt, adhesive and very greasy, containing plenty of fertiliser, called ibriz ("pure gold"). This comes from the Sudan: mixed with the Nile during flood, the mud precipitates and settles. When the water drains away, the earth is ploughed and cultivated, and every layer there comes to it a new layer of mud. This is why there all the earth is cultivable, nothing is left fallow without cultivation as they do in Iraq and Syria, but they plant different crops in rotation each year.

Papyrus, the Paper of Egypt, 1908
Elbert Farman

We started for San at early dawn the next morning with donkeys procured in a neighboring village. It was a ride of only two hours. The country was low and marshy and, at the time of the high Nile, flooded. These marshy lands are mostly unfit for cultivation, but produce tall grasses which are of some value since they constitute the only perennial pasturage in Egypt.

The papyrus, once produced in this section in great abundance, has now entirely disappeared. Like its contemporaries, the crocodile and hippopotamus, it has withdrawn from Egypt to the banks of the Blue and White Nile.

The manufacture of papyrus was for a long period of great importance to Egypt. Commencing early in the reign of the Pharaohs, it continued till the time of the Khalifs. During the Greek and Roman period, Egypt supplied this invaluable article to the whole civilized world and derived from it immense revenues. The rich, wet lands of the Delta, which were once covered with this plant, as with a thicket, are now largely devoted to the culture of rice, indigo and cotton. As a remembrance, we have derived from papyrus our word 'paper' and from the Greek form, biblos, our word 'Bible.'

Papyrus served for many other purposes than that of making the paper on which the ancients wrote. It was used for calking their vessels and for sails and rope. . . . The lower part of the papyrus plant was also used for food.

The Commerce of the Country, c. 1000
al-Muqaddasi
Egypt is a country of commerce; it is an important source of very fine leather, resistant to water, sturdy, and pliant; leather of sheep and asses' skins, leggings and cloth of three-ply yarns of camels' hair and goats' wool—all these are from the metropolis. From Upper Egypt come rice, wool, dates, vinegar, raisins. From Tinnis . . . cloth variegated in colour; from Dimyat, sugar cane. From al-Fayyum, rice, and a linen of inferior quality; from Busir, shrimp, and cotton of superior quality. From al-Farma, fish, and from the towns around it, large baskets, and ropes made of fibre of the finest quality. Here are produced white cloth of the greatest fineness, wraps, canvas, the mats of 'Abbadani style of very fine quality, grains, grass peas, oils of rape, and of jasmine, and of other plants beside these.

Their specialities include reedpens incomparable! and their vitriol, marble, vinegar, wool, canvas, cloth, linen, leathers, shoes, leggings, geese, plantains, wax, sugar candy, fine linen, dyes, apparel, spun yarn, waterskins, *harisa,* the sweet pastry called *nayda,* chick peas, lupin, cloves, arum, mats, asses, cattle, girdles. . . .

The Food of the Country, c. 1200
'Abd al-Latif al-Baghdadi
. . . In Egypt they extract oil from the seeds of the radish, the turnip, and the lettuce and use it for cooking. They also make soap from these oils; the soap made in Egypt is soft, red, yellow and green. It is this soap that the sweetmeat *sapouniyyeh* appears to have some resemblance, and from that it takes its name.

As for the stews of the Egyptians, those which are sour or ordinary have nothing in particular, or very little, different from those used elsewhere; but, on the contrary their sweet stews are of a singular kind, for they cook a chicken with all sorts of sweet substances. Here is how they prepare this food: they boil a fowl, then put it in a julep, place under it crushed hazelnuts or pistachio nuts, poppy seeds or purslane seeds, or rose hips, and cook the whole until coagulated. Then they add spices and remove it from the fire. . . .

As for the sweetmeats, these are indeed various and would need a special book to describe them. There are some kinds which are employed as curatives for certain ailments, and which are given to persons on a diet, the sick, and to convalescent persons, when they want something sweet to eat. Of this number are the *khabis* of pumpkin, *khabis* of carrot, the sweet called *wardiyyeh* in which the rose enters, that called *zindjebiliyyeh* which is made with ginger, the pastilles of aloes wood and of lemon, of musk, and many others.

Travelers in Egypt often wrote of the costume of the people—
for the Europeans, so very different to their own. The Arabic
scholar, Edward Lane, sought to understand the purpose of the
dress of the better-off males, Dr. Meryon described the simple

clothes of the poorer women, while Elizabeth Cooper was fascinated by the lives of women of means.

Dress of the Male, 1844
Edward Lane
The dress of the men of the middle and higher classes consists of the following articles. First, a pair of full drawers of linen or cotton, tied round the body by running a string or band, the ends of which are embroidered with coloured silks, though concealed by the outer dress. The drawers descend a little below the knees, or to the ankles; but many of the Arabs will not wear long drawers, because prohibited by the Prophet. Next is worn a shirt, with very full sleeves, reaching to the wrist; it is made of linen, of a loose, open texture, or of cotton stuff or of muslin, or silk, or of a mixture of silk and cotton, in stripes but all white. Over this, in winter, or in cool weather, most persons wear a *sudeyree,* which is a short vest of cloth, or of striped coloured silk and cotton, without sleeves. Over the shirt and the *sudeyree* or the former alone, is worn a long vest of striped silk and cotton (called *kaftan*), descending to the ankles, with long sleeves extending a few inches beyond the fingers' ends, but divided from a point a little above the wrist, or about the middle of the fore-arm; so that the hand is generally exposed, though it may be concealed by the sleeve when necessary; for it is customary to cover the hands in the presence of a person of high rank. Round this vest is wound the girdle, which is a coloured shawl, or a long piece of white figured muslin. The ordinary outer robe is a long cloth coat, of any colour, called . . . by the Egyptians *gibbeh,* the sleeves of which reach not quite to the wrist. Some persons also wear a *beneesh;* which is a robe of cloth, with long sleeves, like those of the kaftan, but more ample, it is properly a robe of ceremony. . . . In winter also many persons wrap a muslin or other shawl (such as they use for a turban) about the head and shoulders. The head-dress consists, first, of a small, close-fitting, cotton cap, which is often changed; next, a *tarboosh,* which is a red cloth cap, also fitting close to the head, with a tassel of dark-blue silk at the crown; lastly a long piece of white muslin, generally figured, or a Kashmeer shawl, which is wound round the tarboosh. Thus is formed the turban. . . . Stockings are not in use; but some few persons, in cold weather, wear woollen or cotton socks. The shoes are of thick red morocco, pointed and turned up at the toes. Some persons also wear inner shoes of soft yellow morocco, and with soles of the same: the outer shoes are taken off on stepping upon a carpet or mat; but not the inner; for this reason, the former are often worn turned down at the heel.

Dress of the Poorer Women, 1812
Dr. Charles Meryon
The poorer sort of women in Egypt were dressed in a blue shift something like a smock frock, the sleeves being very large. These shifts have at the sides two slits in the place of pocket-holes, so long that it is not unfrequently happened in bending themselves forward that their naked skin was seen. Over their faces was a slip of

black cotton or silk (according to the means of the wearer) tied round the head by a fillet or tape. From the centre of this, in a perpendicular line, pieces of silver or gold, or sometimes pearls, were hung. Over the head passed a long blue or black veil, one end of which had its two corners stitched together for about three inches, and, the corner so stitched being put under the chin, the face came out through an oval opening in it. The sleeves of the shift, which tapered down to a point, were often, when the women were employed, tied by the points behind the back. The arms, thus left bare to the shoulders, showed sometimes as much symmetry of form as would enchant a statuary or a painter.

The World of Women of Means, 1914
Elizabeth Cooper

It is hard to say, outside the little social life among relatives and a few friends, what are the amusements of the Egyptian lady. She sings, she generally plays some musical instrument—now it is the piano for the educated girl, and in nearly every house of means is found the Victrola [gramophone], with songs in Arabic and English, French and Italian. In Cairo she has much more opportunity of being gay, as she can go to the theatre, the opera, and even on little shopping tours to the big European shops or to the tiny bazaars in the native quarter. In the smaller cities and villages she is restricted to the fetes and festivities of her social sphere.

There are many magazines and papers, novels and books of every kind printed in Arabic, for the women who are not advanced enough to read those in French or English, and now, when education for the woman has become such a fetish in Egypt, these popular educators are found in every home. If the mother cannot read them—and few of the women of the older day can read—the daughter and the grand-daughters can read to them the news of the world, and there are few women who have not at least a superficial knowledge of what is passing outside their walls.

Reflecting the mood and style of their times, the Arab traveler and scholar al-Muqaddasi and the British writer Rudyard Kipling summed up Egypt for their contemporaries. Kipling intended to amuse his readers; a thousand years earlier, and a half-millennium after Herodotus, al-Muqaddasi gave a serious interpretation. It is al-Muqaddasi who truly stands the test of time.

Trying to Explain Some History, 1913
Rudyard Kipling

Here is a country which is not a country but a longish strip of market garden, nominally in the charge of a government which is not a government but the disconnected satrapy of a half-dead empire, controlled pecksniffingly by a Power which is not a Power but an Agency, which Agency has been tied up for years, custom and blackmail into all sorts of intimate relations with six or seven European Powers, all with rights and perquisites, none of whose subjects seem directly amenable to any Power which at first, second or third hand is supposed to be responsible. That is the barest outline. To fill in the details (if any living man knows them) would be as easy as to explain baseball to an Englishman or the Eton Wall game to a citizen of the United States. But it is a fascinating play. There are Frenchmen in it, whose logical mind it offends, and they revenge themselves by printing the finance reports and the catalogue of the Bulak Museum in French. There are Germans in it, whose demands must be carefully weighed—not that they can by any means be satisfied, but they serve to block other people's. There are Russians in it, who do not very much matter at present but will be heard from later. There are Italians and Greeks in it (both rather pleased with themselves just now), full of the higher finance and the finer emotions. There are Egyptian Pashas in it who come back from Paris at intervals and ask plaintively to whom they are supposed to belong. There is His Highness, the Khedive, in it, and *he* must be considered not a little, and there are women in it, up to their eyes. And there are great English cotton and sugar interests, and angry English importers clamouring to know why they cannot do business on rational lines or get into the Sudan, which they hold is ripe for development if the administration would only see reason.

Among these conflicting interests and amusements sits and perspires the English official, whose job is irrigating or draining or reclaiming land on behalf of a trifle of ten million people, and he finds himself tripped up by skeins of intrigue and bafflement which may ramify through half a dozen harems and four consulates. All this makes for suavity, toleration, and the blessed habit of not being surprised at anything whatsoever.

The Beneficence of Egypt, c. 1000
al-Muqaddasi

This is the region in ruling which Pharaoh gloried over all mankind *(Qur'an, sura 43, v. 51)*, and supplied at the hands of Joseph sufficient to feed the inhabitants of the world. There are to be found the vestiges of the Prophets, the Wilderness, and Mount Sinai; the monuments of Joseph, the scenes of the miracles of Moses. Thither fled Mary with Jesus. God has mentioned this region repeatedly in the *Qur'an*, and has shown its pre-eminence to mankind. It is one of the two wings of the world, and the excellences of which it can boast are countless. Its metropolis is the dome of Islam, its river the most splendid of rivers. Through its natural prosperity is Hijaz populated, and by its populace the season of Pilgrimage is enlivened. Its beneficence spreads to the East and to the West, for God placed it between the two seas, and has extolled its reputation in the areas of the sunrise and of the place of sunset. Let me tell you that Syria, with all its greatness, is just a rural district of it, and Hijaz, with its inhabitants, depends on it. It is said to be "the height of land" (al-Rabwa) *(Qur'an, sura 23, v. 50),* and its river flows with honey in Paradise. It has become again the abode of the Commander of the Faithful, and Baghdad has been superseded until the day of Judgment; its metropolis has now become the greatest glory of the Muslims. Even so, it has had drought for seven consecutive years, grapes and figs there are dear

2
Arriving in Egypt
At Alexandria and Elsewhere

 Arriving in Egypt, whether coming from the sea to the dry land or from the desert to the kindly land of the Nile, is an experience to be savored. The Nile came out to meet the traveler from the Mediterranean, as the French statesman Chateaubriand noted. To some other travelers, Alexandria was their first meeting with the 'East.' Whether arriving from East or West, Alexandria, with its ancient buildings, its history, and its kaleidoscope of peoples, fascinated all who came.

As the Nile Flows into the Mediterranean, 1806
F.R. Chateaubriand
On 20th October, at five in the morning, I perceived, upon the green and ruffled service of the sea, a line of froth, beyond which the water was pale and placid. The captain came up, and tapping me on the shoulder, said, in the Frank language, *"Nilo!"* It was not long before we entered the celebrated river, whose water I tasted and found salt. Some palm trees and a minaret indicated the site of Roetta, but the land itself was still invisible. This coast resembles the savannahs of Florida: its appearance is totally different from that of the shores of Greece or Syria, and strongly reminds you of the effect of a tropical horizon.

17

At ten o'clock we at length discovered, below the tops of the palm trees, a line of sand running westward to the promontory of Aboukir, which we should have to pass in our way to Alexandria. We were then exactly facing the mouth of the Nile at Rosetta, and were going across the Bogaz. The water of the river in this place is red, inclining to violet, of the colour of a moor in autumn. The Nile, whose inundation was over, had been for some time falling.

It was eleven o'clock at night . . . when we came to anchor in the commercial harbour, in the midst of vessels lying before the city.

Alexandria, c. 960
Ebn Haukal
Eskanderia, Alexandria, is a considerable town, built on the sea-side: the houses, the other edifices, are of marble. And out in the sea there is a *minareh* [lighthouse], or watch-tower, of hard stone, and very lofty. It contains about three hundred houses. No one without a guide can arrive there.

The Day of Our Landing, 1183
Ibn Jubayr
The first day of the month was a Sunday and the day after our arrival in Alexandria. The day of our landing, one of the first things we saw was the coming on board of the agents of the Sultan to record all that had been brought in the ship. All the Muslims in it were brought forward one by one, and their names and descriptions, together with the names of their countries, recorded. Each was questioned as to what merchandise and money he had, that he might pay *zakat,* without any enquiry as to what portion of it had been in their possession for a complete year and what had not. Most of them were on their way to discharge a religious duty and had nothing but the bare provisions for the journey. But they were compelled to pay the *zakat* without being questioned as to what had been possessed by them for the complete year and what had not . . .

Before the building of the Suez Canal, Europeans bound for India either sailed round the tip of southern Africa or took the overland route through Egypt, as the Pratt family did in 1843. Fanny Pratt wrote to her three sons left in England of her experiences in Egypt.

Passing through Egypt, 1843
Fanny Pratt
My darling children,
Since our landing in Alexandria our journeys have been so rapid and fatiguing that

it was out of my powers to write, but now we are safely on board this vessel and have been refreshed with rest and sleep I hasten to give you an account of our adventures. My last letter was closed as we approached the Egyptian coast. It is unlike any country I have seen; it is very brown and flat. Pompey's Pillar stands in solitary splendour and can be seen immediately on entering the harbour, also Mohammed Ali's Palace, manufactories, dockyard and a number of windmills, twelve in one group. The Pasha has a monopoly of the mills. We found difficulty in obtaining rooms as there are but two hotels, but Papa succeeded in doing so. It was the rainy season but we got on shore ere it commenced, passed under the bows of so many fine ships, which have quite the appearance of English vessels.

On entering the hotel we hired a carriage and drove to see Mohammed Ali's Palace. It was a very large building and splendidly fitted up after the French fashion and full of painting and gilding. The floors are beautiful: each room laid in different patterning in mosaic of cedar, satin, rosewood and others. The walls are covered with damask of warm colours, curtains the same, and each room has a couch from end to end. There is a billiard room, and one small boudoir fitted up for cold weather with an English grate—it is called the Fire Room. In spite of having rain to Pompey's Pillar and Cleopatra's Needle they are splendid monuments of antiquity and in excellent preservation—one of the Needles is still lying prostrate [this is the one that now stands on the Thames Embankment in London], and I fear will be covered with the rubbish that abounds on all sides. Alexandria appears but a city of ruins, with the exception of the portions the Pasha has rebuilt.

We dined at the Table d'Hote with 150 persons I should think and at daybreak next day, started off for the Mahmoudieh Canal. . . . There were three commodious boats provided and a steam tug to tow us. We passed the day very pleasantly though there was little country.

Some travelers came to Egypt across the desert—from the south, the west, or, like Friar Felix, from the Holy Land and the east.

Coming from the Desert, 1483
Friar Felix Fabri

Without warning the hoped-for moment arrived. From the edge of a plateau we looked down to where, over against us, far below, lay a country of a different kind . . . from our barren and enormous waste. For we looked down upon a part of Egypt, a kindly land. . . . And seeing it we were seized with both joy and amazement: with joy because we saw the end of the dreadful wilderness, men's dwellings, plentiful water, and many other things we had lacked in the desert. Yet amazement too, because we looked at a strange land. For we saw a great gathering of waters, as if it had been the sea, and high above those waters grew groves of tall palms, and other fruitful trees, and towers and other lofty buildings rose from the waters, towns and villages stood wonderfully in the midst of the waters . . . . For it was the time of the rising of the Nile, which river, leaving his bed, enriches and irrigates the whole of Egypt.

> Western travelers arriving in Alexandria were often seeing for the first time a place truly 'foreign' to them with buildings and people totally unfamiliar, and even with unfamiliar sounds and language. William C. Prime was one such—and his first night was disturbed by all this 'strangeness.'

Sleepless in Alexandria, 1857
William C. Prime

. . . I did not sleep on shore the first night in Egypt. . . . Dogs abound in the city of the son of Philip. They have no special owners, and are a sort of public property, always respected. But such infernal dog-fights as occurred once an hour under our windows no one elsewhere has known or heard of. I counted fifteen dogs in one melée the first evening, each fighting, like an Irishman in a fair, on his own account.

Besides this, the watchmen of the city are a nuisance. There are a large number of them, and some twenty are stationed in and around the grand square. Every quarter of an hour, the chief of a division enters the square and shouts his call, which is a prolonged cry, to the utmost extent of his breath. As he commences, each watchman springs into the square; and by the time he has exhausted his breath they take up the same shout in a body, and reply. He repeats it, and they again reply; and all is then still for fifteen minutes. But as if this was not enough, there was a tall gaunt fellow, who had once been a dragoman, but was a poor and drunken dog now, and, in fact, crazy from bad habits, who slept somewhere in the square every night, and who invariably echoed the watchman with a yell that rang down the square, in unmistakable English, "All right"; and once I heard him add, in the same tremendous tone, "Damn the rascals!"

And just before dawn, when the law of Mohammed prescribed it, at that moment that a man could distinguish between a white thread and a black, there was a sound that now came to my ears with a sweetness that I can not find words to express. In a moment of the utmost stillness, when all the earth, and air, and sky was calm and peaceful, a voice fell through the solemn night, clear, rich, prolonged, but in a tone of rare melody that thrilled through my ears, and I needed no one to tell me that it was the muezzin's call to prayer. "There is no God but God!" said the voice, in the words of the Book of the Law given on the mountain of fire, and our hearts answered the call to pray.

Almost as soon as they arrived, travelers set out to see the country, where so much was ancient or unfamiliar. Two traveling Arab scholars gave loving descriptions of Alexandria in their day—when that wonder of the ancient world, the Pharos lighthouse, still stood.

A Guide to Alexandria, c. 1000
al-Muqaddasi

Al-Iskandariyya (Alexandria) is a delightful town on the shore of the Romaean Sea. Commanded by an impregnable fortress, it is a distinguished city, with a goodly meed of upright and devout people. The drinking water of the inhabitants is derived from the Nile, which reaches them in the season of its flood via an aqueduct, and fills their cisterns. It resembles Syria in climate and customs; rainfall is abundant; and every conceivable type of product is brought together there. The countryside round about is splendid, producing excellent fruits and fine grapes. It is a clean town, and their buildings are of the kind of stone suited for maritime construction; it is also a source of marble. It has two mosques. On their cisterns are doors which are secured at night so that thieves may not make their way up through them. The remaining towns here are very well developed; and in the surrounding area grow locust, olives, and almonds, and their cultivated lands are watered by the rain. It is near here that the Nile debouches into the Romaean Sea. It is the city founded by Dhu al-Qarnayn (Alexander the Great), and has indeed a remarkable citadel. . . .

The lighthouse in Alexandria has its foundations firmly anchored in a small peninsula, and may be approached by a narrow road. It is firmly set in the rock, and the water rises on the lighthouse on the west side. The same is true of the fortress of the city, except that the lighthouse is on a peninsula on which there are three hundred buildings, to some of which a mounted horseman may go; he may go to all of them using a password. The lighthouse is elevated above all the towns along the shore, and it is said that there used to be a mirror there in which could be seen every ship taking off from the shores of the entire sea. A custodian attends to it every day and night, and as soon as a ship comes into his range of sight, he notifies the commander, who dispatches the birds that go to the shore, that those there may be in a state of readiness.

Some Features and Antiquities of Alexandria, 1183
Ibn Jubayr

First there is the fine situation of the city, and the speciousness of its buildings. We have never seen a town with broader streets, or higher structures, or one more ancient and beautiful. Its markets also are magnificent. A remarkable thing about the construction of the city is that the buildings below the ground are like those above it and even finer and stronger, because the waters of the

Nile wind underground beneath the houses and alleyways. The wells are connected, and flow into each other. We observed many marble columns and slabs of height, amplitude and splendour such as cannot be imagined. You will find in some of the avenues columns that climb up to and choke the skies, and whose purpose and the reason for whose erection none can tell. It was related to us that in ancient times they supported a building reserved for philosophers and the chief men of the day. God knows best, but they seem to be for the purpose of astronomical observations.

One of the greatest wonders that we saw in this city was the lighthouse which Great and Glorious God had erected by the hands of those who were forced by such labour as 'a sign to those who take warning from examining the fate of others' [Koran XV, 75] and as a guide to voyagers, for without it they could not find the true course to Alexandria. It can be seen from more than seventy miles, and is of great antiquity. It is most strongly built in all directions and competes with the skies in height. Description of it falls short, the eyes fail to comprehend it, and words are inadequate, so vast is the spectacle.

We measured one of its four sides and found it to be more than fifty arms' lengths. It is said that in height it is more than one hundred and fifty qamahs [one qamah = a man's height]. Its interior is an awe-inspiring sight in its amplitude, with stairways and entrances and numerous apartments, so that he who penetrates and wanders through its passages may be lost. In short, words fail to give a conception of it. May God not let it cease to be an affirmation of Islam and preserve it. At its summit is a mosque having the qualities of blessedness, for men are blessed by praying therein. . . . We went up to this blessed mosque and prayed in it. We saw such marvels of construction as cannot faithfully be described.

Amongst the glories of this city, and owing in truth to the Sultan, are the colleges and hostels erected there for students and pious men from other lands. There each may find lodging where he might retreat, and a tutor to teach him the branch of learning he desires, and an allowance to cover all his needs. The care of the Sultan for these strangers from afar extends to the assigning of baths in which they may cleanse themselves when they need, to the setting up of a hospital for the treatment of those of them who are sick, and to the appointment of doctors to attend them. At their disposal are servants charged with ministering to them in the manner prescribed both as regards treatment and sustenance. Persons have also been appointed who may visit those of the strangers who are too modest to come to hospital, and who can thus describe their condition to the doctors, who would then be answerable for their care.

Travelers of earlier generations who had acquired a classical education were far more at ease with the background to many of the sites they visited than many tourists are today. Eliza Fay, though not an educated woman, on her way through Egypt to India, is a good example of someone with such classical knowledge. Dr. Meryon, Lady Hester Stanhope's doctor, and others saw Alexandria with a more modern eye.

A Tourist's History, 1779
Eliza Fay
24th July, 1779. Having mounted our asses, the use of horses being forbidden to any but Musselmans, we sallied forth preceded by a Janissary, with his drawn sword, about three miles over a sandy desert, to see Pompey's Pillar, esteemed to be the finest column in the World. This pillar which is exceedingly lofty, but I have no means of ascertaining its exact height, is composed of three blocks of Granite: (the pedestal shaft and capital, each containing one). When we consider the immense weight of the granite, the raising such masses, appear beyond the power of man. Although quite unadorned, the proportions are so exquisite, that it must strike every beholder with a kind of awe, which softens into melancholy, when one reflects that the renowned Hero whose name it bears, was treacherously murdered on this very Coast, by the boatmen who were conveying him to Alexandria; while his wretched wife stood on the vessel he had just left, watching his departure, as we may naturally suppose, with inexpressible anxiety. What must have been her agonies at this dreadful event!

We saw also the *outside* of St Athanasius's Church, who was Bishop of this Diocese, but it being now a Mosque were forbidden to enter, unless on condition of turning Mahometans, or losing our lives, neither of which alternative exactly suited my ideas, so I deemed it prudent to repress my curiosity.

Muhammad 'Ali's Alexandria, 1813
Dr. Charles Meryon
Alexandria is a large maritime port, and the vast number of vessels in the harbour gave sure evidence of its commerce. At the time to which this narrative refers, the sale of corn by the Egyptian government to the English brought in an immense profit to the pasha of Egypt, who monopolized that branch of commerce entirely; as he had done, by degrees, every branch that was lucrative. Thus the rice mills, formerly held by industrious individuals, whose separate interest excited a competition in the trade, were . . . all taken into the hand of the pasha. . . .

To house the grain that is brought to Alexandria, the pasha, in 1815, constructed on the strand of the western harbour a vast magazine, the dimensions of which made it an object of curiosity. It is a single room, one hundred and twenty paces long by fifteen broad, and the roof is supported by one hundred and twenty shafts. . . .

As the pasha holds Alexandria to be the key of his dominions, he has fortified its ramparts, which his courtiers may tell him are impregnable. In 1813, he demolished the old Saracen walls, which took in the circuit of what is called the old city. . . .

Alexandrian Sightseeing, 1849
Samuel Bevan
In the evening (Furner) insisted on my taking another lesson on donkey-riding, so selecting two of the best looking from the 'stand' close to our office door, we cantered through the square towards Cleopatra's Needle, which forms a prominent object on the sea-shore, just outside the town. . . .

From the Needles we made a long round to Pompey's Pillar and the Baths of Cleopatra. There is a good view from the base of the former over the Mahmoudieh Canal, which fertilizes in its course a narrow strip of country, and studded as it is mostly with numerous sails, forms a curious feature in the landscape. The pillar stands out in solitary grandeur from a vast plain of ruins and tombs, the site of ancient Alexandria. Hard by is a little building bearing some resemblance to a temple; this is a refuge for hard-pressed debtors, a strong-hold against all pursuit, and so long as they remain under its friendly shelter, neither law nor remorseless creditor has power to lay hands upon them. Our road to what are said to be the Baths of Cleopatra, lay through a bustling and most dirty street of low dwellings, to a kind of quay or shipping place for corn, near to which is a group of quaint looking wind-mills with six or eight sails each, the whole in full motion, spinning round with a rushing noise that sorely alarmed our poor donkeys, although it served to prove to us that there was at least no lack of corn in Egypt. A dusty gallop of another mile then brought us to the shore, where we tethered our beasts, and proceeded to examine the spot where it alleged the "Queen of Beauty" used to perform her ablutions. The Baths consist of three or four rocky caves open to the sea, where sheltered from the scorching rays of the sun, the water acquires an enticing temperature, and ripples in and out at a depth of several feet. Close by the Baths, in a sandy cliff, are some excavations of prodigious size, which an old Arab informed us were Catacombs, but as they contain no bones or relics of mortality, and do not even boast a stray skull or two, he found us somewhat sceptical; the old man conducted us through the outermost apartments, having no candles, and the evening closing in, we could see but little of their dimensions, so pitching him a few paras we hastened homewards.

The crowded streets and bazaars of Alexandria, with their blend of people of all nations and ways of life, astonished the newcomer.

Alexandrian Street, 1833
Robert Curzon
We took possession of all the rooms upstairs, of which the principal one was long and narrow, with two windows at the end, opening onto a covered balcony or verandah: this overlooked the principal street and the bazaar. Here my companion

and I soon stationed ourselves, and watched the novel and curious scene below; and strange indeed to the eye of a European, when for the first time he enters an Oriental city, is all he sees around him. The picturesque dresses, the buildings, the palm trees, the camels, the people of various nations, with their long beards, their arms, and turbans, all unite to form a picture which is indelibly fixed in the memory. Things which have since become perfectly familiar to us were then utterly incomprehensible, and we had no one to explain them to us, for the one waiter of the poor inn, who was darting about in his shirt sleeves in the manner of all waiters, never extended his answers to our questions beyond 'Si, Signore', so we got but little information from him; however, we did not make use of our eyes the less for that.

Among the first thing we noticed was the number of half-naked men who were running about, each with something like a dead pig under his arm, shouting out 'Mother! mother!' (*Moyah!* water) with a doleful voice. These were the *sakis* or water-carriers, with their goat-skins of the precious element, a bright brass cupful of which they sell for a small coin to the thirsty passengers. An old man with a fan in his hand made of a palm branch, who was crumpled up in the corner of a sort of booth among a heap of dried figs, raisins and dates, just opposite our window, was an object of much speculation to us how he got in, and how he would ever manage to get out of the niche into which he was so closely wedged. He was the merchant, as the Arabian Nights would call him, or the shop-keeper as we should say, who sat there cross-legged among his wares waiting patiently for a customer, and keeping off the flies in the meanwhile, as in due time we discovered that all merchants did in all countries of the East.

Soon there came slowly by a long procession of men on horseback with golden bridles and velvet trappings, and women muffled up in black silk wrappers; how they could bear them, hot as it was, astonished us. These ladies sat upon a pile of cushions placed so high above the backs of the donkeys on which they rode that their feet rested on the animals' shoulders. Each donkey was led by one man, while another walked by its side with his hand upon the crupper. With the ladies were two little boys covered with diamonds, mounted on huge fat horses, and ensconced in high-backed Mameluke saddles made of silver gilt. These boys we afterwards found out were being conducted in state to a house of their relations, where the rite of circumcision was to be performed.

Our attention was next called to something like a four-post bed, with pink gauze curtains, which advanced with dignified slowness preceded by a band of musicians, who raised a dire and fearful discord by the aid of various windy engines. This was a canopy, the four poles of which were supported by men, who held it over the heads of a bride and her two bridesmaids or friends, who walked on each side of her. The bride was not veiled in the usual way, as her friends were, but was muffled up in Cachmere shawls from head to foot. Something there was on the top of her head which gleamed like gold or jewels, but the rest of her person was so effectually wrapped up and concealed that no one could tell whether she was pretty or ugly, fat or thin, old or young; and although we gave her credit for all the charms which should adorn a bride, we rejoiced when the villainous band of music which accompanied her turned round a corner and went out of hearing. . . . The prodigious multitude of donkeys formed another strange feature in the scene.

A street in Cairo

There were a hundred of them, carrying all sorts of things in panniers; and some of the smallest were ridden by men so tall that they were obliged to hold up their legs that their feet might not touch the ground. Donkeys, in short, are the carts of Egypt and the hackney-coaches of Alexandria.

> Once arrived, Western travelers had to decide whether to continue to wear their European clothes—which made them stand out—or adopt the local dress, which was naturally more suited to the climate and way of life, and had other advantages too . . .

What to Wear? 1819
John Fuller
The stock of clothes which I had brought with me from Europe being nearly exhausted, I assumed today the Oriental dress, which I continued to wear all the time I remained in the Levant. I do not, however, in general recommend its adoption, except in those places where the prejudices of the people render it necessary: for although the superior dignity and grace which it gives to the figure may flatter the personal vanity of the wearer, its cumbrousness will constantly check his activity, and multiply the temptations to indolence which in a hot country are always sufficiently abundant.

There is one circumstance, however, which may recommend it to *some* travellers: the change of appearance effected by the resumption of the Frank [foreign] costume is so complete, that it will enable them, on their return to Europe, safely to avoid noticing those persons with whom in the East they may have been connected by the ties of familiarity or obligation, but whom it may not be agreeable to recognise in more polite countries.

> Travelers moved up river from Alexandria to observe the rest of Egypt—though often returning once more to embark from Alexandria for home..

On Our Way, 1840
Sarah Haight
When about to set out from our hotel in Alexandria, we had our first initiative in the mode of transporting travelling effects in the East. We sent to engage a platoon of porters to carry our immense *materiel* to the canal; but instead of the troop of noisy Arabs who seized upon it when we first landed at the custom-house quay, and brought up each heavy load one mile for ten *paras*, two huge camels came stalking into the courtyard. Now I had seen at Smyrna the compact bales of

merchandise nicely balanced one on each side of the camel, but it puzzled my ingenuity to conceive how they could dispose, on the round backs of these two animals, such a medley of discordant articles as our travelling equipage is composed of. Round, square or triangular, short or long, straight or crooked, slippery or rough, was the separate quality of each individual article. On a May-morning in Gotham, no little skill is displayed by our ingenious cartmen in stacking up the indefinite sundries of a moving household; but I am much deceived if, set to load a *camel* with such incongruous traps, they would not be completely 'non-plussed'. First, then, the docile animal was made to kneel down. The manner in which this movement is effected is singular, and very painful to behold at first. The beast, at a signal given . . . first utters a groan in anticipation at its expected burden; then stooping, it puts one fore knee upon the ground, then the other; after which, gathering its hind legs under the body, it comes down to the ground with an awkward and apparently painful jerk.

Then commences the operation of loading up. There is a sort of wooden pack-saddle, with projecting sticks on the top whereby to attach ropes. Then a large rope-net (made of the coarse fibres of the palm-tree wood) is spread over this saddle, and several feet on the ground on each side of the animal. Then on the net commences a foundation of boxes, trunks, and other heavy articles, on which is raised a superstructure of hampers, kegs, barrels, *batterie de cuisine,* arms, saddles, and other gear too tedious to mention. The sides of the net are then gathered up and made fast to the pack-saddle horns. The beast is then assisted to rise, not by a kindly shoulder, but by the brawny arm of an Arab wielding the bamboo, who repays with interest the many rough blows which he himself has received from other quarters. When the animal is on his feet again, then comes the surplus cargo of light articles, in the shape of beds thrown across the top of the load, jugs and jars hung round the sides, the whole flanked by innumerable baskets, pails, lanterns, etc, etc.

Thus loaded, two camels carried all our effects. But it is only for short distances that such heavy loads can be carried by the camel. For a regular, long caravan journey, it would have required a dozen of these ships of the desert to transport conveniently and safely the same articles, with fuel and water for a few days.

3
The Nile Delta

 The Nile Delta is one of the fascinating
places in Egypt. In it, travelers encountered history and a way of life that had
remained the same for its inhabitants for
many centuries, despite the continuous
changes in its geology. This chapter presents
different travelers' testimonies about the diverse villages
they visited in the Delta, some of which still stand today,
while others have disappeared. Like the continuous and
alternating flows of sweet and salty water at this point
where the Nile meets the sea, life in the Delta seems to
have been lived as consecutive waves. Al-Muqaddasi and
Naser-e Khosraw take a step back in history and describe
the prosperous city of Tinnis as it once stood. The histories
and geography of Rosetta and Damietta are narrated by
such diverse witnesses as John Fuller and al-Muqaddasi.
Charles Meryon gives a European's account of what nineteenth century travelers encountered there, while Edward
Lane writes of the boats and boatmen and Elbert Farman
actually goes on board, sailing across Lake Manzala.
Meanwhile, A.C. Smith speculates on bird life and
Herodotus complains of insects.

The Delta, c. 960

Ebn Haukal

The sea which borders Egypt is bitter, but where the river Nile pours into it, and overcomes it, the waters of the sea are rendered sweet. Farther out, when the waters of the Nile are confounded with the sea, the bitterness again predominates. In the sea there are islands, to which one may pass over in boats or vessels. Of these islands are Teneis (or Teines) and Damiat. In each of these agriculture is practised and cattle are kept . . . . The waters of this sea are not very considerable, and vessels move on it by help of men. It produces a certain fish, which is called *delfin* (dolphin), and this is a fish which if any person eat, he will be troubled with horrible dreams.

Through the Towns and Villages, 1183

Ibn Jubayr

We left Alexandria by the grace and help of God Most High on the morning of Sunday the 8th of Dhu 'l-Hijjah, the 3rd of April. Our first stage was to a place called Damanhur, a walled town in a large plane which extends from Alexandria to Misr. This plain is wholly cultivated, and is covered by the Nile in flood. Right and left are innumerable villages. The next day, Monday, we crossed the Nile at a place called Sa in a ferry boat, and came to a place called Birmah. It is a large village, with a market and all conveniences. Early on the morning of Tuesday, which was the Festival of the sacrifice of the year 578, we shared in the prayers in a place called Tandatah, a large and populous village, where we observed a vast concourse being addressed by the preacher in an eloquent and comprehensive discourse. Our way then took us to a place named Subk, where we passed the night. That day we had passed a pleasant place called Malij. All along the road were continuous cultivations and orderly villages. Early on Wednesday morning we removed, and came to the best village we had yet passed through. It is called Qalyub, and is six miles from Cairo, with fine bazaars and a large congregational mosque, superbly built. After that came Munyah, also a fine place, and from there we moved to Cairo, the Sultan's magnificent and extensive city.

Visiting a Village, 1812

Dr. Charles Meryon

During the season of the ebb of the river, the banks are so high that nothing whatever can be seen from the boat; it is necessary, therefore, to land to get a view of the country. When landed, the eye roves over an endless plain, the sameness of which is broken by groves of date-trees, and in the midst of them, on low eminences, generally stand villages and towns. The spectator feels a kind of loneliness, and is forced to recall to his mind the productiveness of the land—to balance the useful with the agreeable—before he can bring himself to admit that Egypt in reality equals its renown. When, however, he walks inland a few furlongs, when he beholds the richness of vegetation, the variety of grain, the indescribable fatness of the soil—the whole together, if he reflects, must forcibly strike him as an example of fertility, well worthy of all the praises that poets and historians have bestowed upon it. The miserable villages of the peasants were an assemblage of hovels, made of mud, or of mud bricks baked in the sun. As they are fearful of Bedouins, or of robbers of other kinds, the village is generally shut in a mud wall, more often rudely rectangular than otherwise, of a height sufficient to prevent a man getting over. To this there is one gate. On entering, a street somewhat wide generally leads from it, and here will be found the villagers squatting on their haunches, eyeing with suspicious looks every stranger that enters, lest he should be some government officer, some soldier, or one of those from whom they are accustomed to experience harm or loss. If the stranger, led by the curiosity natural to the European, should endeavour to penetrate farther into this village, he finds himself, at every instant, opposed by a blind alley, or he winds through a lane which, perhaps, brings him out just where he entered: and, in some villages, we found mazes more intricate than the Cretan labyrinth is reported to have been. Then the alarm of the women running to hide themselves, and of the children scampering after them, the jealousy of the husbands, and sometimes the barking of dogs, make it altogether difficult for a European to do more than seat himself in some open space, and limit his curiosity to the sight of what comes before him.

Ramadan in Lataifa, 1992
Amitav Ghosh

From the very first days of the lunar month the normal routines of the village had undergone a complete change: it was as though a segment of time had been picked from the calendar and turned inside out. Early in the morning, a good while before sunrise, a few young men would go from house to house waking everyone for the suhur, the early morning meal. After that, as the day progressed, a changed lassitude would descend upon Lataifa. To ease the rigours of the fast, people would try to finish all their most pressing bits of work early in the morning, while the sun was still low in the sky; it was impossible to do anything strenuous on an empty stomach and parched throat once the full heat of the day had set in. . . . In every house as the sun sank slowly towards the horizon, the women would lay out their trays and serve the food they had cooked during the day. Their families would gather around, ravenous now, with cool, tall glasses of water resting in front of them. They would sit watching the lengthening shadows, tense and still, listening to their radios, waiting for the sheikhs of the mosque of al-Azhar in Cairo to announce the legal moment of sunset. It was not enough to see the sun going down with one's eyes; the breaking of the fast was the beginning of a meal of communion that embarked millions of people and the moment had to be celebrated publicly and in unison.

When the meal was finished and the trays had been cleared away, the men would wash and change and make their way to the mosque, talking, laughing, replete with a sense of well-being which the day's denials had made multiply sweet. I would go to my room alone and listen to the call of the muezzin and try to think of how it must feel to know that on that very day, as the sun travelled around the earth, millions and millions of people in every corner of the globe had turned to face the same point, and said exactly the same words of prayer, with exactly the same prostrations as oneself. A phenomenon on that scale was beyond my imagining.

Evidence of the Past, 1908
Elbert Farman
The sites of the ancient cities of the Delta are marked by mounds of earth which rise above the surrounding country, sometimes to the height of thirty to forty feet, and which are filled with potsherds of the successive generations that have inhabited these places.

Two Sides of Rosetta, 1819
John Fuller
Passing through some low sand-hills interspersed with palm trees, we soon afterwards arrived at Rosetta. This town makes no show on the land side, but on entering it we found that it was much larger and better built than Alexandria. It has, however, a very gloomy appearance; the houses, which in general are four storeys high, being constructed with very small dark-coloured bricks, bedded in thick layers of white mortar, and having a great number of small windows closed with wooden lattices. We passed through the bazaar, which is dark and narrow, to the house of Mr. Lenzi, the English vice-consul, who received us with much cordiality as his extravagant fears of the plague would allow, and procured us a lodging at an inn kept by an Italian, where we would have been comfortable enough, had we not been for the first time greeted by one of the modern plagues of Egypt in the shape of mosquitoes, which swarm upon the banks of the Nile, and are of a more venomous quality there than in any other place I visited. The moment you embark on the river, however, they disappear.

Nothing can be more striking than the difference in the character of the scenery on the land side and on the river side of Rosetta. On the one there is nothing to be seen but heaps of sand and a few straggling palm trees. On the other, the Nile rolls his slow and majestic course through fields and gardens overgrown with luxuriant vegetation, and through groves of palms, orange trees, limes, and bananas. Its stream is divided just below the town by an island covered with lofty sycamores and acacias, among which were now deposited some Egyptian statues, which might have been supposed the tutelary deities of the spot.

Rosetta was at this time a place of great consideration, being the emporium from which all the grain brought from the Delta and from Upper Egypt was shipped for Alexandria. The opening of the canal however, at Rahmanie, must since have much diminished its importance. Its population was estimated as from twenty to thirty thousand. The quay is very fine, extending nearly a mile along the western side of the river. The Pasha's granaries are built upon it, and we saw a great number of 'Fellahs' or peasants employed in carrying the corn to and from the boats. Some of them were fine strong men, but they were almost naked and very miserable in their appearance, their pay being, as we understood, at the rate of five parahs (or about the eighth part of sixpence) per day, a very low scale of wages, notwithstanding the extreme cheapness of food in Egypt. The work however appeared to be done with great alacrity, owing perhaps to the vigilant super-intendence of the Albanian taskmasters, who stood with long sticks in their hands, which they applied without ceremony to every loitering 'operative'.

The gardens round Rosetta are large and productive. The season for dates was nearly passed, but some clusters still remained hanging on the trees, packed up in baskets made of leaves to protect them from the birds.

Damietta, c. 1000
al-Muqaddasi
Dimyat (Damietta): you may travel in this lake for a day and a night, sometimes meeting with fresh water, and narrow straits, until reaching another town, which is better [than Tinnis], more spacious, wider, more open, more frequented; with more fruits, better construction, more water, artisans more skilful, clothes finer, more finished workmanship, better baths, stronger walls, and fewer vexations. Over it stands a fortress built of stone. it has many gates, and a large number of well-garrisoned outposts. A festival is held here every year to which the members of the garrisons come from all around. The Roman Sea is within shouting dis-tance of it, and the houses of the Copts are on the shore. It is here that the Nile flows into the sea.

Damietta, 1908
Elbert Farman
Damietta, once a prosperous town and one of the principal seaports of Egypt, is now in its decay.

Sand-bars have been formed at the mouth of the river to such an extent that only vessels of light draught can enter and its commerce has been principally trans-ferred to Alexandria and Port Said. The numerous minarets and imposing domes of its mosques and the high building along the bank of the river still give to the city an appearance of much importance. The architecture of its crumbling buildings attests its former prosperity and wealth. It still has a population of about forty thousand and is visited annually by several hundred small vessels, many of which come from Greece and Syria. It has interesting and well-stocked bazaars in that part of Egypt and the fish of the neighbouring lake.

Ancient Boats, c. 450 B.C.
Herodotus

The Nile boats used for carrying freight are built of acacia wood—the acacia resembles in form the lotus of Cyrene, and exudes gum. They cut short planks, about three feet long, from this tree, and the method of construction is to lay them together like bricks and through-fasten them with long spikes set close together, and then, when the hull is complete, to lay the deck beams across on top. The boats have no ribs and are caulked from inside with papyrus. They are given a single steering-oar, which is driven down through the keel; the masts are of acacia wood, the sails of papyrus. These vessels cannot sail up the river without a good leading wind, but have to be towed from the banks; and dropping downstream with the current they are handled as follows: each vessel is equipped with a mast made of tamarisk wood, with a rush mat fastened on top of it, and a stone with a hole through it weighing some four hundredweight; the raft and the stone are made fast to the vessel with ropes, fore and aft respectively, so that the raft is carried rapidly forward by the current and pulls the 'baris' (as these boats are called) after it, while the stone, dragging along the bottom astern, acts as a check and gives her steerage-way. There are a great many of these vessels on the Nile, some of them of enormous carrying capacity.

Boats and Boatmen on the Nile, 1844
Edward Lane

The navigation of the Nile employs a great number of the natives of Egypt. The boatmen of the Nile are mostly strong, muscular men. They undergo severe labour in rowing, poling, and towing; but are very cheerful; and often the most so when they are most occupied; for then they frequently amuse themselves by singing. In consequence of the continual changes which take place in the bed of the Nile, the most experienced pilot is liable frequently to run his vessel aground: on such an occurrence, it is often necessary for the crew to descend into the water, to shove off the boat with their backs and shoulders. On account of their being so liable to run aground, the boats of the Nile are generally made to draw rather more water at the head than at the stern; and hence the rudder is necessarily very wide. The better kind of boats used on the Nile, which are very numerous, are of a simple but elegant form; mostly between thirty and forty feet in length; with two masts, two large triangular sails, and a cabin, next the stern, generally about four feet high (but of late made higher to suit the requirements of European travellers), and occupying about a fourth or third of the length of the boat. In most of these boats the cabin is divided into two or more apartments. Sudden whirlwinds and squalls being very frequent on the Nile, a boatman is usually employed to hold the main-sheet in his hand, that he may be able to let it fly at a moment's notice. The traveller should be especially careful with respect to this precaution, however light the wind.

The Sailing Boats of the Nile, 1819
John Fuller
Three different kinds of boats navigate the Nile. The largest are called Germs, and are used exclusively for the conveyance of corn and merchandise. The Cangia is used for passengers only, and almost every person of consideration possesses one of his own. The Mahash is an intermediate rate, capable of carrying a considerable cargo, but fitted up with a large cabin for the accommodation of passengers also. A vessel of this class being on the point of sailing for Cairo, we engaged our passage on board. The cabin was sufficiently large for my companion and myself, and a temporary awning erected on the deck for Nasr-Allah and the servants.

Lake Manzala, 1908
Elbert Farman
It was a beautiful morning with the cloudless sky of an Egyptian summer. The deep crimson that heralded the sun, the yellow light that accompanied it and the clear soft atmosphere, free from the dust of the land, made this early morning sail most enjoyable. It was the more so because there were no waves, although the wind was sufficiently strong to have made an ugly sea, had the water been sufficiently deep to permit an undercurrent.
The lake is very irregular in form, but is approximately forty miles in length and twenty broad and covers an area of eight hundred to a thousand square miles. It is so shallow throughout its whole extent that it is said that one could wade from one side to the other were it not for the miry bottom . . . . The bottom of the lake is covered with a thick matting of coarse grass, which in many places grows to the height of a number of feet. . . .
As we glided quietly but swiftly over the grassy waters, fish were darting from under the bow of the boat, showing that they were very abundant. We passed between Matariyeh (situated upon a point of land projecting from the west many miles into the lake) and a group of islands opposite, on the east. . . . Matariyeh is a town of fishermen. It is all fish and fishing. There is no other business. The occupation of the father has been transmitted to the son from the earliest historic periods. These people, with others about the lake, form a race of fishermen.

Tinnis, a City, c. 1000
al-Muqaddasi
Tinnis, situated between the Roman Sea and the Nile, is a small island in a lake, the whole of which has been built as a city—and what a city! It is Baghdad in

Departure from Old Cairo

miniature! A mountain of gold! The emporium of the Orient and of the West! Markets are elegant, fish cheap. It is the goal of travellers, prosperity is evident, the shore delightful, the mosque exquisite, the palaces lofty. It is a town with resources, and well-populated yet as it is situated on a narrow island, the water encircles it like a ring.

Water and Money, c. 1050

Naser-e Khosraw

When the water of the Nile rises, it pushes the salt water of the sea away from Tennis so that the water is fresh for ten parasangs. For that time of the year, reinforced, underground cisterns called *masna'as* have been constructed on the island. When the Nile water forces the salty seawater back, they fill these cisterns by opening a watercourse from the sea into them, and the city exists for a whole year on this supply. When anyone has an excess of water, he will sell to others, and there are also endowed *masna'as* from which water is given out to foreigners.

The population of this city is fifty thousand, and there are at any given time at least a thousand ships at anchor belonging both to private merchants and to the sultan; since nothing is there, everything that is consumed must be brought in from the outside. All external transactions with the island are made therefore by ship, and there is a fully armed garrison stationed there as a precaution against attack by Franks and Byzantines. I heard from reliable sources that one thousand dinars a day go from there into the sultan's treasury. Everyday the people of the city turn that amount over to the tax collector, and he in turn remits it to the treasury before it shows a deficit. Nothing is taken from anyone by force. The full price is paid for all linen and *buqalamun* woven for the sultan, so that the people work willingly—not as in some other countries, where the artisans are forced to labour for the vizier and sultan! They weave covers for camel litters and striped saddle-cloths for the aristocrats: in return, they import fruits and foodstuffs from the Egyptian countryside.

Bird Life in the Delta, 1868
Reverend A.C. Smith

I shall always regard that railway journey [to Cairo] as the greatest ornithological treat I ever had in my life. I was not altogether a perfect novice in observing the birds of other countries, yet I was quite amazed at the profusion of birds which presented themselves before my astonished eyes on that memorable occasion. I had been told by more than one friend of Egyptian experience, when in England, that with the exception of hoopoes, pigeons and clouds of water fowl to be seen on the sandbanks, but never approached, I should find no variety to reward my exertions; and though I knew . . . that such was by no means the case, but only the opinion of careless travellers, who generally have one eye closed to the objects of nature around them, yet I certainly was not prepared for the abundance as well as the great variety which this first days' journey brought before my eyes.

Immediately after leaving Alexandria, as we skirted the shores of Lake Mareotis, water fowl of many species literally swarmed: *grallatores,* as well as *natatores,* in incredible numbers, well waited on by *raptores.* I shall allude to all these birds again on an after page of this volume; suffice it to say here that vultures of three species, hawks, kestrels, buzzards and harriers were to be seen far and near during our entire passage through the Delta. Here there were dogs on one side, vultures on another, tearing at the carcase of a dead camel, while hooded crows were always at hand to take their share. There were herons and spoonbills in abundance, and flocks of the russet-backed heron fearlessly attending the ploughman, just as rooks are wont to do; though the Egyptian teams were certainly as strange to our eyes as were the birds which followed them, to wit a pair of camels, or a pair of cows, or a camel yoked with a cow, or even a tall gaunt camel with a diminutive donkey, an oddly matched pair indeed. There were sandpipers and little ringed plovers running on the shallows, flocks of geese and ducks roused from the adjoining marshes by the noise of the advancing train, and for the first twenty miles or so, gulls and terns of various sorts.

Night Monsters, c. 450 B.C.
Herodotus

The country is infested by swarms of gnats, and the people have invented various methods of dealing with them; south of the marshes they sleep at night on raised structures, which is of great benefit to them because the gnats are prevented by the wind from flying high; in the marsh-country itself they do not have these towers, but everyone instead, provides himself with a net, which during the day he uses for fishing, and at night fixes up round his bed, and creeps in under it before he goes to sleep. For anyone to sleep wrapped in a cloak or in linen would be useless, for the gnats would bite through them; but they do not even attempt to get through the net.

"The Field of Victory," 1908
Elbert Farman

It was nearly sunset when I arrived at Mansurah, wearied by the heat and dust and by constantly viewing the panorama of the day. The station was on the opposite side of the river from the city. The only way of crossing was by a small boat, although as early as the thirteenth century, at the time of the Crusades, there was a fortified bridge at this place.

Mansurah, though a city of thirty thousand inhabitants, then had no hotel. It is on the right bank of the Damietta branch of the Nile and sixty miles from its mouth. It is a town of medieval origin, historically noted for being the scene of one of the important battles of St. Louis (Louis IX) of France. It was here that this real hero of the middle ages gained at great sacrifice of life, in 1250, an important victory over the Saracens. The Crusaders were soon after defeated at the same place and St. Louis taken prisoner. It is this Saracen victory that is said to have given the place the name of Mansurah, 'the victorious' or, as it has sometimes been rendered, 'field of victory'.

The End of the Mahmudiya Canal, 1836
John Lloyd Stephens

The appearance of the river at the mouth of the canal is worthy of its historic fame. I found it more than a mile wide, the current at that season full and strong; the banks on each side clothed with a beautiful verdure and groves of palm trees (the most striking feature in African scenery), and the village of Fouah, the stopping place for boats coming up from Rosetta and Damietta, with its mosques and minarets, and whitened domes, and groves of palms forming a picturesque object in the view.

Upon entering the Nile we changed our boat, the new one being one of the largest and best on the river, of the class called canjiah, about seventy feet long, with two enormous lateen sails; these are triangular in form, and attached to two very tall spars more than a hundred feet long, heavy at the end, and tapering to a point; the spars or masts rest upon two short masts, playing upon them as pivots. The spar rests at an angle of about thirty degrees, and, carrying the sail to its tapering point, gives the boat when under way, a peculiarly light and graceful appearance. In the stern a small place is housed over, which makes a very tolerable cabin, except that the ceiling is too low to admit of standing upright, being made to suit the cross-legged habits of the Eastern people. She was manned by ten Arabs, good stout fellows, and a rais or captain.

> Robert Curzon traveled on the Mahmudiya Canal through dull sandy flats interspersed with large pools to Atfeh, where it joined the Nile.

The Father of Rivers, 1833
Robert Curzon
. . . we were glad to arrive the next day on the shores of the Father of Rivers, whose swollen stream, although at Atfeh not more than half a mile in width, rolled by towards the north in eddies and whirlpools of smooth muddy water, in colour closely resembling a sea of mutton-broth.

In my enthusiasm on arriving on the margin of this venerable river I knelt down to drink some of it, and was disappointed in finding it by no means good as I had always been told it was. On complaining of its muddy taste I found that no one drank the water of the Nile till it had stood a day or two in a large earthen jar, the inside of which was rubbed with a paste of bitter almonds. This causes all impurities to be precipitated, and the water thus treated becomes the lightest, clearest, and most excellent in the world.

Women along the Banks of the Nile, 1819
John Fuller
The groups of women going to fetch water form a striking feature in the scenery of the Nile.

Thirty or forty of them are frequently seen walking in single file, and at regular distances to and from the river, each with a jar on her head and another on the palm of her hand. From the necessity of preserving their balance in this mode of carrying burdens, to which they are from their childhood habituated, these Egyptian peasants acquire a firmness and grace of step which we scarcely see excelled in the saloons of polished cities. Their erect attitude, simple drapery, and slim figures increased in apparent height by the pitchers on their heads, give them at a distance a very classical appearance, but if you approach the Naiads, you find them pale, dingy, and emaciated. This opportunity, however, very seldom occurs; for whenever a turn in the river or any accidental circumstance brings you suddenly upon them, they muffle their faces in their dress, and retreat as hastily as possible.

Pleasures and Ennui, 1842
W.H. Bartlett

I hastened on board [at Atfeh], the sun had sunk and given place to a rosy twilight, and the moon peeped up above the rich level of the Delta. And here I must
notice, that what reconciles the traveller to this land of plagues—of flies and
beggars, of dogs and dust and vermin, is not alone the monumental wonders on
the banks of the Nile, but the beauty of the climate, the lightness of the air,
inspiring a genial luxury of sensation, the glorious unfailing sun-set and serene
twilight, reflected in the noble river, and casting over the hoary remains of antiquity a glow and gorgeousness of hue which heightens their melancholy grandeur,
and gilding over a mud village until even its filth and misery are forgotten. I
mounted the roof of the little cabin as the broad lateen of the sail swelled smoothly
under the pressure of the Etesian wind, which, at this season of the inundation,
by a wonderful provision of nature, blows steadily from the north, thus alone
enabling vessels to stem the powerful current of the rising Nile.

The boat, with her broad sails and her long wake whitening in the moon, and
her Arab crew, lying upon deck, chanting their peculiar and plaintive songs, flew
rapidly along through historic waters. I sat up to a late hour, so delightful was my
impression of the patriarch of rivers.

But on the following morning the scene was wholly changed. On awaking, we
were close to the alluvial chocolate-coloured bank, the rich deposit of countless
inundations, and the crew on shore were engaged in the toilsome task of tracking
or hauling the boat, (a process represented on the ancient sculptures) to the music
of a monotonous chant, which they seemed scarce able to utter. There was not a
breath of air, and the warm, soft, cloudless sky was reflected back from the glassy
surface of the broad yellow river. The heat was close and overpowering. Hours like
these, of which the traveller on the Nile must make up his mind to not a few, are
indeed awfully wearisome. It is too hot to go on shore and walk through the deep
dust of the unsheltered bank, and cooped up and panting for breath in the narrow
cabin of your boat, you seem doomed, ere the ardours of noon abate, to be roasted
alive, like a crab in its own shell. Every thing inspires listless, restless, irritable ennui,
only to be alleviated, if haply at all, by the fumes of the consoling pipe.

First Sight of the Pyramids, 1848
Harriet Martineau

Till 3 p.m. there was little variety in the scenery. I was most struck with the
singular colouring—the diversity of browns. There was the turbid river, of vast
width, rolling between earthy banks; and on these banks were mud villages, with
their conical pigeon-houses. The minarets and Sheiks' tombs were fawn-coloured
and white; and the only variety from these shades of the same colour was in the
scanty herbage, which was so coarse as to be almost of no colour. But the dis-
tinctness of outline, the glow of the brown, and the vividness of light and shade,
were truly a feast to the eye.

At 3 o'clock when approaching Werdan, we saw large spreading acacias growing out of the dusty soil; and palms were clustered thickly about the town; and at last we had something beyond the banks to look at;—a sandy ridge which extends from Tunis to the Nile. When we had passed Werdan, about 4 p.m., Mr. E. came to me with a mysterious countenance, and asked me if I should like to be the first to see the Pyramids. We stole past the groups of careless talkers, and went to the bows of the boat, where I was mounted on boxes and coops, and shown where to look. In a minute I saw them, emerging from behind a sandhill. They were very small; for we were still twenty-five miles from Cairo; but there could be no doubt about them for a moment; so sharp and clear were the light and shadow on the two sides we saw.

I had been assured that I would be disappointed in the first sight of the Pyramids; and I had maintained that I could not be disappointed, as of all the wonders of the world, this is the most literal, and, to a dweller among mountains, like myself, the least imposing. I now found both my informant and myself mistaken. So far from being disappointed, I was filled with surprise and awe; and so far was I from having anticipated what I saw, that I felt as if I had never before looked upon any thing so new as those clear and vivid masses, with their sharp blue shadows, standing firm and lone in their expanse of sand. In a few minutes they appeared to grow wonderfully larger; and they looked lustrous and most imposing in the evening light.—This impression of the Pyramids was never fully renewed. I admired them every evening from my window at Cairo; and I took the surest means of convincing myself of their vastness by going to the top of the largest; but this view of them was the most moving: and I cannot think of it now without emotion.

Once the railway from Cairo to Alexandria was opened, many travelers took a train for the journey rather than traveling by river boat.

By Train to Cairo, 1883
Gabriel Charmes

I return to Alexandria, to take the train there which is to conduct me to Cairo. Hardly have we crossed the Lake Mareotis, where are produced on fine days the most fairy-like mirages, when we find ourselves really in Egypt. Vast plains, richly cultivated, spread out on all sides as far as the horizon, not closed by a single hill. Canals intersect them everywhere. On the banks of these canals, fellah, with or without costume, raise water by means of a *chadouf* and *nattaleh*. The shelving banks serve for roads, and a considerable crowd may be seen there moving on. Sometimes it is an Arab who is fleeing on horseback at full gallop; sometimes a fellah walking slowly, leaning on a long staff; sometimes a woman covered with a black veil, her head bearing a heavy burthen, which does not hinder her from carrying on her raised hand a *gargoulette* filled with water, and holding a naked child astride her shoulders. A file of camels, with the head of each tied to the tail of the one that precedes, moves on solemnly. Black buffaloes graze in the fields on the giant trefoil called *bersim*. A child watches them while a flock of herons fly around them, and pitch, without ceremony, on their hardened backs.

A series of towns and villages are met with: Damanhour, which the soldiers in Bonaparte's expedition imagined to be a city of the Thousand and One Nights, Tel-el-Barout, Kafr-el-Zaiat, Tantah, whose fair recalls the most scandalous saturnalia of antiquity, etc.

The wide river rolls its yellow waves under a sky of azure through an endless plain covered with the richest products. The temperature changes abruptly; it becomes sensibly warmer; now, we indeed enter Egypt.

By degrees the valley gets narrower; the yellow line of the desert appears; the Pyramids, rose tinted in the morning light, rise in the horizon; at last the mosque of Mehemet Ali, which commands Cairo, lifts its cupola and two-pointed minarets on the summit of the hill of Mokkatam. A forest of cupolas and minarets rise everywhere. We are arrived.

4
Cairo
Mother of Cities

 Cairo changes daily and yet has remained the same for centuries. The Cairo of al-Muqaddasi at the end of the first millennium and that of Ibn Battuta, in 1326, is the Cairo that visitors and residents know today. One only has to step off a busy street into the garden of a mosque or into one of the narrow lanes that run between buildings or pass into the spice market to step back to timeless Cairo.

Cairo, c. 1000
al-Muqaddasi

Al-Fustat [old Cairo] is a metropolis in every sense of the word; here are together all the departments of government's administration, and moreover, it is the seat of the Commander of the Faithful. It sets apart the Occident from the domain of the Arabs, is of wide extent, its inhabitants many. The region around is well cultivated. Its name is renowned, its glory increased; for truly it is the capital of Egypt. It has superseded Baghdad, and is the glory of Islam, and is the market place for all mankind. It is more sublime than the City of Peace [Baghdad]. It is the storehouse of the Occident, the entrepot of the Orient, and is crowded with people at the time of the Pilgrimage festival. Among the capitals there is none more

Cairo & the Valley of the Nile

populous than it, and it abounds in noble and learned men. Its goods of commerce and specialities are remarkable, its markets excellent as is its mode of life. Its baths are the peak of perfection, its bazaars splendid and handsome. Nowhere in the realm of Islam is there a mosque more crowded than here, nor people more handsomely adorned, no shore with a greater number of boats.

It is more populous than Naysabur, more splendid than al-Basra, larger than Damascus. Victuals here are most appetizing, their savouries superb. Confectionaries are cheap, bananas plentiful, as are fresh dates; vegetables and firewoods are abundant. The water is palatable; the air salubrious. It is a treasury of learned men; and the winter here is agreeable. The people are well-disposed, and well-to-do, marked by kindness and charity. Their intonation in reciting the *Qur'an* is pleasant, and their delight in good deeds is evident; the devoutness of their worship is well-known throughout the world. They have rested secure from injurious rains, and safe from the tumult of evildoers. They are most discriminating in the selection of the preacher and the leader in prayer; nor will they appoint anyone to lead them but the most worthy, regardless of expense to themselves. Their judge is always dignified, their *muhtasib* deferred to like a prince. They are never free from the supervision of the ruler and the minister. Indeed were it not that it has faults aplenty, this city would be without compare in the world.

The town stretches for about two-thirds of a *farsakh*, in tiers one above the other. It used to consist of two quarters, al-Fustat and al-Jiza, but late on, one of the khalifs of the house of al-Abbas had a canal cut around a portion of the town, and this portion became known as al-Jaziri (the island), because of its lying between the main course of the river and the canal. The canal itself was named the "canal of the Commander of the Faithful," and from it the people draw their drinking water. Their buildings are of four storeys or five, just as are lighthouses; the light enters them from a central area. I have heard it said that about two hundred people live in one building. In fact, when al-Hassan bin Ahmad al-Qarmati arrived there, the people came out to meet him; seeing them, as he considered, like a cloud of locusts, he was alarmed, and asked what this meant. The reply was: "These are the sightseers of Misr; those who did not come out more numerous still."

> Coming through North Africa from Tangier to make the pilgrimage to Mecca, Ibn Battuta traveled up the Nile from Alexandria to the city of Misr—Cairo.

Mother of Cities, 1326
Ibn Battuta

I arrived at length at the city of Misr, mother of cities and seat of Pharaoh the tyrant, mistress of broad provinces and fruitful lands, boundless in multitude of buildings, peerless in beauty and splendour, the meeting-place of comer and goer, the halting-place of feeble and strong, whose throngs surge as the waves of the sea, and can scarce be contained in her for all her size and capacity. . . .

It is said that in Cairo there are twelve thousand water carriers who transport water on camels, and thirty thousand hirers of mules and donkeys, and that on the Nile there are thirty-six thousand vessels belonging to the Sultan and his subjects, which sail upstream to Upper Egypt and downstream to Alexandria and Damietta, laden with goods and profitable merchandise of all kinds. On the bank of the Nile opposite Old Cairo is the place known as *The Garden* (now the island of Roda), which is a pleasure park and promenade, containing many beautiful gardens, for the people of Cairo are given to pleasure and amusements.

> Rudyard Kipling's powerful skill with words painted Cairo's variety, its sounds, and the spirit of place.

A City of the Earth, 1913
Rudyard Kipling

But I bought nothing. The city thrust more treasure upon me than I could carry away. It came out of dark alleyways on tawny camels loaded with pots; on pattering asses half buried under nets of cut clover; in the exquisitely modelled hands of little children scurrying home from the cook-shop with the evening meal, chin pressed against the platter's edge and eyes round with responsibility over the pile; in the broken lights from jotting rooms overhead, where the women lie, chin between palms, looking out of windows not a foot from the floor; in every glimpse into every courtyard, where the men smoke by the tank; in the heaps of rubbish and rotten bricks that flanked newly painted houses, waiting to be built, some day, into houses once more; in the slap and slide of the heelless red-and-yellow slippers all around, and, above all, in the mixed delicious smells of frying butter, Mohammedan bread, kababs, leather, cooking-smoke, assafetida, peppers and turmeric. Devils cannot abide the smell of burning turmeric, but the right-minded man loves it. It stands for evening that brings all home, the evening meal, the dipping of friendly hands in the dish, the one face, the dropped veil, and the big, guttering pipe afterward.

Praise be to Allah for the diversity of His creatures and for the Five Advantages of Travel and for the glories of the Cities of the Earth! Harun-al-Raschid, in roaring Baghdad of old, never delighted himself to the limits of such delight as was mine, that afternoon. It is true that the call to prayer, the cadence of some of the street cries, and the cut of some of the garments differed a little from what I had been brought up to; but for the rest, the shadow on the dial had turned back twenty degrees for me, and I found myself saying, as perhaps the dead say when they have recovered their wits, 'This is my real world again.'

Some men are Mohammedans by birth, some by training, and some by fate, but I have never met an Englishman yet who hated Islam and its people as I have met Englishmen who hated some other faiths. *Musalmani awadani*, as the saying goes—where there are Mohammedans, there is a comprehensible civilisation.

Then we came upon a deserted mosque of pitted brick colonnades round a vast courtyard open to a pale sky. It was utterly empty except for its own proper spirit, and that caught one by the throat as one entered. Christian churches may compromise with images and side-chapels where the unworthy or abashed can traffic with accessible saints. Islam has but one pulpit and one stark affirmation—living or dying, one only—and where men have repeated that in red-hot belief through centuries, the air still shakes to it.

The Cities that Make Up Cairo, c. 960
Ebn Haukal

The chief city of Egypt is called Fostat, situated on the bank of the River Nile to the north. The Nile flows from the east; and this city is situated on one side of it. Near to it are certain edifices, called *Jezireh,* or the Island, to which they pass from Fostat on a bridge; and from this *Jezireh* they have constructed a bridge to the other bank, where there is a place called *Jeirah* [Giza]. The extent of the city is about two thirds of a *farsang*: it is very well inhabited, and supplied with provisions; all their houses are seven or eight storeys high. . . . *Hamra* is a town situated on the bank of the River Nile. It has two principal mosques: one in the middle of the town built by Amru ben Aas; and the other in the place called Mouekef, erected by Laaher ben Toulon. Without the town is a certain place of about a mile in extent, which that Laaher Toulon called to be built for his troops: this they call Fetaia or Ketaia. . . . On the northern side of the river Nile, near Fostat, there is a certain hill, called

Moazem, in the vicinity of which is found the *khemahein*, and this hill extends to the land of the Ionians (Greeks). And near that hill, in the district of Fostat, is a burying place, where the tomb of Shafaei is situated,—the Lord be merciful to him!

In the vicinity of Fostat, there grows a plant, called *balsam*, from which the oil is extracted. This is not to be found in any other part of the world.

Somewhere to Stay, 1855
Richard Burton

The "Wakálah", as the Caravanserai or Khán is called in Egypt, combines the office of hotel, lodging-house, and store. It is at Cairo, as at Constantinople, a massive pile of buildings surrounding a quadrangular "Hosh" or court-yard. On the ground-floor are rooms like caverns for merchandise, and shops of different kinds—tailors, cobblers, bakers, tobacconists, fruiterers, and others. A roofless gallery or a covered verandah, into which all the apartments open, runs round the first and sometimes the second story: the latter, however, is usually exposed to the sun and wind. The accommodations consist of sets of two or three rooms, generally an inner one and an outer; the latter contains a hearth for cooking, a bathing-place, and similar necessaries. The staircases are high, narrow, and exceedingly dirty; dark at night, and often in bad repair; a goat or donkey is tethered upon the different landings; here and there a fresh skin is stretched in process of tanning, and the smell reminds the veteran traveller of those closets in the old French inn where cats used to be prepared for playing the part of jugged hare. The interior is unfurnished; even the pegs upon which clothes are hung have been pulled down for fire-wood: the walls are bare but for stains, thick cobwebs decend in festoons from the blackened rafters of the ceiling, and the stone floor would disgrace a civilised prison: the windows are huge apertures carefully barred with wood or iron, and in rare places show remains of glass or paper pasted over the framework. In the court-yard the poorer sort of travellers consort with tethered beasts of burden, beggars howl, and slaves lie basking and scratching themselves upon mountainous heaps of cotton bales and other merchandise.

This is not a tempting picture, yet is the Wakalah a most amusing place, presenting a succession of scenes which would delight lovers of the Dutch school—a rich exemplification of the grotesque, and what is called by artists the "dirty picturesque".

I could find no room in the Wakálah, Khan Kahlíl, the Long's, or Meurice's of native Cairo; I was therefore obliged to put up with the Jamáliyah, a Greek quarter, swarming with drunken Christians, and therefore about as fashionable as Oxford Street or Covent Garden. Even for this I had to wait a week. The pilgrims were flocking to Cairo, and to none other would the prudent hotel keepers open their doors, for the following sufficient reasons. When you enter a Wakálah, the first thing you have to do is to pay a small sum, varying from two to five shillings, for the Miftáh (the key). This is generally equivalent to a month's rent; so the sooner you leave the house the better for it. I was obliged to call myself a Turkish

pilgrim in order to get possession of two most comfortless rooms, which I afterwards learned were celebrated for making travellers ill; and I had to pay eighteen
piastres for the key and eighteen ditto per mensem for rent, besides five piastres
to the man who swept and washed the place. So that for this month my house-
hire amounted to nearly four pence a day.

Above the seething city of Cairo the minarets continue to
point heavenward, still dominating the skyline, and, unless
one is too dazed by the traffic-covered veneer of the city, the
visitor can still be as astonished by Cairo as Reverend Smith
was in 1868. Many have felt in Cairo that they had wandered
into the world of the *Thousand and One Nights*.

Water and Minarets, 1868
Reverend A.C. Smith
Then the strange architecture, the really handsome fountains, which abound at the
corners of the bazaars for the continual refreshment of this water-loving people; the
mosques, many of which have no slight pretensions to beauty,—above all the
minarets, the most graceful and elegant of buildings, and which catch the eye at the
distant ends of the streets; the light and airy lattice-work of the windows, which
admits the air, but keeps out prying eyes from the rigidly secluded interior; these
and many a charming bit of detail, on which one continually stumbles in the more
retired part of this extensive city, made our daily rides through the streets of
Cairo fascinating and amusing during the whole of our stay. At intervals, and
more especially at the quieter hours of evening and night, came the musical
chant of the Muezzins from the galleries of the tall minarets, calling the faithful
to prayer; and as the solemn sound of these aerial invitations to devotion float
over the city, it seems like the melodious voice of angels calling out of heaven:
"God is great. God is merciful. There is no Deity but God: Mahommed is the
Apostle of God. Come to prayer, come to prayer. Prayer is better than sleep. There
is no Deity but God."
    But what continually came uppermost in the minds of us all, and I suppose of
most of my fellow countrymen in Cairo, was the strong feeling we had that we
were living in the midst of the scenes so familiar to us in childhood from that
favourite book, *The Arabian Nights Entertainments,* but never realised till now.

Canals Cut through the City, 1039
Naser-e Khosraw
In the midst of the houses in the city are gardens and orchards watered by wells. In
the sultan's harem are the most beautiful gardens imaginable. Waterwheels have
been constructed to irrigate these gardens. There are trees planted and pleasure parks

built even on the roofs. At the time I was there, a house on a lot twenty by twelve ells was being rented for fifteen dinars a month. The house was four stories tall, three of which were rented out. The tenant wanted to take the topmost floor also for [an additional] five dinars, but the landlord would not give it to him, saying that he might want to go there sometimes, although, during the year we were there, he did not come twice. These houses are so magnificent and fine that you would think they were made of jewels, not of plaster, tile and stone! All the houses of Cairo are built separate one from another, so that no one's trees or outbuildings are against anyone else's walls. Thus, whenever anyone needs to, he can open the walls of his house and add on, since it causes no detriment to anyone else.

Going west outside the city, you find a large canal called al-Khalij [Canal], which was built by the father of the present sultan, who has three hundred villages on his private property along the canal. The canal was cut from Old to New Cairo, where it turns and runs past the sultan's palace. Two kiosks are built at the head of the canal, one called Lulu [Pearl] and the other Jawhara [Jewel].

> Cairo is huge, yet from almost every part of it one can glimpse the Citadel high above the city, built there by Salah al-Din, or Saladin, and now dominated by the twin minarets and dome of the mosque of Muhammad 'Ali.

The Citadel above Cairo, 1819
John Fuller
The Citadel is built on a rock detached from the chain of the Moccatam mountains, which approach very near to the town on the eastern side. Before the invention of gunpowder its position was considered very strong, but it is commanded from the neighbouring ridges. This circumstance, however, has not hindered the Pasha from expending large sums of money in repairing the walls and approaches, which had become much dilapidated by time, and by the several cannonadings which the castle had suffered during the occupation and after the expulsion of the French. The works were not yet completed, but the Pasha's Seraglio, built on the side of the rock which is steepest and which overlooks the city, was finished, and occasionally occupied by him. It consists of a very spacious hall, communicating with several large apartments, which besides the usual Turkish luxuries of cushions and divans, are furnished with mirrors, clocks and other specimens of European refinement, and are ornamented with some tolerable landscapes, painted in fresco on the walls by Greek and Armenian artists from Constantinople. Without, the prospect is vast and impressive, combining the extremes of prosperity and desolation. The governor of Egypt may view with pride from the windows of his palace the city of Cairo, with its countless domes and busy population, the rich fields of the Delta, and the Nile which brings him the tribute of twenty provinces; but the

Pyramids on one side, and the deserted tombs of the Mameluke sultans on the other, memorials of dynasties which have passed away before their works have perished, may remind him of the instability of his power. The other curiosities of the Citadel have been fully described by every traveller who has written on Egypt for the last two hundred years. The Well of Joseph as it is called, whatever may have been its origin, is a very remarkable excavation, being cut nearly three hundred feet deep in the solid rock, with a spacious gallery round it, extending spirally from top to bottom. The Hall of Joseph or Yussuf, is now referred to the prince of that name, better known as Sultan Saladin; . . . a large and lofty oblong building, constructed with what we would call Saxon arches, supported on granite pillars. Though it has long been roofless, yet such is the serenity of the climate that some inscriptions in the ancient Cusic character on a wooden frieze which runs round the interior, remain almost unimpaired. It is now used as a magazine for artillery, of which we saw a great variety of different ages and countries, from the Venetian of the fifteenth to the French and English of the nineteenth century [this magazine blew up in 1824]. In front of the Seraglio was stationed a large body of the cavalry of the Pasha's guard, whose appearance reminded us of what we had read of Mameluke splendour, and exceeded in picturesque effect any military display which I have seen in Europe. From the bright and varied hues of the dresses and turbans, and the richness of the equipments, the square which they occupied when seen from a distance looked like a bed of the gayest flowers.

Looking down across Cairo, 1834
Hon. W.E. Fitzmaurice
The two following days we amused ourselves by seeing the various mosques and curious buildings about Cairo; in the evening I strolled up to Sifa, which over-looks the Citadel. It is a scene that one would never tire of: standing on a bed of high rocks you have a most beautiful panorama before you of every description of scenery. In the foreground are the Tombs of the Mamelukes, Old Cairo stretching out beyond the river; here and there the eye rests on an Arab village with its minaret and grove of palms; in the distance the Pyramids seem to increase in size as the sun sinks behind them in the gloom of the desert, and occasionally you catch a turn of the majestic river, as it winds its way down this beautiful valley, bearing verdure and fertility on its dimpled waters; reminding one of the beautiful lines in the opening of *Rasselas* [the novel by James Bruce, the Scottish explorer], where truly may it be styled, 'The Father of Waters', and as truly does it scatter over half the world the harvest of Egypt.

> The most splendid and charming among the buildings of the city are the mosques—some grand and dominant in their neighborhoods; others a homely part of a small community. Other great buildings, too, have made their impact on travelers.

The Mosques of Cairo, c. 1000
al-Muqaddasi
This particular mosque is known as al-Sufflani (the Lower). It was founded by
'Amr bin al-'As, and within it stands his pulpit. The building is well constructed, with some mosaics set into the walls. It stands on pillars of marble,
and is bigger than the mosque at Damascus, and the crowding in it is greater
than that of six other mosques here. The markets are all around it, except that
between them and the mosque, on the side towards the *Qibla*, is the Dar al-
Schatt, as well as storage spaces, and a place for performing the ablution. This
district is the most flourishing in Misr; to the left is the Zuqaq al-Qanadil (the
Corridor of the Lamps)—but one can have no idea of what Zuqaq al-Qanadil is
like!

The Fawqani (Upper Mosque) was built by the House of Taylūn—it is
larger and more magnificent than the Sufflani mosque. It is built on massive
pillars adorned with stucco, its roofs are lofty. In its centre is a vaulted structure resembling that of Zamzam, and therein is a drinking fountain. The
mosque overlooks both the mouth of the canal and some part of it. Some
extensions have been added to it, while behind it are some handsome resi-
dences. Its minaret is of stone; it is small and the steps to the top of it are on
the outside.

The Great Mosque of Sultan Hassan, 1857
William C. Prime
In one of our rambles about town, going up one street and down another, without heeding wither they led us, we found ourselves one day at the great entrance
of the mosque of the Sultan Hassan, and dismounted to enter it. Outside the
door were vendors of trifles of various sorts; a kind of old junk dealers, second-
hand clothiers, and sellers of paste and imitation jewellery. Among them were
vendors of Meccan curiosities—sandal-wood beads, and the wood, dipped in the
holy well of Hagar, which they use to clean their teeth with. All, or nearly all,
the Moslems have good teeth, kept white with this wood, a small stick of which,
chewed at one end, forms a soft brush, which they use till the whole is worn
away.

The mosque is a grand structure, chiefly interesting from being built of the
stone which was the casing of the great Pyramid of Ghizeh. It is the most
imposing structure in all the Mohammedan countries I have visited, and probably
the most in the Moslem world. The lofty walls surround a rectangular court,
one side of which opens by a grand arch into an immense alcove, in the rear of
which is the enclosed chamber around the tomb of Sultan Hassan, who was
murdered and buried here. . . . On the tomb lie, as is the custom, a copy of the
Koran in a strong box, and sundry old coverings of silk, that were once heavy
and gorgeous. The days are past when any one lived to cover the Sultan Hassan
with cashmere.

Mosque of Sultan Hassan

The Splendid Mosque, 1846
Isabella Romer

This mosque, (the name of which signifies the "Splendid Mosque", and not, as has erroneously been stated, the "Mosque of Flowers"), may be termed the University of the East, for in the numerous Colleges attached to it are educated all the youths destined in this part of the world for the priesthood and the profession of the law, which are always combined in Mahometan countries, where he who best understands the Koran is the best lawyer. Formerly El Azhar sent out its pupils throughout the whole of Africa and part of Asia, and it contains separate colleges under the same roof for the natives of the different provinces of Egypt, or of other Mahometan nations who come to study there, and pay nothing for the instruction they receive. But the number of these has greatly diminished since Mohammed Ali seized upon the cultivable lands that belonged to the mosques, which in the case of El Azhar, formed a considerable portion of its revenues. It now contains from one to two thousand students, three hundred of whom form a college of the blind, which is maintained from funds bequeathed for that purpose by pious Moslems.

The mosque is situated in the very heart of the city, and in such a labyrinth of thickly populated and narrow streets that no good view of its exterior is to be obtained from any side. It has five entrances, the principal one leading into the vast court paved with marble, which we found full of students, seated upon the pavement in little groups, and studying with their professors. I confess that I trembled as I walked through them, and fancied that every one who looked up at me would discover, from the colour of my eyes and the absence of *khol* round them, that I was an European, and, even an Englishwoman;—but nothing of the sort happened, and I got safely into the interior of the mosque. Its great space, and the innumerable quantity of low slender columns with which it is supported, spreading in all directions like a forest, reminded me of the descriptions I have read of the Moorish Mosque of Cordova; but there is no great beauty in El Azhar beyond that which magnitude and airiness produce. We seated ourselves at the foot of one of the columns, and I there made the best use I could of my eyes.

The interior of the mosque was quite as full as the great court, and the groups were highly characteristic and exceedingly picturesque; the base of each column being surrounded by a little turbaned conclave deep in either the study of, or dissertations on, the Koran.

The Buildings of Cairo, c. 1200
'Abd al-Latif al-Baghdadi

One notices in the buildings of the Egyptians a marvellous art and a very wise disposition of the parts; it is very rare to leave any place unused which has no purpose. Their palaces are vast: usually they make their abode in the upper floors, and are practical enough to make the openings of their houses exposed to the agreeable winds from the north. One sees hardly any houses which have not their ventilators. Their ventilators are tall and wide and open to every action of the wind; they are placed carefully with much skill.

The markets and streets in Egypt are very wide and the buildings very high. They construct them of hewn stone and red bricks. . . . They construct the latrine drains very solidly, and I found in a ruined palace these drains still existing in good condition. They dug the trenches until water was found, in a manner so that for a very long time there was no need to clean them out.

When they build a tenement house, a palace for a prince, or a covered market, they get an engineer and entrust its execution to him. He comes to the place, which is on a slight elevation or platform, devises a plan in his mind, and arranges all the parts of the plan, following the kind of building required. After this he undertakes successively the various parts one after the other, and finishes the whole in a way so that as each part is finished it is inhabited, until all is completed. One part finished, he undertakes another, and so on till the whole building in all its parts is united, without their being any fault or omission to be remedied afterwards.

Streets, Houses, and Palaces of Cairo, c. 1612
George Sandys
Some of those streets I have found two miles in length, some not a quarter so long; every one of them is locked up in the night, with a door at each end, and guarded by a musketeer, whereby fire, robberies, tumults, and other disorders are prevented.

Without the city, towards the wilderness, to stop sudden incursions of the Arabs from abroad, there watch on horseback four Sanjiaks, with each of them a thousand horsemen.

This city is built after the Egyptian manner, high, and of large rough stone, part of brick, the streets being narrow. It hath not yet been above one hundred years in the Turks' possession, wherefore the old buildings remain; but, as they decay, the new to be after the Turkish manner, poor, low, much of mud and timber; yet, of the modern fabrics, I must except diverse new palaces which I have seen, both of Turks, and such Egyptians as most engage against their own country and so flourish in its oppression. I have oft gone to view them and their entertainments, . . .

The palaces I found vast and high, no state or flourish outwardly; the first court spacious, set with fair trees for shade, where are several beasts or rare birds, and wonderful even in those parts; the inner court joined to delicious gardens, watered with fountains and rivulets; beside the infinite variety of strange plants, there wanted no shade from trees of cassia, oranges, lemons, figs of Pharaoh, tamarinds, palms, and others, amongst which pass very frequently chameleons.

The entry into the house, and all the rooms throughout, are paved with many several-coloured marbles, put into fine figures; so likewise the walls, but in mosaic of a less cut; the roof laid with thwart beams, a foot and a half distant, all carved, great and double gilt; the windows with grates of iron, few with glass, as not desiring to keep out of the wind, and to avoid the glimmering of the sun, which in those hot countries glass would break with too much dazzling upon the eye. The floor is made with some elevations a foot high, where they sit to eat and drink; those are covered with rich tapestries; the lower pavement is to walk upon, where in the chief dining chamber, according to the capacity of the room, is made one or more richly gilt fountains in the upper end of the chamber, which, through secret pipes, supplies in the middle of the room, a dainty pool, either round or four-square, triangular or of other figure, as the lace requires . . . so neatly kept, and the water so clear, as make apparent the exquisite mosaic at the bottom; herein are preserved a kind of fish of two or three feet long, like barbells, which have often taken bread out of my hand, sucking it from my fingers at the top of the water.

But that which to me seemed more magnificent than all this was my entertainment. Entering one of these rooms, I saw at the upper end, amongst others sitting cross-legged, the Lord of the Palace, who beckoning me to come, I first put off my shoes, as the rest had done, then bowing very often, with my hand on my breast, came near; where he making me sit down, there attended ten or twelve handsome young pages, all clad in scarlet, with crooked daggers and scimitars, richly gilt; four of them came with a sheet of taffety and covered me; another held a golden incense with rich perfumes, wherewith being a little smoked, they took all away; next came two with sweet water, and sprinkled me; after that, one brought a porcelain dish of coffee, which when I had drunk, another served up a glass of excellent sherbet. Then began our discourse. . . . In their questions and replies, I noted the Egyptians to have a touch of the merchant or Jew, with a spirit not so soldier-like and open as the Turks, but more discerning and pertinent.

Interior of a house, at Cairo

The Sultan's Banquet, c. 1050
Naser-e Khosraw

It is customary for the Sultan to have a banquet twice a year, on the two great holidays, and to hold court for both the elite and the common people: the elite in his presence and the commoners in other halls and places. Having heard a great deal about these banquets, I was very anxious to see one with my own eyes, so I told one of the Sultan's clerks, with whom I had struck up a friendship, that I had seen the courts of the Persian sultans, such as Sultan Mahmud of Ghazna and his son Mas'ud, who were great potentates enjoying much prosperity and luxury, and now I wanted to see the court of the Prince of the Faithful. He therefore spoke a word to the chamberlain, who was called the Saheb al-Setr.

The last of Ramadan 440 (8 March 1049) the hall was decorated for the next day, which was the festival, when the Sultan was to come after prayer and preside over the feast. Taken by my friend, as I entered the door of the hall, I saw constructions, galleries and porticos that would take too long to describe accurately. There were twelve square structures, built one next to the other, each more dazzling than the last. Each measured one hundred cubits square, and one was a thing one hundred metres square with a dais placed the entire length of the building at a height of four ells, on three sides all of gold, with hunting and sporting scenes depicted thereon and also an inscription in marvellous calligraphy. All the carpets and pillows were of Byzantine brocade and *buqalmun,* each woven exactly to the measurements of its place. There was an indescribable lattice-work balustrade of gold along the sides. Beside the dais and next to the wall were silver steps. The dais itself was such that if this book were nothing from beginning to end but a description of it, words would still not suffice.

They say that fifty thousand maunds of sugar were appropriated for the Sultan's feast. For decoration on the banquet table I saw a confection like an orange tree, every branch and leaf of which had been executed in sugar, and thousands of images and statuettes in sugar. The Sultan's kitchen is outside the palace, and there are always fifty slaves attached to it. There is a subterranean passageway between the building and the kitchen, and the provisioning is such that every day fourteen camel-loads of ice are sued in the royal sherbet-kitchen.

Most of the emir's and Sultan's entourage received emoluments there, and if the people of the city make requests on behalf of the suffering they are given something. Whatever medication is needed in the city is given out from the harem, and there is also no problem in the distribution of other ointments, such as balsam.

The Ever-changing Streets, 1865
Lady Herbert

The streets are a never-ending source of amusement and interest to the party—not only from their intrinsic beauty, but from the indescribable variety and novelty of the bazaars and of the costumes of the people. Ladies of whom nothing is visible but the eyes, the rest of their bodies being enveloped in gorgeous-coloured silks, and over all a cloak of black silk called a *habarah;* dervishes with their long black robes, and green turbans; picturesque water-carriers, with their water-skins, and others with long sticks of sugar cane, the chewing of which is general amusement to people of all ages and classes; Arabs and fierce Bedouin in burnous, and Kaffirs with long guns; Syrians with red caps and flowing robes; fat Turks in flowered silk dressing-gowns and ample turbans; peasant women draped from head to foot in the blue dress and black veil which are their only covering, with a child generally sitting, monkey-like, on their shoulder; and in the midst of this motley crowd thronging the narrow streets, which are latticed over with matting to keep out the sun, strings of camels and donkeys beautifully caparisoned with crimson and emboroidered trappings, closely followed by their owners, screaming out *'riglak'* (beware), *'shimlak'* (to the left), *'Ya Sitt'* (O Lady) etc., etc. (to warn the passengers out of the way), in every conceivable key and pitch of shrillness, the whole combining to form a picture unrivalled in any other Eastern town.

Now and then they came on a marriage procession; the bride, in crimson and covered with jewels, walking under a canopy, supported by four men, and preceded by musicians, producing the most wonderful melody out of the most curious instruments. This kind of procession was often immediately followed by a group of little boys, dressed in red, with gold-embroidered jackets, on horseback, going to be circumcised; or else a funeral would block the way; that is, a long string of hired mourners, men and women, veiled and howling, the coffin richly covered with silk trappings, and a diamond 'aigrette' at the head, testifying to the rank of the deceased.

> Still, as ever, the bazaars of Cairo offer excitement and variety to citizen and visitor alike. The vendors' cries that rose to the windows of Edward Lane's house have changed but continue—as has the coinage used in some transactions. James Capper, 'Abd al-Latif, and many citizens and visitors enjoyed the pleasures of the Bagnio.

The Bazaars of Cairo, 1839
P.D. Holthaus

The finest part of eastern cities are the bazaars or markets; that in Cairo is on a remarkably large scale. Here all the glories of the world are exhibited for sale: gold, ivory, gum, silks, balsams, pearls of great value, carpets, Persian shawls, singular shells from the Red Sea, corals, ostrich feathers and ostrich eggs, Nile whips cut from the hides of the hippopotamus, and besides these the precious fruits of the torrid zone, all in separate departments. In these bazaars I purchased a variety of articles. These wares are brought from the Nile, and by the countless caravans which from Cairo traverse all the East, and which take thence in exchange provisions and articles of dress. In the bazaars are the shops also of the Arab artisans, who have liberty to sit here and work, and expose their wares to sale. . . .

Ancient Coins, 1801
Edward Daniel Clarke

Who would have believed that ancient *Roman* coins were still in circulation in any part of the world? Yet this is strictly true. We noticed *Roman* copper medals in *Cairo* given in exchange in the markets among the coins of the city, and valued at something less than our halfpenny. What is more remarkable, we obtained some of the large bronze medals of the *Ptolemies* circulating at higher value, but in the same manner.

Cries in the Market, 1844
Edward Lane

Bread, vegetables, and a variety of eatables are carried about for sale. The cries of some of the hawkers are curious, and deserve to be mentioned. The seller of tirmis (or lupins) often cries, "Aid! O Imbabee! Aid!" This is understood in two senses—as an invocation for aid to the sheyk Imbabeh (in the village from which the best tirmis is grown) and also implying that it is through the aid of [this] saint that the tirmis of Imbabeh is so excellent. . . . The seller of sour limes cries, "God make them light (or easy of sale)! O limes!" . . . A curious cry of the seller of a kind of sweet-meat (halaweh) composed of treacle fried with some other ingredients is "For a nail! O sweetmeat!" indicating that children and servants often steal implements of iron etc from the house in which they live, and give them to him in exchange for his sweetmeat. The hawker of oranges cries, "Honey! O oranges! Honey!". . . . A very singular cry is used by the seller of roses: "The rose was a thorn; from the sweat of the Prophet it blossomed." This alludes to a miracle related to the Prophet. The fra-grant flowers of the henna-tree (or Egyptian privet) are carried about for sale, and the seller cries. "Odours of paradise! O flowers of the henna!"

Cries in the Streets, 1970
Elizabeth Warnock Fernea

Was I lonely? Yes, I admitted to myself, I was, a bit. Being a mother and a *sitt* took a little getting used to, after my years as a career girl, a working wife and a companion-helper to my husband in his research. I sat there in unaccustomed leisure, and while the children shouted on the swings and the nannies scolded them and wiped their noses and kept them out of the drinking fountain and gossiped, the lush produce of the Delta and the services of the city were hawked along the street and carried up and down the back stairs of the apartment houses fronting the *ganeena*.

The bazaar

"Crazy tomatoes! Jewels! Jewels!" Yes, the tomato peddler came and the lettuce vendors, crying *"Khass! Khass!* Fresh lettuce!" for although open-air markets,
grocery stores and government food cooperatives are found throughout Cairo, the
individual peddlers still make the rounds, hoping for a tiny profit on a barrow of
produce, bought early in the morning on the outskirts of the city from the carts
arriving from the countryside.

Onions, potatoes, radishes (*"Fijl! Fijl!"*), garlands of garlic, braces of pigeons,
crates of live chickens, tiny eggs in grass baskets were offered for sale on our street
and, in season, fresh artichokes and narrow sweet strawberries. Oranges and grape-
fruit came in the winter, pomegranates and prickly pear in the spring, with Persian
melons and mangoes, and in early summer, the great red watermelons for which
Egypt is justly famous.

The Bagnio, 1783
James Capper
After your arrival at Cairo, I would advise you as well for your health as for pleasure, almost immediately to repair to the Hummam or Bagnio. The Turkish manner
of bathing is infinitely superior to any thing of the kind that is now known, or at
least practised, in any part of Europe, for even most of the inhabitants of Italy,

once so famous for the magnificence of their baths, have long neglected this luxurious but salutary custom. As some of your friends may never have seen a Turkish bagnio, I shall attempt a description of what I used, which was one of the common sort, such as are to be met with in every city of the Levant.

The first room is the undressing chamber which is lofty and spacious. Near the wall is a kind of bench raised about two feet from the floor, and about seven or eight feet wide, so that after bathing a person may lie down upon it full length; the windows are near the top of the room, as well that the wind may not blow upon the bathers when undressed, as for decency's sake.

After undressing a servant gives you a napkin to wrap round you, and also a pair of slippers, and thus equipped you are conducted through a narrow passage to the steam room or bath, which is a large round room of about twenty-five feet diameter paved with marble, and in the centre of it is a circular bench where you are seated until you find yourself in a profuse perspiration, then your guide or attendant immediately begins rubbing you with his hand covered in a piece of coarse stuff called *keffay,* and thereby peels off from the skin a kind of scurf, which cannot be moved by washing only.

When he has rubbed you a few minutes he conducts you to a small room, where there is a hot bath about four feet deep and ten feet square, in which he will offer to wash you having his hand covered with a smoother stuff than before; or you may have some perfumed soap given you to wash yourself. After you have remained here as long as is agreeable, you are conducted to another little side room, where you find two cocks of water, the one hot the other cold, which you may throw over yourself with a basin, the water being tempered to any degree of warmth, or perfectly cold if you prefer it.

This being the last ablution, you are then covered with a napkin, and from hence conducted to the undressing room, and placed upon the before-mentioned bench, with a carpet under you and, being extended upon it full length, your attendant again offers to rub you dry with napkins. Some people have their nails cut, and also are shampooed; the Turks generally smoke after bathing and the operation of shampooing; and in about an hour, a few minutes more or less, they commonly dress and go home.

The Baths of Cairo, c. 1200
'Abd al-Latif al-Baghdadi

The Egyptian baths are also worthy of admiration. I have never seen better constructed or better positioned, nor more excellent for beauty and wisdom. Their pools, to begin with, are capable of each containing two to four corner basins or more. The water is conveyed by two taps, one for hot water, the other for cold water. Those who would bathe themselves descend into the basin and plunge into the water.

Inside these baths are cabinets furnished with doors, where one undresses; there are special cabinets for persons of distinction so that they do not mix with common persons, and do not appear naked in public. This room for undressing is well arranged and constructed. In the middle is a marble basin ornamented with columns which support a dome. The ceilings of all these places are ornamented with paintings; the walls are divided by white panels. The pavement is of marbles of various colours and sections, those of the interior being always more beautiful than those of the exterior. These baths are very light, the roofs are very high. All the vases are of various brilliant colours, clear and very elegant. In a word, when one enters one wishes never to leave, and in fact, when a prince at enormous expense builds himself a house, he spares nothing to embellish his dwelling, and he never fails to make a most beautiful bath.

> Cairo's gardens and parks are an inheritance from the past—
> the green lungs of a throbbing metropolis. Elizabeth Fernea
> acclaimed the gardens and the people who created them; the
> German journeyman Holthaus found in the gardens, as else-
> where, sites that link Cairo to the infant Jesus.

A Changing City, 1970
Elizabeth Warnock Fernea

Along the river the changes are even more dramatic. Standing on the steps of the Museum of Antiquities, it is difficult to imagine that the view across Liberation Square to the river did not exist twenty years ago, that this central section of modern Cairo was occupied by the British Army. By cutting a riverside highway through the old army compound and building beside the highway the pleasant tree-shaded esplanade of the Corniche, the president gave to his people the view and the freedom of the Nile banks, which had once been reserved for a few British officials and titled Egyptians. He extended Maidan Ismailia across the British parade grounds, planted trees and grass and flowers, erected mobile film screens, folk art museums. In a decade the focus of the modern city has shifted to this maidan, renamed Liberation Square; a cluster of new buildings has risen to encircle it. Beside the old Museum of Antiquities, long still pools reflect the blue and orange mosaic tiles flaring across the façade of the Nile Hilton; nearby stand the Arab League headquarters, the new Shepheard's Hotel, the Cairo town hall, and the Egyptian radio and television studios.

He may not have realised it, but President Nasser was only carrying one step further the tradition of other leaders and conquerors throughout the history of the Near East, who in times of peace have used their power to create gardens, surroundings of beauty in which to enjoy their leisure. The Arabic word for paradise is *El Genneh,* literally, the garden, and what could be more heavenly than a lush garden in a region of the world where eighty percent of the land is dry, arid desert?

In the past, of course, the leaders pleasured only themselves. As early as the sixth century, in Fustat, the original army camp from which Cairo proper grew, Khumarawayh, son of Ibn Tulun, was busy silvering and gilding the trees in his palace grounds.

The Mameluke lord, Emir Ezbek, home from the wars in the fifteenth century, built a pleasure lake in Cairo, where "floated the flowers of the yellow water lily." Later, beside this lake Napoleon set up his headquarters and here the first Shepheard's Hotel of whodunit fame was eventually built.

It was the great Albanian Mohammed Ali who was responsible for the first "public" garden. He filled in the lake, landscaped it and opened it to the fashionable citizens of Victorian Cairo.

But the Ezbekiyah Gardens, commemorating the old emir who watched the yellow water lilies, charged an entrance fee, which effectively screened its clientele. President Nasser's idea of free gardens for everyone's enjoyment is relatively modern; we were glad that one such garden was so close to us.

The Gardens of Cairo and Memorials of Jesus, 1839
P.D. Holthaus

[Returning from the Pyramids] . . . we again reached the Nile, opposite to Old Cairo. We sailed for the Nile island, Roda, and saw the ancient building in which the Pharaohs once resided. On this island are very beautiful gardens and walks, which belong to Ibrahim Pasha, and particularly a splendid botanic garden. Foreign plants and flowers of all kinds adorn it, and diffuse around their precious odours. Many slender palms and fountains give shade and coolness. Through the middle flows a broad canal, with several islands; and in a large pond are many singular gold and silver fish. There is also a lovely shell grotto, by which a sentinel is constantly posted. Several other gardens extend themselves close up the Harem of Ibrahim Pasha, which, on that account, you are not allowed to enter. At the southern end of the island is the Nile Meter [Nilometer], a white column of marble, on which are marked the heights of the Nile's risings. The height of the water is every day proclaimed through the streets of grand Cairo. . . .

In successive days I visited all the remarkable objects of Cairo, and those several places that are memorable through their connection with the Sacred records. The very next morning I mounted an ass and rode again with a guide to Old Cairo. In a Coptic Christian church, I saw under ground, in a rocky cave, the place where Mary and Joseph, when they were persecuted by Herod, are said to have lived with the child. A cradle hewn in the stone, marks the spot where the young child Jesus slept. They show also the sleeping place of Mary, and the well from which she drew water, as well as a little bath.

The next day I rode with a guide, nine miles to the north of Cairo, to the tree where the parents of Jesus, with their child, passed the night, as they fled into Egypt. This tree stands not far from a village, in a citron thicket, and in a garden full of balsams, and where many other precious plants grow. This, called the Tree of the Mother of God, is an old fig-tree, which has divided in the middle, and has thus two stems. Its boughs still put forth green leaves, and still bear fruit. After I had cut my name and place of birth in this oldest tree in the world, I returned through a beautiful and romantic country, and through two villages surrounded by palm-trees, and orchards, towards Cairo.

Through a singular avenue of acacias and fig-trees, we arrived, six miles from the city, at Shubra. Here Mehemed Ali has his pleasure-palace, and a wonderfully beautiful botanic garden. The paths are all paved with mottled stones; the flowers, plants and fruits, extremely diversified. There are spice, pepper and cinnamon trees. In a magnificent and richly-wrought fountain, you see lions and crocodiles, out of whose jaws the water springs, and a gas-light is suspended above it.

Today, one of the little frequented treats of Cairo is the wonderfully restored Nilometer on Roda Island. In Robert Curzon's day it still measured the prosperity of the whole country from the flood of the Nile—as it had nearly a millennium earlier. A 'bad Nile' spelled hardship and poverty for all the people of Egypt. Curzon visited it at low water; Captains Irby and Mangles when high water gave prosperity. In 1826, John Carne was fortunate enough to witness the day of the cutting of the Nile bank, allowing the river to flow into the city, while G.A. Hoskins enjoyed another Cairo festival.

The Rise of the Nile: The Nilometer, 1833
Robert Curzon

In England everyone talks about the weather, and all conversation is opened by exclamations against the heat or the cold, the rain, or the drought; but in Egypt, during one part of the air at least, the rise of the Nile forms the general topic of conversation. Sometimes the ascent of the water is unusually rapid, and then nothing is talked of but inundations; for if the river overflows too much, whole villages are washed away; and as they are for the most part built of sunburned bricks and mud, they are completely annihilated; and when the waters subside, all the boundary marks are obliterated, the course of canals is altered, and mounds and embankments are washed away. On these occasions the smaller landholders have great difficulty in recovering their property; for few of them know how far their fields extend in one direction or the other, unless a tree, a stone, or something else remains to mark the separation of one man's flat piece of mud from that of his neighbour. But the more frequent and the far more dreaded calamity is the deficiency of water. This was the case in 1833, and we heard nothing else talked of.

"Has it risen much today?" inquires one.

"Yes, it has risen half a pic since the morning."

"What! no more? In the name of the Prophet! what will become of the cotton?"

"Yes, and the doura will be burnt up to a certainty if we do not get four pics more."

In short, the Nile has it all its own way; everything depends on the manner in which it chooses to behave, and El Bahar (the river) is in everybody's mouth from morning till night. Criers go about the city several times a day during the period of the rising, who proclaim the exact height to which the water has arrived, and the precise number of pics which are submerged on the Nilometer.

The Nilometer is an ancient octagon pillar of red stone in the island of Rhoda, on the sides of which graduated scales are engraved. It stands in the centre of a cistern, about twenty-five feet square, and more than that in depth. A stone staircase leads down to the bottom, and the side walls are ornamented with Cufic inscriptions beautifully cut. Of this antique column I have seen more than most people; for on 28th of August, 1833, the water was so low that there was a great apprehension of a total failure of the crops, and of the consequent famine. At the time nine feet more water was wanted to ensure an average crop; much of the Indian corn had already failed; and from the Pasha in his palace to the poorest fellah in his mud hovel, all were in consternation; for in this country, where it never rains, everything depends on irrigation—the revenues of the state, the food of the country, and the life and death of the bulk of the population.

The Nilometer, c. 1000
al-Muqaddasi

The Nilometer: a pond in the middle of which is a tall column whereon are the marks in cubits and fingers; in charge of it is a superintendent, and around it are doors that fit together tightly. A report is presented to the Ruler every day of the amount the water has risen, whereupon the herald proclaims, "God hath augmented today the blessed Nile by so much; its increase last year on this day was so much; and may God bring it to completeness!" The rise is not proclaimed until after it has reached twelve cubits, it is announced to the Ruler only, for at twelve cubits the water does not extend to the cultivated villages of the countryside. However, when the height of the water reaches fourteen cubits, the lower portion of the region is watered; but if it reaches sixteen cubits, there is a general rejoicing, for there will be a good year. When the water has gone down, the people begin ploughing and sowing.

Celebration, 1826
John Carne

The 16th August was the day fixed on for the celebrated cutting of the bank of the Nile; a time of great rejoicing with the Egyptians, the inundation being now at its height.

It is the custom for a vast number of people of different nations to assemble and pass the night at the appointed spot. We resolved to go and mingle among them, not doubting that something highly interesting would occur. We arrived at the place about eight at night, it being a few miles distant from the city: there was a firing of canon, illuminations in their way and exhibitions of fireworks. The shores of the Nile for a long way down from Boulac were covered with groups of people, some seated beneath the large spreading sycamores, smoking; others gathered around parties of Arabs, who were dancing with infinite gaiety and pleasure, and uttering loud exclamations of joy, affording an amusing contrast to the passionless demeanour and tranquil features of their Muslim rulers. . . .

Perpetually moving over this scene which (both shores and river, and groups of palms), was illumined by the most brilliant moonlight, were seen Albanian soldiers in their national costume, Nubians from the burning clime of farther Egypt, Mamelukes, Arabs and Turks. At a number of small sheds, each of which had its light or small fire, you might have meat, fish etc ready dressed. . . . The other side of the beautiful river which shone like glass in the splendid light, still presented a gay appearance; lights moving to and fro amid the trees, boats pushing off with new-comers, and sounds of gaiety, with the firing of musquetry being still heard.

At last day broke, and soon after the report of the cannon announced that the event so ardently wished for was at hand. We proceeded to the spot, around which immense crowds were rapidly gathering. The high and shelving banks of the canal to which the Nile was to be admitted, were crowded with spectators. We obtained an excellent situation for observing the ceremony, by fortunately meeting with Osmin, a Scottish renegade, but a highly respectable man, and the confidential servant of Mr. Salt.

The Kiaya Bey, the chief man of the Pasha, soon arrived with his guards, and took his seat on the summit of the opposite bank. A number of Arabs now began to dig down the dyke which confined the Nile, the bosom of which was covered with a number of pleasure boats, full of people, waiting to sail down the canal into the city. Already the mound was only partly demolished, when the increasing dampness and shaking of the earth induced the workmen to leave off. Several Arabs then plunged into the stream, and, exerting all their strength to push down the remaining part, some openings were soon made, and the river broke through with irresistible violence. For some time it was like the rushing of a cataract.

According to custom, the Kiaya Bey distributed a good sum of money, throwing it into the bed of the canal below, where a great many men and boys scrambled for it. Several of them had a sort of net, fastened on the top of a pole, to catch the money as it fell. It was an amusing scene, as the water gathered fast round them, to see them struggling and groping amidst the waves for the coin; but the violence of the torrent soon bore them away; and there were some who had lingered to the last, and now sought to save themselves by swimming, still buffeting the waves, and grasping at the money showered down, and diving after it as it disappeared. Unfortunately this sport every year costs a few lives, and one young man was drowned this morning.

The different vessels, long ere the fall had subsided, rushed into the canal and entered the city, their decks crowded with all ranks, uttering loud exclamations of joy. The overflowing of the Nile is the richest blessing of Heaven to Egypt: as it finds its way gradually into the various parts of the city and neighbourhood, the inhabitants crowd to drink of, and wash in it, and rejoice in its progress.

The Country Prospers, 1817
Captains Charles Irby and James Mangles
We went the other day to the island of Rhoda to see the Mekias, but the column of graduation was wholly covered by water; so that we might have spared ourselves the trouble. The island, however, now presents a complete carpet of verdure, with beautiful sycamore trees and well recompensed us. There are no barns in Egypt: the peasant being sure of fair weather at harvest-home, the corn is immediately threshed, and the grain is piled up in immense hills, encircled by a wall.

The birds are freely allowed their share, though, during the time it is ripening, their claims are disputed by children, who are placed on elevated mud-hillocks, scattered in all directions throughout the plains; here they bawl and fling stones by means of a sling, to deter the feathered robbers from their depredations.

The other day we went to Boulac, situated on the banks of the Nile; it is, properly speaking, the port of Cairo, and the best scene it presents at this time of year, is not exceeded by any of our quays in Europe. The large *djerms* some of forty and fifty tons, make an immense profit during the overflowing of the Nile; the stream brings them down with great rapidity, and the strong north breeze takes them up again with equal speed. It is said these boats sometimes clear half their original cost the first season; a great part of the year, when the Nile is in its bed, they are laid up in ordinary, as their great draught of water prevents them navigating at that season.

Cairo in Festive Mood, 1863
G.A. Hoskins
The festivals of Cairo are very interesting, but travellers, spending almost all their time on the Nile, have seldom an opportunity of seeing them.

The Mooled el Hassaneyn is a grand festival to celebrate the birth of El Hassaneyn, whose head is buried in his mosk, and, except the Mooled of the Prophet, excels everything of the kind celebrated in Cairo. I witnessed it on the last and best night—Tuesday, the 7th of November. It was almost a scene from the Arabian Nights.

After driving through dark and narrow streets, deserted, except by a few straggling passengers, each with his long paper lantern, carried by himself or his servant, we burst into long bazaars, brilliantly illuminated by a line of entirely glass chandeliers, lighted with oil; the smallest had from thirty to forty lights, the largest about two hundred. I observed two with fourteen rows of lights, having the appearance of so many chandeliers, one above another. The stems and designs of these chandeliers were almost always beautiful. At the base there was generally a large globe of glass, pure as crystal, about six to nine inches in diameter. Above these were similar globes, or sometimes half-globes, coloured gold, blue and red. The chandeliers appeared to be what we should call in Europe old Venetian glass, and lighted up admirably the beautiful street architecture, the glorious white and red mosks with their picturesque doors and minarets, and the elegant fountains. Awnings of various colours covered portions of the bazaars, giving a gay and tent-like appearance to the scene.

It was, however, the people that interested me most. The bazaars and streets appeared a sea of white turbans, not one in a hundred wearing only the red tarboosh. The shops or stalls were all lighted up, and the citizens were seated on the benches before them, often on Persian carpets, smoking their pipes. Fickees were reciting the whole of the Koran; many were listening, whilst grey-beards, with spectacles on their noses, were reading portions of the sacred volume, making prayers and recitals for the sake of El Hassaneyn.

Beyond the gates of Cairo are the Tombs of the Caliphs in the City of the Dead, the Northern Cemetery, where the Mamluk sultans have been laid in great splendor since the fifteenth century. In 1326 the Moroccan traveler Ibn Battuta visited another great cemetery to the south of Cairo.

The Tombs of the Caliphs, 1873
Gabriel Charmes
All at once, between the two walls of sand, appear the Tombs of the Caliphs. Nothing can give an idea of this sight, the most melancholy and the finest I have ever met with in my life. The background of the picture is formed on the left by a fiery-red hill, named the Montagne-Rouge; it joins the bluish escarpments of the Mokatam, bathed in a transparent vapour, which gives them a fairy aspect; on the right, the Citadel, more gloomy, lifts its great walls into the azure of the sky. Before the girdle of rocks, which seem to be arranged like reflectors of light, an immense group of minarets and cupolas, crowded together, glitter like a magic apparition. It is the Necropolis of the Caliphs—a city of tombs, a cemetery of a special kind, that resembles in no way Turkish cemeteries, since it does not contain a blade of verdure, since one sees there only walls and dust, but the debris of construction scattered in the desert. The Arabs desired to place their tombs in the solitude, far from the eyes of the world, in the centre of a valley of sand, as if to hinder the busy noise of life from troubling their last sleep.

The environs of the Caliphs are formed of mounds, amid which one often loses himself without seeing any other object around than a yellowish rampart that surrounds him everywhere. I remember having tarried for a long time in one of

Tomb of Sultan Kaitbay

these numerous promenades at the Tombs of the Caliphs, in the bottom of a sort of funnel of an intense colour, like the brightest gold; the sky, of an intense blue, seemed superposed on the summit of this funnel, which it closed in hermetically. This contrast of two tones equally violent, deprived of any shade, would have been anywhere else offensive and insufferable; it was there, without knowing why, of marvellous harmony. Nature alone can permit herself such liberties; Art would be impotent to imitate them. But when one encounters them in reality, they produce a mixture of inexpressible surprise and admiration; they are impressions that partake of a dream, the remembrance of which, though always intense, leaves on the mind the sentiment of a prodigious illusion.

When you advance amid the Tombs of the Caliphs, you soon find yourself surrounded by a crowd of children, who frolic merrily on these sepulchral ruins. Through a sort of caprice of fortune, dawning life bursts forth everywhere in this great cemetery; never has the antithesis of youth and death taken a more tangible or striking form. They are the guardians of the tombs and the few inhabitants of this mortuary city that people it with this numerous offspring. Surrounded with the desert, without wants like all other Arabs, working consequently seldom, they bring forth children, it seems, in order to pass away the time. I asked one day a guardian of one of the tombs, who was walking about, surrounded with an immense family, whence came the prolific ardour, the results of which I witnessed.

"What should I do?" he replied. "It is so wearisome here."

Visiting the Dead, 1326
Ibn Battuta
At Cairo too is the great cemetery of al-Qarafa, which is a place of peculiar sanctity, and contains the graves of innumerable scholars and pious believers. In the Qarafa the people build beautiful pavilions surrounded by walls, so that they look like houses. They also build chambers and hire Koran-readers, who recite night and day in agreeable voices. Some of them build religious houses and madrasas beside the mausoleums and on Thursday nights they go out to spend the night there with their children and women-folk, and make a circuit of the famous tombs. They go out to spend the night there on the 'Night of mid-Shaban', and the market-people take out all kinds of eatables.

Cairo in the Evening, 1873
Gabriel Charmes
An incessant murmur rises from the streets and other places of Cairo. In the evening, at sunset, the colours are still more brilliant. A vast blood-red curtain sets off the dark mass of the Pyramids of Gizeh; the tops of the palms and sycamores appear gilded; the desert, far yonder, passes through every gradation of grey, blue, violet and opal. On the Nile the white sails of the dahabiehs resemble the wings of great swans spreading their plumage over the water; the noise of the city has become so intense that it seems almost like the rolling of a distant thunder.

It is thus that Cairo should be contemplated morning and night, and if one would admire it freely and inspire himself deeply with the poesy of this wonderful city, that history, art, and nature have done everything to embellish.

5
Pyramids and Sphinx

The man-made mountains that are the Pyramids, and the great crouching figure of the Sphinx—even when we come to them with present-day knowledge—stun us. From the distance they are immediately familiar; close to, they become far huger than in our imaginations. The writer and broadcaster Leonard Cottrell summed up in 1949 and on later visits what many travelers have felt and feel about the Pyramids.

The Spell of the Pyramids, 1956
Leonard Cottrell
"The Giza Pyramids are beyond doubt the supreme expression of Pharaonic majesty and power, whether one sees them far across the valley, lifting their golden tips above the morning haze, or at glaring mid-day, when their huge limestone sides lean against the sky like a flight of heavenly stairs. . . ."

Since I wrote those words, six years ago, I have had the opportunity to read far more about the Pyramids, and to revisit them on several occasions. In spite of the importunate dragomans and the troops of tourists, in spite of the touts and the souvenir-sellers, in spite of the efforts—by scholars, cranks, by religious fanatics—to explain away their mystery, each visit to the Pyramids only serves to deepen their spell.

71

The Wonders of the Country, c. 1200
'Abd al-Latif al-Baghdadi

Of all the countries, that I ever visited myself, or ever acquired any knowledge of
from the researches of others, there are none that can compare with Egypt, in regard
to the immense number of ancient monuments, that it contains. Among the wonders of that country are the Pyramids, which have attracted the attention of many
authors, whose works are filled with descriptions and dimensions of these buildings.
There are many of them; and they are all situated upon the same side of the river as
Gizeh, upon the same line with the ancient capital of Egypt, and at the distance of about
two days' journey from it. There are also others at Bousir. They vary much in size.
Some are constructed with earth and bricks, but the greater number of them are built
of stone, in a form exactly pyramidal, and with a smooth and even surface; others are
constructed in steps or degrees. There were formally at Gizeh a considerable number
of small pyramids, which were destroyed, in the time of Salah-eddin Youssef . . . by
Karakousch, an emir in that prince's army. He had the superintendence of all the buildings in the capital, and constructed the stone wall, which surrounds Fostat, Cairo, and
all the ground between these two places, and the Citadel upon the Mokatam. He also
built the Citadel itself, and the two wells, which exist to this day, and are considered
among the wonders of Egypt; a staircase of nearly three hundred steps leads to the bottom of them. . . . In proceeding to describe the Three Pyramids, which are distinguished above all the others by their immense and wonderful size, it is to be remarked,
that they are situated in a line at Gizeh, in front of Fostat, and at short distances from
each other, facing the east. Two of the three are of enormous magnitude, and are built
of white stone. These are nearer together than the Third; which is one quarter less than
the others, and is constructed of red speckled granite so extremely hard that it is worked
with great difficulty. The monument appears small when compared with the others;
but when viewed by itself, and at a little distance, it is truly magnificent.

The form of the Pyramids, and their extreme solidity, are indeed well worthy
of admiration; and have enabled them to resist the effects of time for so many ages,
that it might almost be considered that it is Time, that experiences the eternal
duration of these extraordinary edifices; and the more they are considered, the
more convincing is the proof, that the most consummate genius and skill were
employed in their construction.

Travelers constantly pondered how the Pyramids could have
been constructed, and even today they remain an engineering
wonder and mystery. The Greek historian Herodotus recorded
the account given to him of the building of the Great Pyramid.

The Construction and Cost of the Pyramids, c. 450 B.C.
Herodotus

This pyramid is built in steps, and, as the work proceeded, the stones were raised

The Pyramids

from the ground by means of machines made of short pieces of wood. When a block had been brought to the first tier, it was placed in a machine there, and so on from tier to tier by a succession of similar machines, there being as many machines as tiers of stone; or perhaps one served for the purpose, being moved from tier to tier as each stone was taken up. I mention this because I have heard both stated.

When completed in this manner, they proceeded to make out the form of the pyramid, beginning from the top, and thence downwards to the lowest tier. On the exterior was engraved in Egyptian characters the sum expended in supplying the workmen with radishes, onions and garlic; and he who interpreted the inscription told me, as I remember well, that it amounted to 1600 talents. If these things be true, how much must have been spent on the *iron* tools, the food and clothing of the workmen, employing as they did, all the time the above mentioned, without counting that occupied in cutting and transporting the stones and making the subterranean chambers, which must have been considerable!

How a Pyramid is Built and Unbuilt, 1825
Edward Lane
During the afternoon of the 19th [March], a favourable wind enabled us to continue the voyage. . . . For several miles . . . we had a view of the Pyramid of

Meydoo'n; a grand object being little inferior in height to the two pyramids of Dahshoo'r.

Early on the 20th I set off to visit the Pyramid of Meydoo'n. It is situated on the low Libyan ridge. . . . This monument is called *El-Har'am el-Kedda'b* or 'the False Pyramid', from its having the appearance of a pyramidal building raised on a round hill. Such I thought it to be until I arrived quite near to it; when I perceived that the supposed hill was really part of the structure, and that the materials thrown down from above had accumulated so high as nearly to cover one half of the pyramid. I found some labourers employed in pulling down and removing upon camels some of the stones from the lower part, to employ them in the construction of some new works ordered by the government (of Mehemet Ali). One benefit to be gained from this work of destruction (independent of the use thus made of the displaced materials) is an insight into the manner in which the edifice was constructed. We find it to be similar in construction to the principal pyramid of Saccara, but displaying much more care and skill. It appears that a slender pyramid (almost like an obelisk) was first raised. This was then cased, or covered, with a circumstructure of masonry, about sixteen feet in thickness, and which rose within fifty feet of the top. This again was built around in the same manner; and so on until the work was completed. . . . The whole must have had the appearance of seven stages of masonry, in the form of truncated pyramids, one raised on top of another.

Extravagance, c. 50
Pliny the Elder
We will mention also cursorily the Pyramids, which are in the same country of Egypt,—that idle and foolish exhibition of royal wealth. For the cause by most assigned for their construction is an intention on the part of those kings to exhaust their treasures, rather than leave them to successors or plotting rivals, or to keep the people from idleness. Great was the vanity of those individuals on this point.

> This account by al-Muqaddasi is interesting—both linking with and diverging from other accounts. One wonders whether the scholar was reporting what others had reported to him without actually visiting the site.

Wonders of the World, c. 1000
al-Muqaddasi
Among the remarkable things in this region are al-Haraman (the two pyramids), which are one of the wonders of the world. Of stone, and resembling two edifices, they rise, each, to a height of four hundred cubits—the cubit of King

Khosraw—its width the same. They are covered with Greek inscriptions, and within both of them are two passages in the highest part of each; there is, too, a remarkable vaulted passageway underground, excavated in the sand.

Varying accounts have been given me about both structures, some saying that they are both talismans, others that they were the granaries of Joseph; others say, no, rather they are his burial grounds. I have read in the book of Ibn al-Faqih that they are both bequeathed to the sand. It is said moreover, that on both of them is written: "I built them both, and whoever claims power in his possession of them, let him destroy them both, for destroying is easier than building." One of the kings purposed to destroy them both, but the revenue of Egypt did not suffice to do that, so he left them both. They are both smooth like big buildings, and may be seen from a distance of two or three days' journey. One does not ascend them unless he is agile. Around about them both is a number of smaller structures, and this indicates that they are graves. Do you not notice about the kings of al-Daylam in al-Ravy, how they have, in imitation, put tall domes over their graves? They made them as strong and as high as they could, so that they would not be obliterated. These are even smaller than these lesser ones. Here also is an idol which some assert Satan used to take possession of and make to speak, with the result that he broke its nose and lips.

Abu'l Haul, the Sphinx, c. 1200
'Abd al-Latif al-Baghdadi

A little more than a bowshot from these pyramids is a colossal figure of a head and neck projecting from the earth. The name of this is Abu'l Haul [the Sphinx] and the body to which the head pertains is said to be buried under the earth. To judge from the dimensions of the head, its length must be more than seventy cubits. On the face is a reddish tint, and a red varnish as bright as if freshly put on. The face is remarkably handsome, and the mouth expresses much grace and beauty: one might fancy it smiling gracefully.

A sensible man enquiring of me as to what, of all I had seen in Egypt, had most excited my admiration, I answered: "The nicety of proportion of the head of the Sphinx." In fact, between the different parts of this head, the nose, for example, the eyes, and the ears, the same proportion is remarked as is observed by nature in her works. Thus, the nose of a child is suitable to its stature, and proportioned to the rest of its frame, while if it belonged to the face of a full-grown man it would be reckoned a deformity. The nose of a grown man on the visage of a child would be an equal disfigurement. The same holds good with respect to all the other members. There are none but should have a certain form and dimension in order to bear such relation to such and such a face, and where these proportions are not observed, the face is spoiled. Hence the wonder that in a face of such colossal size the sculptor should have been able to preserve the exact proportion of every part, seeing that nature presented him with no model of a similar colossus or any at all comparable.

The Sphinx, 1852
Dean Arthur Penrhyn Stanley
. . . if . . . the Sphinx was the giant representative of Royalty, then it fittingly guards the greatest of Royal sepulchres, and, with its half human, half animal form, is the best welcome and the best farewell to the history and religion of Egypt.

The Sphinx and the Sepulchres, 1882
Samuel Cox
We alight amid the sandy heaps, and look down into the rock-cut taverns, and up to the half-hid genius of the Unknown.

The Sphinx is sunk in the lime rock. It is a part of it. The tombs about it are lined with immense granite blocks, laid imperfect courses, and with joints as true and handsome as any modern masonry. These blocks come from the cataract eight hundred miles above. They form an antique cemetery, covered by forty feet of sand. The temple is thirty feet beneath the level of the sand. From it a roadway, paved with white flagstones, leads up to the pyramids. They seem to have been connected religiously. The nose of the Sphinx is broken or worn off. It detracts from his dignity. It is a mistake to call the Sphinx *her*. His head-dress is partly demolished. Once the head was crowned with the royal helmet of Egypt; but his feet and form remain—for solution. Let its Oedipus stand forth! There is no satisfactory guess yet as to any of these gods of Egypt. Only one thing is surmised, that in the gods we see the men who made them. We read in their calm features aspirations after the other world—Immortality!

Pyramids and Sphinx, 1835
Alexander Kinglake
Familiar to one from the days of early childhood are the forms of the Egyptian Pyramids, and now, as I approached them from the banks of the Nile, I had no print, no picture before me, and yet the old shapes were there; there was no change; they were just as I had always known them. I straightened myself in my stirrups, and strived to persuade my understanding that this was the real Egypt, and that those angles which stood between me and the West were of harder stuff and more ancient than the paper pyramids of the green portfolio. Yet it was not until I came to the base of the great Pyramid that reality began to weigh upon my mind. Strange to say, the bigness of the distinct blocks of stones was the first sign by which I attained to feel the immensity of the whole pile. When I came, and trod, and touched with my hands, and climbed, in order that by climbing I might come to the top of one single stone, then, and almost suddenly, a cold sense and understanding of the Pyramid's enormity came down overcasting my brain. . . . And near the Pyramids more wondrous and more awful than all else in the land of Egypt, there sits the lonely Sphinx. Comely the creature is, but the comeliness is not of this world; the once worshipped beast is a deformity and a monster to this generation, and yet you can see that those lips, so thick and heavy, were

The Sphynx

fashioned according to some ancient mould of beauty, some mould of beauty now forgotten—forgotten because that Greece drew forth Cytherea from the flashing foam of the Aegean, and in her image created new forms of beauty, and made it a law among men that the short and proudly wreathed lip would stand for the sign and the main condition of loveliness through all generations to come. Yet still there lives on the race of those who were beautiful in the fashion of the older world, and Christian girls of Coptic blood will look on you with the sad, serious gaze, and kiss your charitable hand with the big pouting lips of the very Sphinx.

> Entering one of the pyramids is an experience that cannot fail to effect the most travel-hardened person. Climb a few of the great stones to reach the entrance—and you marvel. Within, the whole structure becomes more and more amazing.

The Terrors of the Interior of a Pyramid, c. 1612
George Sandys
A most dreadful passage, and no less cumbersome, not above a yard in breadth, and four feet in height, each stone containing that measure, so that, always stooping

and sometimes creeping by reason of the rubbish, we descended, not by stairs, but as down the steep of a hill a hundred feet, where the place for a little circuit enlarged, and the fearful descent continued, which they say some never durst attempt any further, save that a Pasha of Cairo, curious to march into the secrets thereof, caused diverse condemned persons to undertake the performance well stored with lights and other provision, and that some of them ascended again well nigh thirty miles off in the deserts. A fable devised only to beget wonder.

But others have written at the bottom there is a spacious pit, eighty and six cubits deep, filled at the overflow by concealed conduits; in the midst of a little island, and on that a tomb containing the body of Cheops, a king of Egypt, and the builder of this Pyramid, which with the truth hath a greater affinity. For since I have been told by one of his own experience that, in the uttermost depth, there is a large square place (though without water) into which he was led by another entry opening to the south, known but to few and entered at this place where we feared to descend.

Into a Pyramid, 1737
Captain Frederick Norden

The most agreeable way of seeing the Pyramids is with a party; they mutually excite each other's curiosity. All the prodigies related by those who have seen them before are not to be too credulously swallowed. From Cairo the tour to them may be made in a day or two. Those who have a mind to spend two days, ride off on asses through the city, cross the canal, and afterwards traverse the isle of Rhoda; on the left of which they and their asses embark, and land at Gizeh, a village opposite to Cairo. There no stop is to be made for the curious, not until a league further, where there is the inn with some chambers to let. There a very disagreeable night is passed by the curious, without beds or other convenience, they are tormented by bugs, but one night is soon over and, when curiosity eggs, such difficulties are most easily borne. Next morning the road to the Pyramids is entered on, . . . two Arabs are taken as guides. . . . At the opening of the first Pyramid fire some pistols in order to dislodge the bats, then order the two Arabs to clear away the sand, that almost chokes up the farther entrance to it.

This done, the next precaution is to strip to your shirt, on account of the excessive heat within the Pyramid; in this trim you get through, each person a *bougie* [candle] in his hand, for in this narrow avenue, it would be dangerous to use *flambeaux* [flaming torches] on account of the suffocating smoke. . . . At the end of it there is a passage made by force, whose opening is scarce one foot and a half high, and the two Arabs, who have wriggled themselves through before, seize each leg, and drag their gentleman through this probation cleft, all covered with filth. Happily this narrow passage is not above two yards long, otherwise such tugging would be unsupportable to all . . . then a large space opens, where the traveller takes breath, and some refreshments. . . .

The progress continues with great difficulty until at last the traveller reaches a salon—and their past difficulties are swallowed up with admiration.

Here, by way of amusement, pistols are fired, which excite a noise equal to that of thunder. No further objects to be seen, they return the same way with the same difficulty.

The first care of tourists when they come out of the Pyramid must be to dress instantly, cover themselves warmly, and drink a glass of generous wine, in order to prevent a pleaurisy, which they are very liable to, on account of the sudden transition from a very hot to a temperate air. This precaution observed . . . they ascend the Pyramid to contemplate the landscape all around, which is delightful. Thereon without, as well as in the chambers within, are described the names of many persons who have visited the Pyramid, and by so doing meant that their having travelled thither should be transmitted to posterity.

This first Pyramid well examined, go to the second which, being shut, is soon dispatched.

Where is the Queen? 1882
Samuel Cox

Let us enter: not without hope! The slippery path inward slopes downward until it meets a great gallery, which runs upward at an angle of forty-five degrees. Then, on a level, it runs to the Queen's Chamber. Returning on this level, at the same angle, and about half-way up the inside, you enter the King's Chamber. But it is no time or place for photographing this picture. Nor, if I were a poet, could I set a single airy sentiment in time, under the yawning, cavernous gap which opens as we enter.

"Take care, head!" I hear the Arabs say to my wife. She bows to Cheops. I do the same. We go up and down, sliding on polished stones, and in peril of tumbling into dark vaults. Our tapers give a sort of 'clear obscure' Rembrandtish aspect to the stony horror about us. After much lifting, pushing and tugging, relying upon the prehensile grip of the naked Arab foot, and the grasp of the steady Arab hand, now being carried and now pulled, now groping along perilous and slippery edges, we come to the Queen's Chamber. Its sarcophagus has been removed. But where is the queen? Doubtless the soothsayers told her, five thousand years ago, that she would be safe forever in this grand mausoleum.

Astronomical Correctness, 1834
Hon. W.E. Fitzmaurice

On the 16th I went again to the Pyramids, and was as much pleased as with our former excursion. As a singular and extraordinary proof of the astronomical correctness with which these stupendous piles are constructed, the polar star is visible on the night of 21st of March, when looking from the lower chamber, through the angular passage by which the Pyramid is entered.

The north star, at this period, when on the meridian, would bear due north. An evidence is thus given of the exact direction of the other three sides of the quadrangle—north, east, south and west; and the corners consequently give the other divisions—north-east, south-west, south-east, and north-west.

The exactness of these points, in a structure which there is every reason to believe was built even before the invention of the hieroglyphics (for the sarcophagus in the chamber within being without any characters of this description lead to this supposition) naturally gives rise to a very elevated idea of the knowledge the ancient Egyptians must have possessed of the heavenly bodies; notwithstanding that the Dendera and Esneh planispheres or zodiacs are supposed to be of the time of the Roman Empire.

> One can no longer climb to the summit of the Pyramids. For travelers in the past this was one of the pinnacles of a journey in Egypt.

Lifted to the Summit, c. 1865
Mrs. M. Carey

Three Bedouins accompanied me—Abraham and two companions—one as hearty as himself, the other rather too old for the work, as was soon proved by his remaining behind before we reached the top, as soon as he thought that his services could be dispensed with. For this he incurred considerable raillery from his companions, who spoke of him just as you might speak of a worn out horse—"old fellow," "good for nothing," etc.

Each of the first two guides seized one of my wrists and held them with so tight a grasp that I was obliged to remonstrate upon the subject and to show them the red marks which were appearing in consequence, upon which they condescended slightly to loosen their grip. They first mounted one of the great steps themselves, while the third guide, remaining on a level with me, placed two more hands at my waist, and assisted me to a succession of springs varying from three to five feet in height. Thus by a series of jumps the ascent of the Pyramid was accomplished in a far easier manner than I had anticipated. Cousin Phil and Selina moved to a distance to watch me. They said I looked like a doll as I was lifted up by the Bedouins from one giant step to the other; they could not hear the song with which the guides aided their efforts and mine as we proceeded; but here it is set to a kind of boatman's chorus, to which they sang it.

Solo: Plenty backshish, lady!
Chorus: Haylée, Haylée, sah!
Solo: To take you up to the top!
Chorus: Haylée, Haylée, sah! [interspersed between each solo statement]
Solo: Custom of every nation!
Ah! Bravo, bravo, lady!

Don't tell this man what you give me!
Chorus: (not knowing English) Haylée, Haylée, sah!
Give it to me myself!
Now stop and take rest, lady!

The ascent occupied twenty minutes, and I rested five times on the way, to take breath for the next climb and to look around me and remember where I was. A sixth pause would have been more to my taste, but the wary guide, suspecting signs of approaching fatigue, said, "No, lady, you must go to the top *now*."

I felt he was right though I doubted my powers to proceed. The old guide had halted at the fourth station, and, to say the truth, he was no loss, for although his assistance was of the greatest use at first, he had by this time become fatigued himself, and instead of jumping me up he only assisted in weighing me down. I jumped much better without him now, and the blocks towards the top of the Pyramid are not so high as the lower ones. One last longish effort then, enlivened by the chattering guide, who well-nigh dispersed the remaining breath that was in me by gravely inquiring if the gentleman down below were my husband and why my Mamma was not here with me, and I stood at the top of the Great Pyramid of Gizeh, with the famous view spread around me, of which I had so often heard and read, and so little dreamed of seeing with my own eyes.

After a few moments to recover breath and my senses, the first objects I sought were Cousin Phil and Selina. How grand I felt up there, and how very small indeed they looked as they waved their specks of handkerchiefs up in congratulation to me!

From the Summit of the Great Pyramid, 1825
Edward Lane

The view from the summit of the Great Pyramid is of a most extraordinary nature. On the eastern side, the eye ranges over an extensive, verdant plain, watered by numerous canals, and interspersed with villages erected on mounds of rubbish and surrounded by palm trees. In the distance is the Nile, beyond which are seen the lofty ma'd'nehs and Citadel of Musr [Cairo], backed by the low yellow ridge of Mount Moocku'tum. Towards the hour of sunset, it is curious to observe the enormous shadows of the two principal pyramids stretching across the cultivated plain.—Turning towards the opposite side, we behold a scene exactly the reverse of that which we have just been contemplating. Instead of the palm-groves and corn-fields, we have before us the undulating, sandy hills of the great Libyan desert.—The view of the Second Pyramid, from this commanding situation, is extremely grand. . . . A small portion of the Third Pyramid is also seen; with one of the small pyramids on its southern side. The space which lies on the west of the Great Pyramid, and north of the Second, is covered with oblong tombs, having the form of truncated pyramids, which, from this height, appear like patches of gravel.—The head of the Great Sphinx, and the distant pyramids of Ab'oo Seer, Sack'cka'rah, and Dah'shoo'r, are seen towards the south–south-east.

The ascent to the summit of the Great Pyramid is not dangerous; though rather tedious. . . . At, or near, any of the angles, we find, on almost every course, or range of stone, a secure and wide footing. Some of the steps are breast-high; and these, of course, are awkward masses to climb. Rather more than half-way up the north-eastern angle is a gap, formed by the displacing of several stones; from which I often saw vultures fly out. I very frequently observed several of these birds soaring above and around the two principal pyramids.

Many stones have been thrown down from the top of the Great Pyramid: which, consequently, wants about 25 feet (or perhaps more) of its original height; for, without doubt, it terminated in a point. It is worthy of remark that Diodorus Siculus describes the top of the Pyramid as being six cubits (or nine feet) square; Pliny states it to have been, in his time, 25 feet; or, according to some copies of his work, 15 feet; the latter of which readings must be considered the more correct.

I sometimes loitered about the Pyramids until half an hour or more after sunset, when the gloom contributed much to the grandeur and solemnity of the scene; and on one occasion I ascended the Great Pyramid about two hours before day-break, and waited upon the summit until sun-rise. It was extremely cold; and the wind, sweeping up the northern side of the Pyramid, sounded like a distant cataract. The Second Pyramid was at first faintly discernible; appearing of vastly more than even real magnitude. Soon afterwards, its eastern side was lighted up by the rising moon; and the effect was truly sublime. By the side of the pile of stones on top of the Great Pyramid, I found shelter from the wind; and there I sat, muffled up, by my snoring servant, till, I, also, was overcome by sleep.

I awoke a little before sunrise; but was so chilly and hungry that I could not remain much longer to enjoy the prospect, which at that hour is particularly beautiful.

As Old Cheops Has Done, 1843
Countess Hahn-Hahn

Dear Brother,—If any one had said to me up there, between the foundation of this pyramid and that of the railroad at Vienna there were as many thousand years as there are thousands of miles from the planet Earth to the planet Syrius, I should have answered at once, "Of course there are!" I seemed to be standing on an island in the midst of the ether, without the slightest connection with all that hearts are throbbing with below. Time seemed to have rent a cleft around me deeper than the deepest ravine in the highest mountain of the Alps. Then one's very view below becomes so utterly—what shall I say?—so utterly lifeless. In the whole immense plain beneath you there is not one prominent feature. It is merely a geographical map with coloured spaces—blue-green, yellow-green, sap-green— just as the culture may be. Among them palm-woods and gardens like dark spots, canals like silver stripes, and banks like black bars. Far and faint the brownish, formless masses of the city, wrapt in its own exhalations. And last of all, but seemingly quite near, the Desert—here no longer horrible. If in time itself there be such enormous deserts, where hundreds of years lie bare and waste, and only here and there some intellectual building, together with the builder, appear in the midst, like an oasis for the mind, why should not a few hundred miles lie barren here upon earth? But even if Fairyland itself lay smiling round, it would make no difference. The pyramid is everything. Like a great mind, it overpowers all in its vicinity. Even the Nile becomes insignificant. As the mountains attract the clouds, so does the pyramid attract the thoughts, and make them revolve perpetually round it. Dear Brother, it is a wonderful sight when man gets up his creations in a kind of rivalship with Eternity, as this old Cheops has done.

Celebrating on High, 1843
Dr. Richard Lepsius

Yesterday, the 15th October, was our king's birthday, and I had selected this day for the first visit to the Great Pyramids. We would there, with a few friends, commemorate our King and our Fatherland in a joyous festival. . . .

The morning was beautiful beyond description, fresh and festive. We rode in a long procession through the yet quiet city, and through the green avenues and gardens which are now laid out before it. Wherever, almost, that we met with new and well carried out works, Ibrahim Pasha was named to us as their originator. He seems to be doing much in all parts of Egypt for the embellishment and improvement of the country.

[The German party arrived at the Pyramids and pitched a tent] About thirty Bedouins, in the meanwhile, gathered around us, and waited for the moment when we should ascend the Pyramids, in order to raise us, with their strong brown arms, up the steps, which are between three and four feet high. Scarcely had the signal for departure been given, than immediately each of us was surrounded by several Bedouins, who dragged us up the rough, steep path to the summit, as in a whirlwind. A few minutes later and our flag[1] was unfurled on the summit of the oldest and highest of human works that is known, and we greeted the Prussian eagle with three loyal cheers to our king. Flying towards the south, the eagle turned his crowned head towards our home in the north, from which a refreshing wind blew, and diverted the rays of the mid-day sun from off us. We also looked homewards, and each one thought aloud, or silently in his heart, of those who loving, and beloved, he had left behind.

---

1. The great Prussian royal standard, the black eagle with the golden sceptre, the crown and the blue sword on a white background, which artists had sketched, stitched and fastened to a high pole.

After a prolonged tour around Europe and the Middle East, Mark Twain and his party reached Egypt and, on their way to the Pyramids, made their presence loudly felt.

Innocents Abroad, 1870
Mark Twain

The donkeys were all good, all handsome, all strong and in good condition, all fast and all willing to prove it. They were the best we had found anywhere, and the most *recherché*. I do not know what *recherché* means, but that is what these donkeys were, anyhow. Some were of a soft mouse-colour, and the others were white, black and vari-coloured. Some were close shaven all over, except that a tuft like a paint-brush was left on the end of the tail. Others were so shaven in fanciful landscape garden patterns, as to mark their bodies with curving lines, left by the shears. They had all been newly barbered, and were exceedingly stylish. Several of the white ones were barred like zebras with rainbow stripes of blue and red and yellow paint. These were indescribably gorgeous. Dan and Jack selected from this lot because they brought back Italian reminiscences of the 'old masters'.

The saddles were the high, stuffy, frog-shaped things we had known in Ephesus and Smyrna. The donkey-boys were lively young Egyptian rascals who could follow a donkey and keep him in a canter half a day without tiring. We had plenty of spectators when we mounted, for the hotel was full of English people bound overland to India and officers getting ready for the African campaign against the Abyssinian King Theodorus. We were not a very large party, but as we charged through the streets of the great metropolis, we made noise for five hundred, and displayed activity and created excitement in proportion. Nobody can steer a donkey, and some collided with camels, dervishes, effendis, asses, beggars, and everything else that offered to the donkeys a reasonable chance for a collision.

When we turned into the broad avenue that leads out of the city towards Old Cairo, there was plenty of room. The walls of stately date-palms that fenced the gardens and bordered the way threw their shadows down and made the air cool and bracing. We rose to the spirit of the time and the race became a wild rout, a stampede, a terrific panic. I wish to live to enjoy it again. . . . Arrived at Old Cairo, the camp-followers took up the donkeys and tumbled them bodily aboard a small boat with a lateen sail, and we followed and got under way. The deck was closely packed with donkeys and men; the two sailors had to climb over and under and through the wedged mass to work the sails, and the steersman had to crowd four or five donkeys out of the way when he wished to swing his tiller and put his helm hard-down. We had nothing to do; nothing to do but enjoy the trip; nothing to do but shove the donkeys off our corns and look at the charming scenery of the Nile. . . . At a distance of a few miles the Pyramids rising above the palms looked very clean-cut, very grand and imposing, and very soft and filmy as well. . . . A laborious walk in the flaming sun brought us to the foot of the great Pyramid of Cheops.

It was a fairy vision no longer. It was a corrugated, unsightly mountain of stone. Each of its monstrous sides was a wide stairway which rose upwards, step above step, narrowing as it went, till it tapered to a point far aloft in the air. Insect men and women . . . were creeping about its dizzy perches, and one little black swarm were waving postage stamps from the summit—handkerchiefs will be understood . . . . On the one hand a mighty sea of yellow sand stretched away toward the end of the earth, solemn, silent, shorn of vegetation, its solitude uncheered by any forms of creature life; on the other, the Eden of Egypt was spread below us—a broad green floor, cloven by the sinuous river, dotted with villages, its vast distances measured and marked by the diminishing stature of receding clusters of palms. It lay asleep in an enchanted atmosphere. There was no sound, no motion. Above the date-plumes in the middle distance, swelled a domed and pinnacled mass, glimmering through a tinted, exquisite mist; away toward the horizon a dozen shapely pyramids watched over ruined Memphis: and at our feet the bland, impassive Sphinx looked out over the picture from her throne in the sands as placidly and pensively as she had looked upon its life full fifty lagging centuries ago.

> Constance Sitwell creates a sense of endless time in her writing, recognizing times past while giving a very real sense of times present.

Lotus and Pyramid, 1927
Constance Sitwell

I was sitting on the window sill of my room eating sugar cane. It was so juicy and fresh one could go on nibbling at it all day. The Soudanese servant, in a green cap and full green trousers, just now brought in a basket-full cut up into pieces, and set it down on the floor with a wide smile. My window is high above the ground; beneath, the white-washed walls of the hotel ache in the midday glare; across the sand I can see the two great Pyramids, all their colour bleached out by the fierce light. But early this morning they looked very different. Just as the sun rose I came to this window and saw them standing there drowsily splendid, a tigerish gold set on the tigerish sand.

When I first drew near the Great Pyramid it was with a feeling of real shrinking. My mind was bludgeoned and I lifted my bewildered eyes; it was almost painful to realise that this was the work of men's slight hands. One wanders along the base, wondering insanely at the vast blocks so perfectly placed along the bottom courses, one stops at the corners to gaze insanely at the fabulous line that goes slanting up and down into the sapphire blue.

The sun beat down on that stupendous slope of stone, and up on it a scattering of tiny men were crawling like sluggish flies; and presently I too began to climb up; we were making for the small opening that leads downward to the King's

Chamber. We reached it at last and the Bedouin in fluttering garments, who was a guide, slid down the polished shaft, at the bottom of which he lit some magnesium wire which showed a narrow gleaming passage going steeply down into the core. The unnatural light played pallidly upon the smooth dark stone as we followed after him. How hot it was in the thick darkness! As we plunged deeper into that stifling fastness of stone an awful oppression seized me, and at last when we came to the solemn bat-infested chamber which contains the royal sarcophagus the sense of the weight pressing downwards became almost more than I could bear. There was something terrible in the thought of the monstrous walls that surround the little empty tomb of sombre reddish granite.

That was my first impression, but later the pyramids grew very familiar. In the evening of the day before we started up the Nile I found my way to a little pyramid, half ruined, near by, and I climbed on to a rock at its base to sit and draw there. A tiny Arab boy came along behind. He was dressed in black with an old black cloak and had a round dirty-white cap on his head. His face was round too, and his smile always ready. When I sat on the sand he jerked off his ragged cloak in an instant and spread it on the ground, and while I sketched he sat holding my paint-box in one hand and my paint-brush in the other.

He had some friends who joined us: a boy from Tunis with pale golden-brown skin, and a diminutive donkey-boy dressed in a stained garment of yellow who dragged the dusty donkey behind him without even one necklet of beads to adorn it. He was seven years old, he said; his donkey looked a hundred. His small wrinkled face was as yellow as his dress, and his name, he told me with some importance as he lit a cigarette, was Abbas. I thought I should never forget that prematurely old little creature who never smiled but puffed brazenly on his cigarette.

The boy from Tunis said that he could divine the future. He stared at me and then drew the sun's disk with rays spreading all round it in the powdery sand. Stooping lower and lower over the circle of his sun with an absorbed face he kept counting these rays, and muttering words that the others tried to translate. Having reached his conclusion, he straightened himself and pronounced: "Not happy, if too much thinking." I thanked him but replied that I did not agree. For the moment, after taking my coin, he looked at me in silence, then kicking away the traces of his sun with his hard feet, he walked off apparently heading for the empty desert.

6

The Fayoum

Away from the main flow of the Nile, reached today by the desert road from Giza, the Fayoum is an area of verdant cultivation around a wide lake, surrounded by rocky hills and expanses of desert. A thirteenth-century Syrian amir, thinking back to the gardens surrounding his home city of Damascus, wrote of the Fayoum: "Cool are the dawns; prolific are the trees; diverse are the fruits; little are the rains."

The Fayoum, c. 1000
al-Muqaddasi
Al-Fayyum is an important place, with fields of finest rice, and cotton of an inferior quality. It has a number of rich villages.

Cairo to the Fayoum, 1873
Murray's Handbook
By those who have the time to spare for this expedition it is well worth undertaking, as it introduces them to a country differing a good deal from its general aspect from the valley of the Nile. The antiquary will find much to interest him

in the supposed sites of Lake Moeris and the Labyrinth, and the ruins on the shore of Birket el Korn; while to the sportsman the Fayoum in the winter months offers more attractions than any other part of Egypt. . . . The best way of reaching the Fayoum is by railway as far as Medeeneh. There camels and donkeys can be procured for visiting the Birket el Korn and other places.

The province of Egypt called the Fayoum is a natural depression in the Libyan hills, surrounded on all sides by desert, save where a narrow strip of soil borders the canal leading to it from the Nile. It is thus almost an oasis, owing its fertility to the water of the Nile, introduced through a natural isthmus in the desert surrounding it. Its present name, *Fyoom*, is probably derived from the ancient Egyptian word *Pi-om,* "the Sea"—an appellation aptly applied to a country which contained such a splendid system for storing and distributing water, as that with which the Fayoum was endowed by King Amenemhat III, the constructor of Lake Moeris and the Labyrinth. . . . . This reputation for fertility it still enjoys, and though its merits have been greatly exaggerated, it is still superior to other parts of Egypt from the state of its gardens and the variety of its productions; since, in addition to corn, cotton and the usual cultivated plants, it abounds in roses, apricots, figs, grapes, olives, and several other fruits, which grow there in greater perfection and abundance than in the valley of the Nile; and the rose-water used in Cairo comes from the neighbourhood of Medeeneh.

Tradition tells that the Fayoum is not an entirely natural area— it was created in the far-distant past by diverting the Nile.

A Land Created, c. 1000
al-Muqaddasi
The Nile used not to reach to al-Fayyum, so the people complained to Joseph— peace be on him—about it. He built a dam in the river, and at the bottom of it he installed valves, inducts of glass. The dam retained the water, so that it rose until it reached the ground of al-Fayyum, and irrigated it. At present it is the most watered area in Egypt—do you not see that there are the farms of rice, or do you not notice the burden of its land taxes, the greatness of its income? During its flood the water goes over the top of the dam; so sometimes they allow the boats to go over with the flow, and they glide down safely, though sometimes they capsize and turn upside down. When the people no longer need the water, the valves are opened and the water subsides.

All the wells that are close to the Nile are sweet, while those some distance away from it are disagreeable. The best baths are those by the shore. Entering through the town are canals from which they draw their water by means of water wheels. On the Nile itself also are numerous wheels which irrigate the gardens when the river is low. The water at al-Fayyum is unhealthy because it flows over the rice farms.

Joseph's Canal, 1985
William Golding
Then we drove south for about twenty kilometres along the side of the canal in
sugar cane country. I looked at this canal until it became ordinary to me. It was a
canal, that was all. Idly, I asked Alaa which canal it was and he said it was the Bahr
Yusuf. I was moodily and quite illogically vexed. For Joseph's Canal is alleged by
all persons like myself who prefer a good story to literal historical accuracy (whatever *that* may happen to be) is, I say, alleged to be the very canal that Joseph—he
of the coat of many colours—built for Pharaoh. They say—*that lot* say—that it
isn't Joseph's canal but a canal built by a much later Joseph. Did you ever hear
anything so silly? Before I had seen it I had already made my mind that even if it
wasn't biblical Joseph's actual ditch, his must have lain along the same line so
what's the odds? You put a canal in the best place for it so the later one was no
more than a restoration of the original. I had promised myself such a thrill at seeing
it; but now I had been looking at it for twenty kilometres and made it so ordinary
to myself that my promised *frisson* was entirely lacking.

But still, it was Joseph's Canal. It was, I think, a greater, a more impressive, a
wider leap of the imagination than the pyramids. There was and is a great
depression in the desert on the western side of the Nile opposite Cairo. This is
the Fayoum, between twenty and thirty miles square. Right back in the earliest
pharaonic days someone conceived the idea of deflecting surplus flood water from
the river into that depression and then—here is the leap—of letting it out again
into the Nile when the flood was inconveniently low. But this join between the
main stream and the Fayoum could not be made down by Cairo. The main stream
for obvious hydrostatic reasons had to be tapped hundreds of miles to the south
so that the gradient of the canal would be so gradual the water would be control-
lable. So there the canal is, huge in length, vast in scope and breathtaking in the
sheer imaginative size of the conception. Now here it was, a canal like any other
and I found I had to screw my wits up to remember what it was I was looking at.
This was Joseph's artificial river (to match his granaries) which turned the Fayoum
into the first man-made lake.

From the summit of the Pyramid of Amenemhat III, a fine
view is obtained of the fertile province of Fayoum, stretching
to the northward and westward, far into the Western Desert.

Looking down across the Fayoum, 1836
Charles Rochfort Scott
A narrow gorge at its eastern extremity connects the Fayoum with the valley of
the Nile; but, on every other side, it is bounded by arid sandy mountains. The
bottom of this singular basin is nearly flat, and in great part covered with plantations of olive, fig, and other fruit trees; these present a remarkable contrast to the

other cultivated plains of Egypt, on which, save the melancholy palms that shelter the villages scattered over them, there is not a tree to break the wavy horizon of corn and cotton.

The surface of the Fayoum is not, however, less richly carpeted from being thus screened and overshadowed. Vines, rose bushes, and indigo, grow luxuriantly beneath the shade of the olive groves; whilst flax, cotton, and the sugar-cane, thrive well in the more open grounds; but for the last named the climate of Upper Egypt is better suited. The rose water of Fayoum is much and deservedly esteemed.

This province owes its great productiveness—its existence perhaps—to the Birket Keroun, or Lake Moeris, which, receiving the flood of the Nile, by means of a branch canal from the Bahr Yousef, retains a sufficient quantity of water to irrigate the circumjacent country for a considerable time after the inundation of the river has subsided.

A second pyramid stands (where the valley of the Fayoum may be said to commence) about five miles to the east at Illaoum. The gorge, which serves as the link, connecting the cultivation of the Fayoum with that of the valley of the Nile, is about four miles wide.

The area of the Fayoum, according to the best modern geographers, is but six hundred square miles, of which Lake Moeris covers about one hundred and eighty. According to Herodotus, the lake alone was in his time three thousand six hundred stadia (nearly four hundred and fifty miles) in circumference, and two hundred cubits deep!

This immense lake he states to have been entirely a work of human labour, and he naturally became very curious to learn what had been done with the earth that had been excavated in its formation, which he at length satisfied himself had been thrown into the Nile.

Let not those, therefore, who—pinning their faith to the Greek geographer—believe that the Delta is a gift of the Nile, wonder what country furnished the soil to fill up the huge gulph. Herodotus's Lake Moeris solves the mystery, for it alone would have supplied sufficient earth to cover the whole Delta with a much thicker layer than is to be found elsewhere.

Buckingham, a well-read merchant naval captain, wrote in his journal of his visit to the Fayoum and four decades later offered this beautiful description to the world in his autobiography.

Collecting Dewdrops, 1813
James Silk Buckingham

As night approached the captain insisted on mooring the boat, though, as the sky was clear, the moonlight bright, and no serious impediments existed to the navigation of the stream, we might have proceeded with safety; but in the East nothing is done in a hurry; time is deemed of little value, and custom is paramount above all reasoning. I therefore resigned myself to the order, and passed the hours till midnight in entertaining conversation with the veteran reis. Though he had lived upon the water for nearly half a century, he had never descended the Nile below Cairo, or even seen the sea; so that my accounts of the Ocean and its perils had all the terror and all the charm of a romance for him; and he looked upon me with additional veneration for the wonders I had described to him.

As we approached that part of Egypt which includes the province of Fayoum, where the celebrated Lake of Moeris, the Labyrinth, and the Pyramids, visited and described by Herodotus are placed, I devoted a few days to an excursion on horse-back to this celebrated spot. We passed through large tracts of land devoted exclusively to the cultivation of roses, extending for miles, and producing millions upon millions of this queen of flowers, from which nearly all the rose-water, and otto or oil of roses, used in and exported from Egypt to all parts of the world, is distilled.

Let me confess to a piece of romantic or sentimental folly as some will deem it, or affectation as others may regard it, which I began to practise here. I had with me a small cut glass vase or bottle, procured at Cairo, into which I began to collect the dew-drops from roses every morning, wherever I found them,—and there are few gardens in Egypt without a flower,—intending to store them up, till the bottle was full, as collected from my own hand from day to day, and therefore the more worthy of being presented, to my dear wife; to whom I ultimately sent them round the Cape of Good Hope, from India, with some appropriate verses, which will be recorded in their proper place. I can only say, that after my morning's devotions, this was one of the most agreeable occupations of the day; and I should have accounted it as a severe misfortune if I had either broken or lost this little treasure, which increased in worth and importance, in my own estimation at least, every day.

The time of my excursion was sufficient to enable me to see much of the memorable site of the ancient lake and its accessories; and some fifty pages of my Journal are filled with the result of my researches, but there is neither time nor space to record them here. I must content myself with transcribing one solitary passage only.

It is scarcely possible to describe in too glowing colours the riches and fertility of the soil over which we passed in the continuation of our route from Hillahoun to Medineh Faioum. All around us seemed one wide garden, crossed and intersected with a thousand meandering rivulets (for such the smallest of these serpentine canals appeared), realising the expression of Moses, who speaks of Egypt as being "watered like a garden of herbs," and strewed with groves and fields, flocks and hamlets, and a teeming population. The heart expands on witnessing such delightful scenes; and on recurring to the source of all this indescribable fertility, one no longer wonders at the veneration in which the ancients held the Nile: "than whom," said Plutarch, "no god was ever more solemnly worshipped," and the grand annual festival in favour of which, says Heliodorus, "was the most solemn of all those observed by the Egyptians, who regarded their river as the rival of heaven, since, without clouds or rain, he watered and fertilised the land."

Sailing toward the Temple of Jupiter Ammon, 1819
Giovanni Belzoni

. . . we put on board some provisions and made towards the west, where the famous Labyrinth is supposed to have been situated. The water of the lake was good enough to drink, though a little saltish; but it was only this year that it could be drunk at all, owing to the extraordinary overflow of the Nile, which surmounted all the high lands, and, in addition to the Bahr Yousuf, came in such torrents into the lake, that it raised the water twelve feet higher than it ever had been in the memory of the oldest fisherman. We advanced towards the west, and at sunset, saw the shore quite deserted, with nothing to look at but the lake and the mountains on the northern side of it. Our boatman lighted a fire, while the other went to fish with a net, and soon returned with a supper of fish.

The land we were now in, had anciently been cultivated, as there appeared many stumps of palm and other trees nearly petrified. I also observed the vine in great plenty. The scene here was beautiful. The silence of the night, the beams of the radiant moon resting on the still water of the lake, the solitude of the place, the sight of our boat, the group of fishermen, and the temple a little way off (Kassar-el-Karon), . . . Nothing could be more pleasing to my imagination.

[On the next day they continued west to near the end of the lake, where they landed and Belzoni set off with two boatmen to the temple named Kassar-el-Karon, standing in the ruins of a town.]

The temple is placed on a small eminence, bearing marks of having been washed by the lake. At its entrance, which faces south-east, there is a portico unlike any other in Egypt, and bearing a Greek inscription, in which the name of Thermusis occurs. . . . . All its walls have the inclination observable in genuine Egyptian buildings; every part is symmetrical; and the winged globe over the entrance, the only external ornament, is alone sufficient to show by what people it was built. Five halls may be traced, though filled with rubbish; and the walls of the inmost, which is the sanctuary, are adorned with sculptures, among which Apis is clearly recognised. Behind it there is a very lofty and strongly re-echoing chamber, quite dark, and accessible only by a small aperture very easily concealed. This place was designed to hide the person who secretly delivered the oracles which the god was supposed to communicate. On the side of the large chamber, there are five small ones, quite unornamented, and now choked up with rubbish. In the interior of the building, there is a flight of steps leading to an upper storey, on the walls of which human figures appear among the sculptures, and among them Cneph or Cnuphis, the Jupiter Ammon of the Greeks, to whom this temple was dedicated. It was long taken for part of the Labyrinth.

The Labyrinth? c. 450 B.C.
Herodotus

I visited this place, and found it to surpass description; for if all the walls and other great works of the Greeks were put together in one, they would not equal, either for labour or expense, this Labyrinth. Though no one would deny that the temples of Ephesus and Samos are remarkable buildings. The Pyramids too are astonishing structures, each one of them equal to many of the most ambitious works of Greece; but the Labyrinth surpasses them. It has twelve covered courts—six in a row facing north, six south. . . . Inside the building is of two storeys and contains 3000 rooms, of which half are underground, and the other half directly above them. The upper rooms I saw, and it is hard to believe they are the work of men; the baffling and intricate passages from room to room and from court to court were an endless wonder to me, as we passed from a courtyard into rooms, from rooms into galleries, from galleries into more rooms, and thence into more courtyards. The roof of every chamber, courtyard and gallery is, like the walls, of stone. The walls are covered with carved figures, and each court is exquisitely built of white marble and surrounded by a colonnade. The founder of the Labyrinth has been variously named by ancient authors, but it seems probable that its builder was Amenemhat III of the XIIth dynasty, the same who constructed the lake of Moeris. His is the oldest name found among the ruins.

> The Prussian Expedition to Egypt led by Dr. Richard Lepsius excavated what they believed was the elusive Labyrinth.

Working at the Labyrinth, 1843
Dr. Richard Lepsius

Here we have been, on the southern side of the Pyramid of Moeris, since 23rd May, and are settled among the ruins of the *Labyrinth;* for I was certain from the first, after we had made but a hasty survey of the whole, that we are perfectly entitled to designate them under this name: I did not, however, imagine that it would have been so easy for us to become convinced of this.

As soon as Erbkam had measured and noted down a small plan of what is extant, I caused some excavators to be levied from the surrounding villages, through the Mudhir of Medinet el Faium, the governor of the province, and ordered them to make trenches through the ruins, and to dig at four or five places at once. A hundred and eight people were thus occupied today. With the exception of those belonging to the nearest place, Howara, who return home every evening, I allow these people to encamp on the northern side of the Pyramid, and to spend their nights there. They have their overseers and bread brought to them; every morning they are counted, and they are paid every evening; each man receives a piastre, each child half a piastre, sometimes when they have been particularly diligent, as much as thirty paras (there are forty of them in a piastre). Each of the men brings with him a pickaxe, and a shallow woven basket *(maktaf)*. The children, who form the greatest number, are only required to bring baskets. The maktafs are filled by the men, and carried away by the children on their heads. This is done in long processions, which are kept in order and at work by special overseers.

Their chief pleasure and a material assistance in their daily work, is singing. They have some simple melodies, which at a distance, owing to their great monotony, make almost a melancholy impression.

Elizabeth Cooper traveled to and beyond the Fayoum in her search for the Bedouin in their home country—she went as a guest of the Bedouin.

Seeking the Bedouin, 1914
Elizabeth Cooper

To see the Bedouin one must go to his home and see him in his native tents. There are Bedouins in the cities, and one soon learns to distinguish them, with their keen eyes, eager faces, and majestic stride, from the more contemplative, quiescent Egyptian. But in the city he is not his true self, it is among the shifting sands of the desert that these fascinating people are at their best. There the Bedouin carries out his tribal customs, and there one realizes that it is true that the virtue of hospitality is the first and the greatest in the eyes of the Arab. To share food and drink with another is to covenant with him in amity for the period of his stay as a guest in the domain of his host. Even to give a drink of water to a guest is to recognize that he is worthy of peaceable reception, while to partake of salt is to enter into brotherhood. . . . Tourists passing through Egypt hear and read of these people who appeal so to the imagination, and around whom are woven the romances and legends dear to the Western heart, and often with a dragoman they make trips to the desert, living in their hired tents, eating the same food as they would at Shepheard's Hotel, doing the things that the dragoman thinks would appeal to the foreigner, and seeing the desert through the eyes of this clever showman, who makes everything picturesque if it is not already made so by nature. He is determined that his people will feel they have wisely invested their five pounds per day in desert scenery, even if he has to import his Bedouins from the neighboring villages. But we were long enough in Egypt to know that that was not the way to see the desert nor its people, and we were delighted when we received an invitation from a chief of the Bedouin tribe to pass several days with him in his castle at the edge of the desert.

We found a carriage waiting for us at the train; in fact a servant of the household had met us in the railway carriage several stations before our ultimate destination, assuring us in various signs and gestures mixed with Arabic and salaams, that we would very much be welcome at the castle of his chief.

We drove for miles across the well-irrigated lands, dotted with the variegated

gowns of the Fellaheen cutting the wheat with the old-fashioned sickle, the donkey trotting along under his burden of *bersein,* while here and there at the doors
of the mud huts women and children peered at us through their half-veiled faces.

As we drove into this semi-royal enclosure of the really sovereign potentate
who rules with no mean government thousands of Bedouins scattered through
Egypt and Tripoli, we were greeted by men of varying ages and degrees of distinction, all member of this important tribe which boasts of nine hundred years of
ancestry and which had originally come from Arabia, the native land of the
Bedouin.

[Elizabeth Cooper was met by the handsome chief and taken into his rambling
two-storied house. She was soon invited to the harem and was greeted, in English,
by a very pretty lady dressed in a modern French dress, with innumerable bracelets
and rings. Later she was led to one of the tents: the sides piled with valuable hand-
woven blankets, the floor covered with rugs—"and for our benefit some chairs
had been found."]

. . . I sat down and looked at this charming home, never having imagined a
tent could be so specious. The flap was open on two sides, and a strong wind from
the desert blew in, and it was cool, although a burning sun was beating upon it.
Around the sides were draped the gaily coloured blankets, striped red and yellow
and black. It looked like a stage setting.

> Bayard Taylor was visiting Egypt for the second time after
> ¬many years and noticed the changes from the preindustrial
> land he had first seen.

History and Science, 1875
Bayard Taylor

Senhoor is raised upon such lofty piles of ruin that there must have been a town
there, at least five thousand years ago. A part of it is again falling into decay: we
passed through streets where there were empty, roofless walls at one side, and
swarming habitations on the other. In Egypt, one might almost say, there is a
mud-hut barometer, building up in prosperity, and letting fall in a season of want.
The more frequent these fluctuations, the more rapidly the basis, or pedestal, of
the village is elevated; and variations from the general average would indicate the
particular fortune of each locality. This is a hint that I offer to archaeologists. . . .

At the very edge of the town we came upon mounds of debris loftier than any
house in it, and climbed to the summit to enjoy the far, sunny prospects. Below,
at the foot of the mound, stood the dismantled gateway of some old Saracenic
palace, rich with carvings and horse-shoe arches; away to the west rose the tall,
smoking chimney of the Khedive's sugar refinery at Nezleh. It was a confusing
jumble of old history and modern science; but the perfect day united all contra-
dictions in one harmonious blending of form and colour. After all, there is a great

deal of humbug in the assumption that old historic associations are disturbed, or put to flight, by the intrusion of modern (and hence, *of course,* prosaic) features, in a landscape. I rather fancy, that the mind which cannot retain such associations in the presence of steam-engines and stove-pipe hats, is but weakly receptive of them.

7
Arrangements for Traveling up the Nile

Travelers in Egypt in the past had to make careful preparations for their journey up the Nile. The Arab traveler Ebn Haukal made the journey sound a great adventure and a delight; John Fuller found the journey easy, but travelers needed advice and help from others—Harriet Martineau provided special advice for ladies. Early travelers needed a *firman*, or letter of introduction, from an important person in order to travel along the river. All was not always harmony, for, as two travelers told, the wind might not always blow, or it could blow too hard.

Up Nile, c. 960
Ebn Haukal
There is not any person who knows the foundations or source of the river nile; on this account, because it issues from a cavern in the territories of *Zingbar*, from a certain spot, which man may very nearly approach, yet never can arrive at: after this, it runs through the inhabited and desert parts of the Nubians to *Misr* (Egypt); and there where it first becomes a river, it is equal to the *Deljeh* and *Frat* (Tigris and Euphrates). And the water of the river nile is the most pure and delicious of all waters on the face of the earth.

Just an Excursion, 1819
John Fuller

The narrative of a voyage on the Nile cannot be very entertaining, the incidents being little more than a repetition of rowing and towing, far and contrary winds, now and then running on a sandbank, and occasionally a mutiny of the boatmen. The police of the country was at this time good, and such perfect tranquillity prevailed that there were no 'hair-breadth 'capes', no attacks from thieves or banditti to be recorded, as in the times of the older travellers. The voyage from Cairo to the Cataract might be performed with as much security, and almost with as much ease, as an excursion on the Thames; and in my progress up and down the Nile, I fell in with not less than five or six parties of Englishmen, and several other Europeans.

The Firman, 1737
Richard Pococke

To Emir Mahomet Kamali
What I order:
The person that brings this letter is an Englishman, going into Upper Egypt, to see whatever is curious there; so when he delivers this letter take care to protect him from all harm; and I command you again to take care of him. I desire you not to fail of it, for the love you bear us.

Osman Bey Merlue

In 1847, the first Murray's Guide to Egypt had two long pages of things useful for a journey, suggesting where they should be acquired. Many of them were standard items that anyone might consider for such a journey, but many were unexpected, and tell much about the journey itself. Harriet Martineau considered there were further requirements for lady travelers and writes of the particular care she regarded necessary for healthy and comfortable living in the east.

Things Useful for a Journey in Egypt, 1847
Sir John Gardner Wilkinson

Certain things are more or less necessary in Egypt, according to the wants of each individual. His list indicated which things should be brought from Europe [E], which could be bought in Cairo [C].

Two or three blankets [E], or *buttaneeh* [C] Mosquito net [C] Iron bedstead to fold up [E] Potatoes [C] Tobacco and pipes [C] Wire for cleaning pipes, put into reed [C] Some tow for the same purpose [C] Mouth-piece and pipe-bowls [C] Cheese [C], or English cheese [E] *Mishmish* and *Kumrededeen* apricots [C] Tea, wine, brandy [E or C] (White wine I believe to be better in a hot climate than red) Table with legs to fold up, and top to take off at the bottom, in order that it can be kept clean [E or C] Foot-tub and washing-tub [C] Flag [E] (for boat on the Nile) Small pulley and rope for flag [E or C] Tea-kettle [C] Various cutlery, dishes, pans [C] Baskets for holding these and other things [C] Broom called *makasheh*, and a tin for sweeping cabin [C] Gun, pistols [E] Powder and shot, etc [C] Ink, paper and pens, etc [C] Camp-stool and drawing table [E or C] Umbrella lined with dark colour for the sun [C] Drawing paper, pencils, rubber, etc, and colours in tin box of Windsor and Newton [E] Side-saddle [E] It will fit for a donkey also. A light Cairene donkey-saddle, but no bridge, the asses of Upper Egypt not being accustomed to such a *luxury* [C] Curtains for boat, of common or other cotton stuff [C] A packing needle or two, and some string, thin ropes, needles, thread, buttons, etc are useful [C] Candlesticks [C] *Bardaks (Goollel)* or water bottles [C] Zeer, or jar, for holding water [C] A fine sieve for clarifying water Almond paste (*rooag, terweeg*) Some tools, nails and string [C] A *Kadoom* may serve as hammer & hatchet [C] Charcoal in mats [C] Fireplaces (*mungud*) [C] Small bellows or fan [C] Fez caps (*tarboosh, tarabeesh*) [C] Cafass, a coop for fowls, with moveable drawer White or light coloured boots or shoes, being cooler, and not needing blacking [E or C] Biscuit or bread twice baked [C] bread in the villages in Upper Egypt will not please everyone; but very good bread is to be had at Thebes, and that of Sioot and some other large towns is by no means bad. *Baliasi*, or earthen jars for flour, rice, butter, and other things rats might eat, are useful. [C] Candles in boxes, or in tin cases, but if in the latter not to be exposed to the sun. [C] In going to the Tombs, or caves, in Upper Egypt, it is well to remember always to have candles, and the means of lighting them. An iron rat-trap for the boat [C] A small boat should also be taken from Cairo, if there be not one belonging to the dahabaeh; It is useful for landing, for shooting, for sending a servant ashore to make purchases. Telescope, thermometer, aneroid barometer, if required [E] Measuring-tape and foot ruler [E] For observations, a sextant and artificial horizon. [E]

Hints to Ladies, 1846
Harriet Martineau

As the very disagreeable subject of the vermin which abound peculiarly in Egypt,—lice,—it is right to say a few words. After every effort to the contrary, I am compelled to believe that they are not always,—nor usually,—caught from the people about one: but they appear of their own accord in one's clothes, if worn an hour too long. I do not recommend a discontinuance of flannel clothing in Egypt.

I think it quite as much wanted there as anywhere else. But it must be carefully watched. The best way is to keep two articles in wear, for alternate days,—one on, the other hanging up at the cabin window,—if there is an inner cabin. The crew wash for the traveller; and he should be particular about having it done according to his own notions, and not theirs, about how often it should be. This extreme care about cleanliness is the only possible precaution, I believe: and it does not always avail; but it keeps down the evil to an endurable point. As far as our experience went, it was only within the limits of Egypt that the annoyance occurred at all. Fleas and bugs are met with: but not worse than at bad French and Italian inns.

The traveller should carry half a dozen gimlets, stuck into a cork, and daily at hand. They serve as a bolt to doors which have no fastening, as pins to anything he wants to fasten or keep open, as pegs to hang clothes, or watch, or thermometer upon; as a convenience in more ways than could be supposed beforehand.—Two or three squares of Mackintosh cloth are a great comfort,—for keeping bedding dry,—and for ablution, and for holding one's clothes in bathing. By substituting them for carpets, also, in Nile boats, there is a relief from danger or vermin.

As for dress,—the first consideration, both for gentlemen and ladies is to have every possible article, made of material that can be washed:—gloves, among the rest. Cotton or thread gloves are of no use, unless of the stoutest kind. The hands are almost as much burned with these as with none. Woodstock gloves (which bear washing well) are good, though, of course, they do not look very handsome.—Brown Holland is the best material for ladies' dresses; and nothing looks better, if set off with a little trimming of ribbon, which can be put on and taken off in a few minutes.—Round straw hats, with a broad brim, such as may be had at Cairo for four or five shillings, are the best head-covering. A double ribbon, which bears turning when faded, will last a long time, and looks better than a more flimsy kind. There can hardly be too large a stock of thick-soled shoes and boots. The rocks of the Desert cut up presently all but the stoutest shoes: and there are no more to be had.—Caps and frills, of lace or muslin are not to be thought of, as they cannot be 'got up', unless by the wearer's own hands. Habit-shirts of Irish linen or thick muslin will do; and, instead of caps, the tarboosh, when within the cabin or tent, is the most convenient, and certainly the most becoming headgear; and the little cotton cap worn under it washed without trouble. Fan and goggles,—goggles of black woven wire,—are indispensable.

No lady who values her peace on the journey, or desires any freedom of mind or movement, will take a maid. What can a poor English girl do who must dispense with home-comforts, and endure hardships that she never dreamed of, without the intellectual enjoyments which in her mistress compensate (if they do compensate) for the inconveniences of Eastern travel? If her mistress has any foresight, or any compassion, she will leave her at home. If not, she must make up her mind to ill-humour or tears, to the spectacle of wrath or despondency, all the way. If she will have her maid, let her, at all events, have the girl taught to ride,—and to ride well: or she may have much to answer for. To begin to ride at her years is bad enough, even at home, where they may be a choice of horses, and the rides are only moderate in length. What is a poor creature to do who is put upon a chance horse, ass, or camel, day by day, for rides of eight hours' long, for weeks together? The fatigue and distress so caused are terrible to witness, as I can testify,— though we were happily warned in time, and went unencumbered by English servants altogether.

> When travel in Egypt became well organized, particularly after steamships could bring people from Europe quickly and easily, a good trade grew up in hiring out large comfortable sailing boats, *dahabiyas.*

The Dahabiya, 1873
Amelia Edwards
A dahabeeyah, at the first glance, is more like a civic or an Oxford University barge than anything in the shape of a boat with which we in England are familiar. It is shallow and flat-bottomed, and is adapted for either sail or rowing. It carries two masts: a big one near the prow, and a smaller one at the stern. The cabins are on deck, and occupy the after-part of the vessel; and the roof of the cabins forms the raised deck, or open-air drawing-room. This upper deck is reached from the lower deck by two little flights of steps, and is the exclusive territory of the passengers. The lower deck is the territory of the crew. A dahabeeyah is, in fact, not very unlike the Noah's Ark of our childhood, with this difference—the habitable part, instead of occupying the middle-part of the vessel, is all at one end, top-heavy and many-windowed; while the fore-deck is not more than six feet above the level of the water. The hold, however, is under the lower deck, and so counterbalances the weight at the other end. Not to multiply comparisons unnecessarily, I may say that a large dahabeeyah reminds one of old pictures of the Bucentaur, especially when the men are at their oars.

The kitchen—which is a mere shed like a Dutch oven in shape, and contains only a charcoal stove and a row of stewpans—stands between the big mast and the prow, removed as far as possible from the passengers' cabins. In this position the cook is protected from a favourable wind by his shed; but in the case of a contrary wind he is screened by an awning. How, under even the most favourable circumstances, these men can serve up the elaborate dinners which are the pride of a Nile cook's heart, is sufficiently wonderful; but how they achieve the same results when wind-storms and sand-storms are blowing, and every breath is laden with the fine grit of the desert, is little short of miraculous.

Thus far, all dahabeeyahs are alike. The cabin arrangements differ however, according to the size of the boat; and it must be remembered that in describing the Philæ, I describe a dahabeeyah of the largest build—her total length from stem to stern being just one hundred feet, and the width of her upper deck at the broadest part being little short of twenty.

Our floor being on a somewhat lower level than the men's deck, we went down three steps to the entrance door, on each side of which there was an external cupboard, one serving as a storeroom and the other as a pantry. This door led into a passage out of which opened four sleeping-cabins, two on each side. These cabins measured about eight feet in length by four and a half in width, and contained a bed, a chair, a fixed washing-stand, a looking-glass against the wall, a shelf, a row of hooks, and under each bed two large drawers for clothes.

At the end of this little passage another door opened into the dining saloon— a spacious, cheerful room, some twenty-three or twenty-four feet long, situate in the widest part of the boat, and lighted by four windows on each side and a sky-light. The panelled wall and ceiling were painted in white picked out with gold; a cushioned divan covered with a smart woollen rep ran along one side; and a gay Brussels carpet adorned the floor. The dining-table stood in the centre of the room; and there was ample space for a piano, two little book-cases, and several chairs. The window-curtains and the portières were of the same rep as the divan, the prevailing colours being scarlet and orange. Add a couple of mirrors in gilt frames; a vase of flowers on the table (for we were rarely without flowers of some sort even in Nubia, where our daily bouquet had to be made with a few bean blossoms and castor-oil berries); plenty of books; the gentlemen's guns and sticks in one corner; and the hats of all the party hanging in the spaces between the windows; and it will be easy to realise the homely, habitable look of our general sitting-room.

Another door and passage, opening from the upper end of the saloon, led to three more sleeping rooms, two of which were single and one double; a bath-room; a tiny back staircase leading to the upper deck; and the stern cabin saloon. This last, following the form of the stern, was semicircular, lighted by eight windows, and surrounded by a divan. Under this, as under the saloon divans, there ran a row of deep drawers, which, being fairly divided, held our clothes, wine, and books. The entire length of the dahabeeyah being exactly a hundred feet, I take the cabin part to have occupied about fifty-six or fifty-seven feet—and the lower deck to have measured the remaining forty-three feet.

For the crew there was no sleeping accommodation whatever, unless they chose to creep into the hold among the luggage and packing-cases. But this they never did. They just rolled themselves up at night, heads and all, in rough brown blankets, and lay about the lower deck like dogs.

Nile-boat Prayers, 1842
Sophia Poole

A custom which is always observed by the Arab boat-men at the commencement of a voyage much pleased me. As soon as the wind had filled our large sail, the Reis [captain] exclaimed: "El-Fat-Hah." This is the title of the opening chapter of the Koran (a short and simple prayer), which the Reis and all the crew repeated together in a low tone of voice. Would to Heaven that in this respect the example of the poor Muslim might be followed by our countrymen, that our entire dependence on the protecting providence of God might be universally acknowledged, and every journey, and every voyage, be sanctified by prayer.

Esprit du Nil, 1873
Amelia Edwards

And now we are on board and have shaken hands with the captain, and are as busy as bees; for there are cabins to be put in order, flowers to arrange, and a hundred little things to be seen to before the guests arrive. It is wonderful, however, what a few books and roses, an open piano, and a sketch or two, will do. In a few minutes the comfortless hired look has vanished, and long enough before the first comers are announced, the Philæ wears an aspect as cozy and home-like as if she had been occupied for a month.

As for luncheon, it certainly surprised the givers of the entertainment quite as much as it must have surprised their guests. Being, no doubt, a pre-arranged display of professional pride on the part of dragoman and cook, it was more like an excessive Christmas dinner than a modest midday meal. We sat through it unflinchingly, however, for about an hour and three quarters, when a startling discharge of firearms sent us all running upon deck, and created a wholesome diversion in our favour. It was the French boat signalling her departure, shaking out her big sail, and going off triumphantly.

I fear that we of the Bagstones and Philæ—being mere mortals and Englishwomen—could not help feeling just a little spiteful when we found the tricolor had started first; but then it was a consolation to know that the Frenchmen were going only to Assuân. Such is the *esprit du Nil*. The people in dahabeeyahs despise Cook's tourists; those who are bound for the Second Cataract look down with lofty compassion upon those whose ambition extends only to the First; and travellers who engage their boat by the month hold their heads a trifle higher than those who contract for the trip. We, who were going as far as we liked and for as long as we liked, could afford to be magnanimous. So we forgave the Frenchmen, went down again to the saloon, and had coffee and music.

At last all is ready. The awning that has all day roofed in the upper deck is taken down; the captain stands at the head of the steps; the steersman is at the helm; the dragoman has loaded his musket. Is the Bagstones ready? We wave a handkerchief of inquiry—the signal is answered—the mooring ropes are loosened the sailors pole the boat off from the bank—bang go the guns, six from the Philæ, and six from the Bagstones, and away we go, our huge sail filling as it takes the wind!

Happy are the Nile travellers who start thus with a fair breeze on a brilliant afternoon. The good boat cleaves her way swiftly and steadily. Water-side palaces and gardens glide by, and are left behind. The domes and minarets of Cairo drop quickly out of sight. The mosque of the citadel, and the ruined fort that looks down upon it from the mountain ridge about, diminish in the distance. The Pyramids stand up sharp and clear.

And now, as the afternoon wanes, we draw near to a dense, wide-spreading forest of stately date-palms on the western bank, knowing that beyond them, though unseen, lie the mounds of Memphis and all the wonders of Sakkârah. Then the sun goes down behind the Libyan hills; and the palms stand out black and bronzed against a golden sky; and the Pyramids, left far behind, look grey and ghostly in the distance.

Presently, when it is quite dusk and the stars are out, we moor for the night at Bedreshayn. Such was our first day on the Nile.

At Home on the Nile, 1849
Florence Nightingale

9 December: We shall have been on board a week tomorrow, and are now thoroughly settled in our house, all our gimlets up, our divans out, our Turkish slippers (mezd) provided, and everything on its own hook, as befits such close quarters. Now, if you ask me how I like the dahabieh life, I must say I am no dahabieh bird, no divan incumbent. I do long to be wandering about the desert by myself, poking my nose into all the villages and running hither and thither, and making acquaintances *où bon me semble*. I long to be riding on my ass across the plain, I rejoice when the wind is foul, and I can get ashore. They call me 'the wild ass of the wilderness, snuffing up the wind,' because I am so fond of getting away. I dearly love our dahabieh as my home, but if it is to stay in it the whole day, as we are fain to do when the wind is fair, that is not my way at all. However, I must tell you what walks I have had. This morning I went ashore with one of the crew at sunrise: it was cold, as cold as an English morning in October, and there was even a touch of hoar frost. But when I got under the shelter of the palm trees it was warmer. We went inland to a village, the situation of which was marked to us by its fringe of palms. Whenever you see these, you are sure of finding houses. We met a woman leading out her flock to water at a pool left by the inundation of the Nile, her black goats and white sheep. A little further on, we came to a brick-field, mud bricks laid out to bake in the sun, and full of chopped straw to make them adhere. It made one think of Rebekah and the Hebrews' task, at every turn. Then we walked round the village. But no European can have the least idea of the misery of an African village; if he has not seen it, no description brings it home. I saw a door about three feet high, of a mud hut, and peeping in, saw in the darkness nothing but a white-horned sheep, and white hen. But something

else was moving, and presently crawled out four human beings, three women and a child; they made a miserable pretence of veiling their faces before my Efreet. The only reason why they had not their camel with them was because he could not get in; next door was a maize enclosure, which differed from the first only by being cleaner, and having no roof. I looked over, and saw him. My Efreet is so careful of me that he won't let anybody come near me. If they do, he utters some dreadful form of words, which I don't understand, and they instantly fall back.

All the houses in the village were exactly like this, the mud walls very thick, nearly three feet. There appeared to me to be only one den inside, but I did not go in because I had promised not. Some little things were setting out to fetch water from the Nile, each with his amphora on the head, each with a rag which scarcely descended over the body, but shrouded the head (the Arab always covers his head). The dogs, who are like foxes, descended from the roofs at sight of me and my Efreet, but, awed by a similar charm, fell back.

The village, which seemed a considerable place, with a governor and a governor's house, possessed a khan. I peeped in. Strings of camels lay round the walls—a few inner cells behind them, roofless and floorless, showed tokens of travellers. But I was afraid of a commotion: so I veiled my face and passed on. A tray covered with the Turkish thimblefuls of coffee (which we also drink) was coming out—the only refinement the Arab possesses. In every village you see a coffee-house; generally a roofless cabin built of maize stalks, with mud benches around the inside, but always the thimblefuls of coffee, made, not like ours, but pounded, boiled for a moment, and poured off directly and drunk black. You cannot drink our coffee in this climate with impunity; it is too heating. We walked round the village, the huts all tumbled together up and down, as animals build their nests, without regularity or plan. The pigeons seemed better lodged: they had round mud cones provided for them, taller than the houses, stuck full of pots at the top for them to build in, and sticks for them to perch on. There was not much curiosity about me, though they (the Arabs, not the pigeons) could never have seen a European woman before; but they looked on with the same interest which the dogs did,—no more. By the time I came back and overtook the dahabieh, which had been tracked meanwhile for some distance (there was little wind, and that was south), the sun was high, but it was still too cold to breakfast on deck, as we have done once.

After breakfast we all five went ashore together for the first time. Paola and Mr. B. took their guns to shoot us our dinner and soon killed seven quails. We meanwhile wandered about in a desert place, or sat under what shelter we could find beneath a tuft of grass (the grasses grow as high as reeds), for the sun had by this time risen with a burning heat. A troop of mounted police, fine looking fellows, rode past us, turbaned and trousered, with guns and pistols.

It is rather tiresome always to have an Efreet with one on land, which I am never allowed to go without, and to be dogged by him everywhere, but it is a most courteous Efreet, and almost too afraid of my coming to harm. It will not let me even climb the dyke without helping me.

All my work since I came on board has been making the pennant (the flag and name of every boat are obliged to be registered at Cairo) blue bunting with swallow tails, a Latin red cross upon it, and ΠΑΡΘΕΝΟΠΗ [*Parthenope,* her sister's name and the name of their boat] in white tape. It was hoisted this morning at the yardarm, and looks beautiful. It has taken all my tape and a vast amount of stitches, but it will be the finest pennant on the river, and my petticoats will joyfully acknowledge the tribute to sisterly affection,—for sisterly affection in tape in Lower Egypt, let me observe, is worth having. The Union Jack flies at the stern, Mr. B.'s colours half-way up the rigging, all made by ourselves. For two days we had no wind, and tracked or rowed or pushed all day. On the third day the north wind rose and we stood away for Benisouef.

Onboard a River Steamer, 1863
Lucie Duff Gordon

After infinite delays and worries, we are at last on board, and shall sail tomorrow morning. After all was comfortably settled, Ismail Pasha sent for *all* the steamers up to Rhoda, near Minieh, and at the same time ordered a Turkish General to come up instantly somehow. So Latif Pasha, the head of the steamers, had to turn me out of the best cabin, and if I had not come myself, and taken rather forcible possession of the forecastle cabin, the servants of the Turkish General would not have allowed Omar to embark the baggage. He had been waiting all the morning in despair on the bank; but at four I arrived, and ordered the *hammals* to carry the goods into the fore-cabin, and walked on board myself, where the Arab captain pantomimically placed me in the right eye and on the top of his head.

Once installed, this became a harem, and I may defy the Turkish Effendi with success. I have got a good-sized cabin with good, clean divans round three sides for Sally [Lucie Duff Gordon's English maid] and myself. Omar will sleep on deck and cook where he can. A poor Turkish lady is to inhabit a sort of dusthole by the side of my cabin; if she seems decent, I will entertain her hospitably. There is no furniture of any sort but the divan, and we cook our own food, bring our own candles, jugs, basins, beds and everything. If Sally and I were not such complete Arabs we should think it very miserable; but as things stand this year we say, *Alhamdulillah*—it is no worse!

Luckily it is a very warm night, so we can make our arrangements unchilled. There is no door to the cabin, so we nail up an old plaid, and, as no one ever looks into a harem, it is quite enough. All on board are Arabs—captain, engineer and men. An English Sitt [lady] is a novelty, and the captain is unhappy that things are not *alla Franca* for me. We are to tow three dahabiehs—M. Mounier's, one belonging to the envoy from the Sultan of Darfur, and another. Three steamers were to have done it, but the Pasha had a fancy for all the boats, and so our poor little craft must do her best. Only fancy the Queen ordering all the river steamers up to Windsor!

At Minieh the Turkish General leaves us, and we shall have the boat to ourselves, so the captain has just been down to tell me. I should like to go with the gentlemen from Darfur, as you may suppose. See what strange combinations of people float on old Nile. Two English women, one French (Mme Mounier), one Frenchman, Turks, Arabs, Negroes, Circassians, and men from Darfur, all in one party; perhaps the third boat contains some other strange element. The Turks are from Constantinople and can't speak Arabic, and make faces at the muddy river water, which, indeed, I would rather have filtered. . . .

I am quite surprised to see how well these men manage their work. The boat is quite as clean as an English boat as crowded could be kept, and the engine in beautiful order. The head-engineer, Ahmed Effendi, and indeed all the crew and captain too, wear English clothes and use the universal, 'All right, stop her—*fooreh* [full] speed, half speed—turn her head,' etc. I was delighted to hear, 'All right— go ahead—*el-Fathah*' in one breath. Here we always say the *Fathah* (first chapter of the Koran, nearly identical with the Lord's Prayer) when starting on a journey, concluding a bargain, etc. The combination was very quaint.

Instructions to the Managers of Cook's Nile Steamers, 1892
John Mason Cook

> A flimsy little booklet with this title was issued to each manager and had to be returned "to the Chief Office in Cairo at the end of the season, or whenever the holder of it is called to some other position." One hears the voice of John Mason Cook as one reads. Examples of instructions include:

II Captain and Pilot (Reis barroni) must know the exact draught of the boat on which they are working.

IV Boats coming down the river must always take the Summer Channel, or the best Channel, and meet, on the western side, boats going up.

IX Steamers coming down and meeting another steamer or sailing boats going up and being in a strong current, must decrease her speed, but if the channel is very narrow she must, if necessary, turn round south again and go to shore.

XIV Steamers on starting from the shore must go slow.

XXII Steamers must anchor, stop or go on shore if there is a thick fog which prevents the Reis seeing the way, and the whistle must blow at intervals.

XXXI Should one steamer be following another, she must, at a distance of about 1/4 mile, give two long whistles by way of warning. . . . The Manager is the responsible person on board the steamer; he has full control of every department, and he is also responsible for every description of servants on board, but must not interfere with the navigation or the working of the engine.

In addition to the 'Instructions,' there are certain 'Rules.'
Among these were:

IV In case of steamers going aground the Captain must work in harmony with the
Reis as to the best means of getting off.

XIV Steamers to salute all Government steamers and Khedival yachts they meet
or pass, with whistle three times.

XV To salute our own steamers by dipping the Egyptian flag.

XVIII In *returning* the salute to a competitive steamer our steamer to dip Egyptian
flag three times.

Saluting steamers: Under no circumstances are our steamers to salute a
steamer of a competing company; but should the competing steamer salute
ours first, we must return the salute out of respect for the Egyptian flag.

Signal flags: Code for using them.

Blue: Make to shore or drop anchor mid-stream for important communication.

Green: Go easy or stop mid-steam, and wait for our felucca.

Yellow/white/blue and green is a code for where mail has been left.

Yellow and white: Can you spare provisions? If so, give one long whistle and wait
for our felucca.

Two long whistles means 'No'.

Under no circumstances are our steamers to stop, even if called upon to do so by
the reis of any competing steamers, even if they are badly stuck and require special
assistance. The only case under which our steamers can be allowed to assist would be
in the event of there being any danger to the passengers on board; but under no other
circumstances are our steamers to stop or render the slightest assistance to them.

Instructions for the 'housekeeping' side of the manager's duties:

A book must be kept by the Manager to enter all the menus of both luncheon and
dinner every day. [Such books are still kept by Nile steamers today.]

Now comes a warning:

Mr. J. M. Cook will most likely be on the river during the season. Managers to
keep a look out for him signalling any boat to stop at any point on the river, and
when he comes on board, to report to him any special matter of importance that
may have arisen during the voyage.

South by Train, 1873
Gabriel Charmes

Still I did not follow the Nile in order to go to Syout; I took the railway. The journey lasts twelve hours across a country singularly spoilt by the manufactories of Ismaïl Pacha and his sugar-cane plantations. On leaving Cairo at about eight in the morning, you enjoy the spectacle, always marvellous, of the first hours of the day in Egypt. On the right, the Lybian desert, guarded by the great Pyramids, extends beyond eye-reach its gilded undulations; in the centre, the green valley of the Nile awakes full of freshness and grace; further, the centre still, the Nile, dyed blue by the reflexion of the sky, unrolls far away its majestic curves gay with vivid colours. But what is particularly admirable, what partakes of the dream and fairy-land, it is the second line of the desert on the left, on the side of the rising sun. Every one of the softest shades of rose, blue, and violet shines over a range of hills united by slight depressions of ground; the colours pale away little by little on the slopes of these hills which lower gradually as far as the Nile, wrapping it there in great white sheets. Unfortunately, when the last Pyramids of Sakkarah are passed, and you arrive in Central Egypt, the picture changes completely. The valley of the Nile enlarges so much, that the desert on each side appears no longer like a light border on a blue sky. The plain is covered with fields of sugar-cane that resemble most deceptively fields of maize. Sometimes the crop is gathered, and then nothing more is distinguished than a blackish earth which the fellahs are turning over and over again. Immense factories, soiled with dust, rise here and there. These factories, the machinery of which comes from the workshops of the firm of Cail, are, it seems, most complete as sugar factories. But they, nevertheless, spoil the landscape in a manner most disagreeable. Nothing is more ugly than their thick columns of smoke rising in the transparent atmosphere of Egypt. The light cannot play on these opaque masses, that produce the effect of great blots on a brilliant picture. But then, if this part of Egypt is the least beautiful of all, it is in return the richest; it is there where are the daïras of Ismaïl Pacha; therefore everything there is wonderfully organized for the cultivation: canals run in every direction; the railway crosses flood gates of architectural pretension, but of a frightful Gothic style, whose construction has cost millions of francs, without mentioning the forced labour. A little agricultural railway serves to convey the sugar-cane. To see the smoke and dust rising everywhere in the sky, one would fancy, he was no longer in Egypt, but in Flanders. At last it comes to an end; at Thenéh, Minieh, Manfalout, etc., one sees Egypt again—Upper Egypt still more beautiful than the Delta. One runs along for hours a canal that irrigates all the country; it is filled with bathers clad solely in the sun-burnt bronzing that covers them; they are there by hundreds swarming in the water like frogs, and the passage of the train troubles in no way a modesty so little disposed to be scared. In fact, they do not appear naked to European eyes, so does their colour clothe them; they seem like figures of the kind that decorate chimney timepieces; their flesh looks like bronze, and if you did not see them move, you would take them really for statues beautifully sculptured.

It is about eight in the evening when the train arrives at Syout.

On the Boats, 1990
Deborah Manley

Today, unless you are adventurous enough to sail down the Nile by felucca, your journey will be in one of the 200 or so river boats that act like floating hotels between Luxor and Aswan. Hemmed in by the barrages and the 'British' dam at Aswan, they move up and down between the two all year long. They glory in great classical names like *Rameses, King of the River*, or *Nefertiti, King Tut, Ra* even, or have names which compete for today's dreams like *Moon River* or *Nile Splendor* (note the US spelling). Our boat was the MV *Atlas*, one of the smaller, less grandiloquent crafts, but comfy, well run and of a pleasing size. Sadly for the company which owned it (these floating hotels are owned by tourist companies or by the hotel chains who own the land-based hotels too), but pleasantly for us, it was hardly more than half full. When at capacity the *Atlas* would hold eighty-five passengers and a crew of sixty. These crew members would encompass a manager and two assistant managers (the manager is effectively the captain and chief executive, purser and PR manager rolled into one); a pilot and two assistants, an engineer and five assistants, a *maitre d'* and ten stewards, a housekeeper with ten staff, three barmen and nine sailors who doubled as porters, and ten service staff. In addition each tourist language group is accompanied by its own tour guide.

At any one time about a fifth of this hierarchy will be on ten days' leave after six weeks on the river. Many of them are able to visit their homes when the boats dock at Luxor or Aswan, but others come from as far away as Cairo.

How do all these people come to their jobs on the boats? For all except the manual workers there are various forms of apprenticeships. Some will have gone to hotel-management school; the guides will have done a university tourist course; the stewards come from long lines of Nubian domestic staff with experience passed down through the families. The pilots learn the river on feluccas and graduate up through work boats to the helm of a floating hotel, learning as they go. There is a lot of camaraderie among the pilots, who wave and shout across to one another from boat to boat as they pass—and give blasts of their horns.

We joined the helmsman one morning as he zig-zagged along past a village at the bend of the river. Despite his pointing them out to us, we could barely discern the slight ripple that warned of a sandbank below the surface, and guided the assured skill of his actions. Nowadays, since the High Dam, the river at least stays in one place. No longer do unexpected shoals catch unwary boats as they frequently did in the past.

At Aswan each company has its own anchorage. The Nile side is lined by arches on which are listed each company's boats, with steps dropping down the steep bank to the mooring. In Luxor and along the river it is a free for all, but the *Atlas* appears to have clout and seniority and often moors beside Luxor temple.

The boats may be lined up two or more deep. We briefly were boat eight on the outer edge. All the boats have a wide central reception area, and to reach an outside boat you walk straight through all of them from the shore.

Only on the River, 1836
John Lloyd Stephens

I have heard all manner of opinion expressed in regard to a voyage on the Nile; and may be allowed, perhaps, to give my own. Mrs. S. used frequently to say that, although she had traveled in France, Switzerland, Germany, Italy, and Sicily, she had never enjoyed a journey so much before, and was always afraid that it would end too soon. Another lady's sentiments, expressed in my hearing, were just the contrary. For myself, being alone, and not in very good health, I had some heavy moments; but I have no hesitation in saying that, with a friend, a good boat well fitted up, books, guns, plenty of time, and a cook like Michel, a voyage on the Nile would exceed any traveling within experience. The perfect freedom from all restraint, and from the conventional trammels of civilized society, form an episode in a man's life that is vastly agreeable and exciting. Think of not shaving for two months, of washing your shirts in the Nile, and wearing them without being ironed. True, these things are not absolutely necessary; but who would go to Egypt to travel as he does in Europe? "Away with all fantasies and fetters" is the motto of the tourist. We throw aside pretty much everything except our pantaloons; and a generous rivalry in long beards and soiled linen is kept up with exceeding spirit. You may go ashore whenever you like, and stroll through the little villages, and be stared at by the Arabs, or walk along the banks of the river till darkness covers the earth; shooting pigeons, and sometimes pheasants and hares, besides the odd shots from the deck of your boat at geese, crocodiles, and pelicans. And then it is so ridiculously cheap an amusement. You get your boat with ten men for thirty or forty dollars a month, fowls for three piasters (about a shilling), a pair, a sheep for half or three-quarters of a dollar and eggs almost for the asking. You sail under your own country's banner; and, when you walk along the river, if the Arabs look particularly black and truculent, you proudly feel that there is safety in its folds. From time to time you hear that a French or English flag has passed so many days before you, and you meet your fellow-voyagers with a freedom and cordiality which exist nowhere but on the Nile.

> **Although John Fuller was assured of the security of the journey, earlier travelers were not so safe—and even within one's boat there could be trouble. . . .**

Melancholy and Invaders, 1851
George Melly

The huge sails were loosed, and expanded to a mild evening breeze, with just strength enough to blow out the folds of our Union Jack, which flew proudly over us. It was an exciting moment, but I cannot say that it was wholly free from melancholy; for while we looked up the mighty river with eager impatience for the wonders it was to disclose, we could not but feel that, when

anchor was hauled up, we threw off our last hold of society, completely sev-
ered ourselves from all communication with our friends, and crossed the
confines of barbarism. But this impression was not allowed to deepen, and
speedily gave way before our earnest longing for new objects and other
regions.

It was late before I went to bed, and I had scarcely fallen asleep, when I was
aroused by a pressure on my feet. At first, I thought some one must be sitting
upon me, and was about to remonstrate, but a sudden squeaking undeceived
me, and I discovered that the intruders were three enormous rats, who had
stretched themselves very comfortably on the coverlet. Fortunately my boots
were at hand, and I flung one into the midst of them, on which they scampered
off in great dismay, vehemently protesting against such uncourteous treatment.
I then got up, and barricaded the door, which I was assisted in doing by one of
our servants.

A Nile journey can sound idyllic, but the weather is not
always ideal, and sailboats are dependent on a fair wind. The
wind on the Nile can be both too little and too great.

Tracking, 1873
Amelia Edwards

The good wind continued to blow all that night; but fell at sunrise, precisely when
we were about to start. The river now stretched away before us, smooth as glass,
and there was nothing for it, said Reïs Hassan, but tracking. We had heard of
tracking often enough since coming to Egypt, but without having any definite
idea of the process. Coming on deck, however, before breakfast, we found nine
of our poor fellows harnessed to a rope like barge-horses, towing the huge boat
against the current. Seven of the M.B.'s crew similarly harnessed, followed at a
few yard's distance. The two ropes met and crossed and dipped into the water
together. Already our last night's mooring-place was out of sight, and the
Pyramid of Ouenephes stood up amid its lesser brethren on the edge of the
desert, as if bidding us good-bye. But the sight of the trackers jarred, somehow,
with the placid beauty of the picture. We got used to it, as one gets used to
everything in time; but it looked like slaves' work, and shocked our English
notions disagreeably.

Thus the morning passes. We sit on deck writing letters; reading; watching the
sunny river-side pictures that glide by at foot's pace and are so long in sight. Palm-
groves, sandbanks, patches of fuzzy-headed dura and fields of some yellow-
flowering herb, succeed each other. A boy plods along the bank, leading a camel.
They go slowly; but they soon leave us behind. A native boat meets us, floating
down side-wise with the current. A girl comes to the water's edge with a great
empty jar on her head, and waits to fill it till the trackers have gone by. The

pigeon-towers of a mud-village peep above a clump of lebbek trees, a quarter of a mile inland. Here a solitary brown man, with only a felt skull-cap on his head and a slip of a scanty tunic fastened about his loins, works a shâdûf, stooping and rising, stooping and rising, with the regularity of a pendulum. It is the same machine which we shall see by and by depicted in the tombs at Thebes; and the man is so evidently an ancient Egyptian, that we find ourselves wondering how he escaped being mummified four or five thousand years ago.

By and by, a little breeze springs up. The men drop the rope and jump on board—the big sail is set—the breeze freshens—and, away we go again, as merrily as the day we left Cairo.

The Khamsin, 1849
Florence Nightingale

About three, the khamsin increased; it was a wind like this which destroyed six years ago a caravan of 300 camels belonging to Mehemet Ali. The air became filled with sand. The river seemed turned upside down, and flowing bottom upwards, the whirlwind of sand from the desert literally covering it. We could not see across the river; and when we could stand upon deck, which was not often, our eyes were completely filled and our faces covered with sand. As to the critic making Thames *not* to walk between his banks, he does not deserve the credit of originality for that idea, for Nile invented the plan first, and today instead of walking between his banks, his banks walked between him. I saw the sand blown up into the *ridge* upon the water, and it looked as if you could have passed the river on dry ground, only the dry ground was on the top. I am glad to have seen it, for I should never have believed in it if I had not, and I give you leave not to believe. By this time Nile seemed to be walking with his bed on his head; but it was no beneficent miracle, like the paralytic man's, for it looked as if earth, air, and water had been blasted together into one whirlwind of sand. We could not wash, for it was no use fishing for water in the Nile; instead of water he gave us a stone, i.e. a sand-bank. The waves were as high as when there is a moderate sea in the Channel, and the wind was hot. It grew dark, and the blast increased so, that we drove a stake into the bank and fastened a rope to it for the night.

Presently Paolo rushed in for one of the guns, which was always kept loaded. He said he saw a strange boat coming in sight. I ran out on deck after him and sure enough, in pitchy darkness, I saw one of the dahabiehs which had overtaken us in the afternoon, floating past us, bottom upwards; nothing to be seen of her passengers. She stuck in the sand just astern of us, and remained fast there. By this time the wind increased so much, and we bumped so incessantly that we were afraid the rope would not hold, and we put out another. I could not help laughing, in the middle of all this, at the figure of our Reis, who had squatted himself at the bottom of our little boat (which was between the dahabieh and the bank), and sat there smoking his pipe, and taking no further interest in the question. If the rope wouldn't hold it wouldn't, and why should he be disturbed?

I did not go to bed—we bumped incessantly, and at the stern especially so hard that we thought we must spring a leak. It was so dark that we could see nothing, but in the morning we found that our boat had been astride of the poor wreck all night, which had been whirled round by the eddy under us. At dawn I looked out, she had entirely gone to pieces,—nothing was left of her but a few of the cabin planks, which our boat picked up, a chest of clothes which we saved, and her oranges floating in the whirlpool. I never saw anything so affecting as those poor oranges, the last luxury of their life in the midst of death.

Torrents of rain were falling—our cabin roof was completely soaked through—the sky was still one heavy mass, but the wind had a little fallen, and we struggled on, towed by the wretched crew, their teeth chattering, dripping with wet, and evidently thinking of the Day of Judgement, the end of the world, was come (for to them rain is much what to us English an earthquake might be) to Manfaloot, which we reached about twelve. There we learnt the fate of the five boats which passed us yesterday to windward: four had gone down, and of their passengers, twenty (including women and children) had been lost.

Wind-bound, 1836
John Lloyd Stephens

On the eighth I had not made much more than fifty miles, and the wind was still ahead, and blowing stronger than ever; indeed, it seemed as if this morning, for the first time, it had really commenced in earnest. I became desperate and went ashore, resolved to wear it out. We were lying along the bank, on the Libyan side, in company with fifteen or twenty boats wind-bound like ourselves. It was near a little mud village, of which I forget the name, and several Bedouin tents were on the bank, in one of which I was sitting smoking a pipe. The wind was blowing down with a fury I have never seen surpassed in a gale at sea, bringing with it the light sand of the desert, and at times covering the river with a thick cloud which prevented my seeing across it. A clearing up for a moment showed a boat of the largest class, heavily laden, and coming down with astonishing velocity; it was like the flight of an enormous bird. She was under bare poles, but small portions of the sail had got loose, and the Arabs were out on the very ends of the long spars getting them in. One of the boatmen, with a rope under his arm, had plunged into the river, and with strong swimming reached the bank, where a hundred men ran to his assistance. Their united strength turned her bows around, upstream, but nothing could stop her; stern foremost, she dragged the whole posse of Arabs to the bank, and broke away from them perfectly ungovernable; whirling around, her bows pitched into our fleet with a loud crash; and tore away several of the boats, and carrying one off, fast locked as in a death-grasp, she resumed her headlong course down the river. They had gone but a few rods when the stranger pitched her bows under and went down in a moment, bearing her helpless companion also to the bottom.

8
The Journey to Luxor

 After the watery tenderness of the Delta and the strident grandeur of Cairo and the almost overwhelming magnificence of the Pyramids and Sphinx, travelers up the Nile met new experiences as they were transported toward Upper Egypt. The fascination of life along the Nile was reflected in the wall-paintings at Beni Hassan, and all around the travelers saw what Ibn Jubayr described in 1183 as "wondrous things."

The Constant Change of Scene, 1833
Robert Curzon

Nothing can be more secure and peaceable than a journey on the Nile, as everyone knows nowadays. Floating along in a boat like a house, which stops and goes on whenever you like, you have no cares or troubles, but those which you bring with you. . . . I can imagine nothing more delightful than a voyage up the Nile with agreeable companions in the winter, when the climate is perfection. There are the most wonderful antiquities for those who interest themselves in the remains of bygone days; famous shooting on the banks of the river; capital dinners, if you know how to make proper arrangements, comfortable quarters, and a constant change of scene.

Egyptian Harmony, 1868
Howard Hopley

There is a profound charm in this landscape; a beauty that grows slowly upon you. The climate also indisposes you for violent contrasts and excitement, you fall in with the prevailing tendency to the tranquil and solemn. All seems to harmonise with the inner impression of *Egypt* on your mind. And although as to mere size there exists nothing here to emulate the majesty of Alpine scenery, there is nevertheless a pervading sentiment and admixture of the sublime. A feeling of mystery may explain this. Looked upon from that point of view, no scenery, save perhaps the awful group of Sinai, can be grander or more severe than this; for the element of mystery tinctures everything in Egypt. Every vestige of its architecture, too, that you meet adds to the feeling. A great critic speaks of structures characterized by 'a severe and, in many cases, mysterious majesty, which we remember with an undiminished awe, like that felt at the presence and operation of some great Spiritual Power.' That is eminently true of the great piles of Egypt. Somehow you instinctively speak low when the Great Pyramid looms into sight. I have seen laughter stopped in an instant by that unexpected apparition.

Gradually, as you travel on, you come to perceive from whence spring the first glimmerings of Egyptian art. The relation of art to nature is nowhere so strongly marked as here. It was the landscape, ever rich in tropic beauty, the sweep of the majestic river, the eternal silence of the desert hills, that engendered in the minds of the early Egyptians feelings which were developed in their art. Most of what you now discover of mysterious yearning, of calm power, of pathos, of stability, as suggested in the paintings, sculpture, and architecture of Egypt, was first mirrored on the artist's soul by a contemplation of what he saw around him. This is manifest even in respect of outward form. The grand ideal of the Egyptian temple is to be found in the stratified cliff. On that fantastic wall you may define pylons, porticoes, pillared arcades without number. A very dull imagination might there build up temples grander than Karnak and more colossal than the pyramid. A chamber cut in the rock, vaulted as the heavens are vaulted, and sown over with golden stars on a field of azure—that was the beginning of all architecture. The very earliest column known is a twisted sheaf of water-lilies, of which the closed flowers form the capital, while the shaft was wreathed with paintings of the same. Lastly, by the pillar side, the artist placed Man, the master—or rather his representative, Osiris—shrouded and silent, bearing in his folded arms the symbols of power and judgment, but speechless. Nature could tell no more.

You can never in your thoughts detach the Egypt of the past from the Egypt of today; neither, indeed, can you ever quite exclude it from sight. Temples, scattered ruins on the plain, tombs sown thick along the mountain cliff on either hand, arrest your eye in succession. And with every thoughtful mind this undercurrent of feeling, as regards the past, must tincture the landscape with colourings of its own. It is a background never lost sight of. The incidents of the near landscape, those change, but that travels on with you. From the pyramids—which stand as man's handwriting upon Egypt, his autograph which Time cannot obliterate—onward to far Syene [Aswan] it is there.

Nile by Night and Dawn, 1845
Eliot Warburton

This sailing on the moon-lit Nile has an inexpressible charm; every sight is soft-ened, every sound is musical, every air breathes balm. The pyramids, silvered by the moon, tower over the dark palms, and the broken ridges of the Arabian hills stand clearly out from the star-spangled sky. Distant lights, gleaming faintly among the scarce seen minarets, mark the site of Cairo, whose voices come as the gargle of some huge fish as he wallows in the water, may disturb the silence for a moment, but it only makes the calm that follows more profound.

All nature seems so tranced, and all the world wound in such a dream, that we can scarcely realise our own identity: vainly we try to think of Europe and gas lamps and new police, and politics. Hark! to the jackal's cry among the Moslem tombs! See where the swarthy pilot sits, statue-like with his turban and flowing beard; those plains before us have been trod by Pharaohs; these waters have borne Cleopatra; yonder citadel was the home of Saladin! We need not sleep to dream.

The night is gone—gone like a passing shadow; the sun springs suddenly into the throne of purple and rose-coloured clouds that the mist has left for him. There is scarcely a dawn—even now it was night—then day—suddenly as a cannon's flash.

Our boat lay moored to the bank. Mahmoud started to his feet, and shouted *Yallough!* like a trumpet. Till then the deck seemed vacant; the crew were sleep-ing in grave-like apertures between the planks, wrapped in their white capotes. These were very shroud-like, and gave their resurrection a rather ghastly appearance. All nature seems to waken now; flocks of turtle-doves are rustling round the villages; dogs are barking the flocks to pasture; cocks are crowing; donkeys are braying; water wheels are creaking; and the Moslems prostrate themselves in prayer, with their forehead to the ground, or their hands crossed upon their bosoms, their eyes motionless, and their lips quivering with the first chapter of the Koran.

For my own part, a plunge into the Nile, constitutes the principal part of the toilette in which razor or looking-glass are unknown. Re-dressed, re-turbaned, and re-seated on my carpet, Abdallah, with a graceful obeisance, presents a chi-bouk of fragrant *latakeea*, as different from our coarse English tobacco as a pastille is from burnt feathers; and Mahmoud offers a little cup of coffee's very essence. In the meantime the crew are pitching the tent upon a little lawn beneath some palm-trees, for yonder forest shadows the ruins of Memphis, and the gardens wherein Moses used to wander with Pharaoh's daughter. Here then I shall wait for my good friend and fellow voyager, who lingers at Grand Cairo, while I haunt the ancient city of the Pharaohs, shooting quails, and questioning the past.

Travelers were struck above all with the monuments of ancient Egypt—so huge and so beautiful—but the people too were a significant part of their experience of Egypt.

Communications with the People, 1814
Henry Light
In some villages I was able to assist the sick by medicines and advice; in others, I added to the catalogue of charms by writing Arabic sentences in praise of God and the Prophet at the request of the villagers. These placed in the turban or hung around the neck, were to preserve the wearer from the evil angel. In one village, called Abou Gaziz, I was requested by a party of women to hold my drawn sword on the ground, while they went through the ceremony of jumping across it, with various motions, to correct the well known Eastern curse of barrenness, and was rewarded by blessings and offerings of durra cake.

So Much to See, 1848
Harriet Martineau
And when on board, there was so much to be seen on the ordinary banks that I was rarely in the cabin. Before breakfast, I was walking on deck. After breakfast, I was sewing, reading, or writing, or idling on deck, under the shade of the awning. After dinner, we all came out eagerly, to enjoy the last hour of sunshine, and the glories of the sunset and the after-glow, and the rising o'the moon and constellations. And sorry was I every night when it was ten o'clock, and I must go under a lower roof than that of the dazzling heavens. All these hours of our first days had their ample amusement from what we saw on the banks alone, till we could penetrate further. . . . There was the pretty sight of the preparation of the drying banks for the new crop;—the hoeing with the short, heavy antique hoe. And the harrow, drawn by a camel, would appear on the ridge of the bank. . . .

Then, there were the endless manoeuvres of innumerable birds, about the islets and rocks: and buffalo, here and there, swimming from bank to bank, and finding it at last, no easy matter to gain the land.—Then, there was the ferryboat, with its ragged sail, and its motley freight of turbaned men, veiled women, naked children, brown sheep, frightened asses, and imperturbable buffalo.—Then, there the long palisades of sugar canes edging the banks; or the steep slopes, all soft and bright with the springing wheat or the bristling lupins. Then, there were the villages, with their somewhat pyramidal houses, their clouds of pigeons, and their shelter of palms: or, here and there, a town, with its minarets rising out of its cincture of acacia.

And it was not long before we found our sight sharpened to discern holes in the rocks, far or near,—holes so squared at the entrance as to hint of sculpture or painting within.—And, then, as the evening drew on, there was the sinking of the sun, and the coming out of the colours which had been discharged by the glare in the middle of the day. The vast and dreary and hazy Arabian desert became yellow, melting into the purple hills; the muddy waters took a lilac hue; and the shadows of the sharp-cut banks were as blue as the central sky. As for the moon, we could, for the first time in our lives, see her the first night;—the slenderest thread of cup-like form, visible for a few minutes after sunset; the old moon being so clearly marked as to be seen by itself after the radiant rim was gone. I have seen it behind a palm, or resting on the ridge of a mountain like a copper ball. And when the fuller moon came up from the east, and I, forgetting the clearness of the sky, have been struck by the sudden dimness, and have looked up to watch her passing behind a cloud, it was delicious to see, instead of any cloud, the fronds of the palm waving upon her disk.

Tombs of Beni Hassan, 1852
Dean Arthur Penrhyn Stanley
These tombs of Beni Hassan are amongst the oldest monuments of Egypt . . . yet exhibiting, in the liveliest manner, hunting, wrestling and dancing,—and curious as showing how gay and agile these ancient people could be, who in their architecture and graven sculptures appear so solemn and immoveable. Except a doubtful figure of Osiris in one, and a mummy on a barge in another, there is nothing of death or judgement here.

Life in the Grottoes, 1860
Mrs. M. Carey
We reached the Grottoes at last. They are cut along the side of the hill, at a distance of about two miles from the village. Those to the south pleased us extremely. They are of the oldest style of Egyptian architecture, and very elegant. The columns represent four stems of water plants, supporting a capital in the form of lotus or papyrus buds. The transverse section of these grottoes is very elegant, and the architecture resembles a depressed pediment, extending over the columns, and resting at either end on a low pilaster. The simplicity and elegance of the style and device strike the eye at once. The walls of all the grottoes are covered with various interesting coloured devices.

When the eye has become accustomed to the partial light within, these can be gradually made out, and we took great delight in tracing the following subjects:— the tillage of the ground; making of ropes; weaving of linen cloth; the manufacture of jewellery and pottery; various hunting scenes; men tending sick cattle; feeding the oryx; fishing-nets; clap-nets; pressing wine in a wine-press; men wrestling; women playing at ball, and performing various feats of agility in a most unwomanlike manner; both sexes receiving the bastinado, the men laid on the ground, the women sitting; playing the harp; games of draughts and 'mora'; a barber shaving a customer; some cranes; a very curious procession of strangers, supposed, from their dress, beards and sandals, and boots, to be some Asiatic people, being presented, probably, to the owner of the tomb, and offering him presents of the produce of their country; finally, boats bearing the dead body to its place of sepulture; these, and many others, we examined with interest, by the assistance of *Murray's Handbook* and Wilkinson's *Ancient Egyptians*. The curious custom is also seen here of writing over the subject represented the name of what it was intended to represent. In one instance, in particular, it appeared very desirable; if the artist did intend in this case to represent kids feeding upon a vine, we should certainly have wished to see written up over them, "This is a vine, these are kids."

> In 1930, Mary Chubb accompanied an expedition to Egypt to investigate and excavate the site of Tell al-Amarna, city of the 'heretic' pharaoh Akhenaten and his wife, the beautiful Nefertiti. Her description of the lifting of a heavy stone might have been given at any time throughout the millennia.

Nefertiti Lived Here, 1930
Mary Chubb

The sand had been cleared down to ground level. Right across the outside of the doorway lay a great oblong of limestone, quite seven feet long by three feet wide. It was far too big and rough to be a doorstep, and in any case, this was not the outer wall of the house.

"Another lintel, I think," said John [Pendlebury]. "Fallen on its face. Perhaps the other side is painted too."

It must have weighed several hundredweights. Four short poles were found, and these were worked very carefully under the outer long side. Sweating and straining, four of the workmen began to raise the outer edge inch by inch, pivoting it up on the inner edge. Stones were slipped in to hold it when they paused for breath or to work the levers further in. A few chunks of limestone, cracked probably by the first crash when the lintel fell, broke away from the edges and lay in the sand. Would the whole thing crack to pieces as the great weight left the support of the ground?

At a word from Ali Sheraif, the Gufti in charge, the men bent to the poles again, marvellously slow and careful, grunting to each other words of warning. We were all in it together somehow. They were just as keen to get it up intact as we were—and I am perfectly certain it wasn't only the prospect of good backshish ahead. As for us, we stood round in a sort of desperate tension of silence. When the front edge was about six inches off the ground and more supports had been wedged in, Tommy slid his long length alongside and got as much of his head as he could into the narrow space.

"Are those supports all right?" Hilda murmured uncomfortably.

A strangled, very sandy *"Gosh!"* floated up from the depths.

"Is there—anything?" asked John, moving about anxiously.

Tommy withdrew his head and, with maddening deliberation, folded himself up again, rather like a camel, looking up at us. His beaming countenance, sunburned by now to a rich tomato, was beaming, and his spectacles flashed in the sun.

"It's covered in bright colours," he said, in a rather shaky voice, and then, bringing out his trump card: "and simply smothered with inscriptions!" . . .

No one knew where Nefertiti's remains were laid, or indeed if any honour was paid her in death. But now I knew this—that Nefertiti had lived close to this old house where we now sat talking about her; had passed the remaining few bitter years of her life, in the place that she made the last defiant stronghold of Atenism (the religion formed by her husband).

Our house, quite close to her northern dwelling that she named 'Castle of the Aten', was very large in comparison to many of the other private houses; perhaps it had belonged to one of her friends, or to a Minister of the new young Pharaoh [Tutankamun].

Nefertiti must have known this house. It's not too fantastic to think that sometimes, long ago, people sitting as we were now, in this very room, may have heard the murmur of servants' voices out beyond the Central Room, speaking the lovely name as she drew near: "Nefertiti. It is Nefertiti. The Beautiful Lady comes!" And in a moment she may have passed through this doorway, trodden this floor, and perhaps sat talking to her host with a small sandalled foot resting on this column base by my chair.

The Temple of Hermopolis at Minya, 1813
James Silk Buckingham

Returning to the boat, we continued our course on the Nile, landing at Minieh, a populous and flourishing town on the western bank, and thence onward to the ruins of Antinoe, on the eastern: a city built by the Roman Emperor Adrian, and so called after his favourite, the beautiful Antinous, who was drowned in the Nile. I passed a whole day within these ruins, which have all the grandeur of Roman times, the architecture being chiefly Corinthian; and the number of edifices, colonnades, and partially dilapidated public structures that still remain, make up a scene of great beauty, though in desolation.

On the following day I visited the first Egyptian architectural monument to be seen on ascending the Nile, namely, the portico of the Temple of Hermopolis. It was like passing from St Paul's Cathedral to Westminster Abbey; the former well calculated to excite admiration for its noble proportions and fine architectural effect, but the latter inspiring feelings of awe and devotion, amid the 'dim religious light' of its coloured glass, lofty aisles, and fretted roof.

A single paragraph from my journal of that day will express this more fully:

When I dismounted and approached its gigantic columns, I know not whether their colossal size, their rich invention, or their exquisite finish attracted my regard more strongly; but this I perfectly remember that—while lost amidst the commingled feelings which the pillared portico of this massive pile inspired, regretting the lost language of its inscriptive figures, and admiring the happiest union of pure simplicity, luxuriant ornament, and everlasting strength,—I felt, beneath its awe-inspiring roof, a sensation of humility and devotion, which Antinoe, with all its beauties of the picturesque, or all the sadness of its desolating ruins, had not the power to create.

Asyut and Explorations, 1836
John Lloyd Stephens

Asyut stands about a mile and a half from the river, in one of the richest valleys of
the Nile. At the season of inundation, when the river rolls down with all its
majesty, the whole intermediate country is overflowed; and boats of the largest
size, steering their course over the waste of waters by the projecting tops of the
palm-trees, come to anchor under the walls of the city. A high causeway from the
river to the city crosses the plain, a comparatively unknown and unnoticed, but
stupendous work, which for more than three thousand years has resisted the headlong current of the Nile at its highest, and now stands, like the Pyramids, not so
striking, but an equally enduring, and perhaps more really wonderful monument
of Egyptian labour.

A short distance before reaching the city, on the right, are the handsome
palace and garden of Ibrahim Pasha. A stream winds through the valley, crossed
by a stone bridge, and over this is the entrance-gate of the city. The governor's
palace, the most imposing and best structure I had seen since the Citadel at Cairo,
standing first within the walls, seemed like a warder at the door. . . . I do not
believe that the contents of all the bazaars in Asyut, one of the largest towns in
Egypt, were worth as much as the stocks of an ordinary dealer in dry goods in
Broadway, New York. But these are not the things for which the traveller stops
at Asyut. On the lofty mountains overlooking this richest valley of the Nile, and
protecting it from the Libyan Desert, is a long range of tombs, the burial place of
the ancient Egyptians; and looking for a moment at the little Mohamedan burying-
ground, the traveller turns with wonder from the little city he has left, and asks:
"Where is the great city which had its graves in the sides of yonder mountain?
Where are the people who despised the earth as a burial-place, and made for
themselves tombs in the eternal granite?"

The mountain is about as far from the city as the river, and the approach to
it is by another strong causeway over the same beautiful plain. Leaving our donkeys at its foot, and following in the nimble footsteps of my little Arab girl, we
climbed by a steep ascent to the first range of tombs. They were the first I had
seen, and are but little visited by travellers and though afterward I saw all that
were in Egypt, I still consider these well worth a visit. . . . The ceilings were
covered with paintings, finished with exquisite taste and delicacy, and in some
places fresh as if just executed; and on the halls were hieroglyphics enough to
fill volumes. . . . The back chambers were so dark, and their atmosphere was
so unwholesome, that it was unpleasant, and perhaps unsafe, to explore them;
if we went in far there was always a loud rushing noise, as if their innermost
recesses might now be the abode of wild beasts. Wishing to see what caused
the noise, and at the same time to keep out of harm's way, we stationed our
selves near the back door of the entrance-chamber, and I fired my gun within;
a stream of fire lighted up the darkness of the sepulchral chamber, and the
report when grumbling and roaring into the innermost recesses, rousing their
occupants to frenzy. There was the noise like the rushing of a strong wind; the

light was dashed from my companion's hand; a soft skinny substance struck against my face; and thousands of bats, wild with fright, came whizzing forth from every part of the tomb to the only avenue of escape. We threw ourselves down 'and allowed the ugly frightened birds to pass over us, and then hurried out ourselves. For a moment I felt guilty; the beastly birds, driven to the light of day, were dazzled by the glorious sun, and, flying and whirling blindly about, were dashing themselves against the rocky side of the mountain and falling dead at its base.

> Many of the travelers were also 'sportsmen' and duck shooting and hunting other game was great sport along the river.

Timseach! Timseach! 1845
Eliot Warburton

The first time that a man fires at a crocodile is an epoch in his life. We had only now arrived in the waters where they abound, for it is a curious fact that none are ever seen below Mineyeh, though Herodotus speaks of them as fighting with the dolphins at the mouths of the Nile. A prize had been offered for the first man who detected a crocodile, and the crew had now been for two days on the alert in search of them. Buoyed up with the expectation of such game, we had latterly reserved our fire for them exclusively, and the wild duck and turtle [doves], nay, even the vulture and the eagle had swept past, or soared above us in security.

At length the cry of "Timseach! Timseach!" was heard from half a dozen claimants of the proffered prize, and half a dozen black fingers were eagerly pointed to a spit of sand, on which were strewn apparently some logs of trees. It was a Covey of Crocodiles! Hastily and silently the boat was run on shore. R. was ill, so I had the enterprise to myself, and clambered up the steep bank with a quicker pulse than when I first levelled a rifle at a Highland deer. My intended victims might have prided themselves on their superior nonchalance; and, indeed, as I approached them, there seemed to be a sneer on their ghastly mouths and winking eyes. Slowly they rose, one after the other, and waddled to the water, all but one, the most gallant or most gorged of the party. He lay still until I was within a hundred yards of them; then, slowly rising up on his fin-like legs, he lumbered towards the river, looking askance at me with an expression of countenance that seemed to say: "He can do me no harm; however, I may as well have a swim." I took aim at the throat of the supercilious brute, and, as soon as my hand steadied, the very pulsation of my finger pulled the trigger. Bang! went the gun; whiz! flew the bullet; and my excited ear could catch the *thud* with which it plunged into the scaly leather of his neck. His waddle became a plunge, the waves closed over him, and the sun shone on the calm water, as I reached the brink of the shore, that was still indented by the waving of his gigantic tail. But there is blood upon the water, and he rises for a moment to the surface.

"A hundred piastres for the timseach," I exclaimed, and half a dozen Arabs plunged into the stream.

There he rises again, and the men dash at him as if he hadn't a tooth in his head. Now he is gone, the waters close over him, I never saw him since.

The Love of Abydos, 1908
Douglas Sladen

It was clear that our dragoman loved Abydos better than any other place he took us to. He bubbled over with information and high spirits. This is the sort of dialogue to which he treated us.

He clapped his hands and began: "This way, this way, ladies, see procession round the walls—men carrying can-shaped vessels of beer—Mohammed knows the numerals 106 barrels. Each column have a figure of Osiris bearing the name of Ramses the Great."

While I was examining the lovely black granite door-jambs, he began to spell out the cartouches in the way he had: "Ramses beloved of Amen—the great son of Ptah elected by Ra—the son of the sun—Amen beloved of Ra."

And while I was examining the gay colours on the smooth, fine limestone he babbled on: "Ramses beloved of Amen."

The colours and the paintings were delightful, and there were such pretty people in the processions. I liked everything about this sumptuous temple. While I was photographing the place where the minor Abydos tablet, now in the British Museum, was cut off, in the way they had in the good old days when finding was keeping and anybody who liked could help himself to ancient monuments, Mohammed began again: "Ladies, ladies and gentlemen, here is Osiris in the Hades accompanied by Isis, Nephetes, and Amnte—one, two, three—receiving the homage. The homage is of a rather practical kind."

"I, your son Seti the First, am burning incense before you, and I pray you to give me a good Nile." The figure of Seti was gloriously dignified and beautiful. Mohammed was witheringly sarcastic to a lady who ventured to suggest that Seti's hands were in a rather strained position. "Madam—hands not wrong—if artist makes any mistakes Seti will cut off his head."

Luncheon with Osiris, 1904
William Jarvie

After visiting the second temple we went back to Abydos and in the Hypostile Hall found our dragoman had arranged a most sumptuous repast, which he had brought from our boat. He had one of our tablecloths spread upon a table around which were our chairs. The first course was sardines, olives, bread and butter; second, eggs; third, cold tongue and ham; fourth, chicken and salad; fifth, pudding; sixth, oranges, bananas, dates and figs; seventh, coffee. With this were various condiments, such as Cross and Blackwell's mustard pickles, chutney, etc., wine for

Mrs. Thayer and myself, Poland water and vichy celeste for James and Maggie. A fine spread, was it not?

We made quite a caravan coming back, for in addition to our four, there were our dragoman, our head waiter and four of the crew. We had also a dashing Egyptian cavalryman upon a superb horse. He had been on duty at the temple and seemed to take a fancy to us, for he rode with us all the way back to Belianah, and occasionally would clear the way of camels, which he sometimes thought were taking up too much of the road and might squeeze us as we passed.

Donkeys to Dendera, 1822
Frederick Henniker
Donkeys and saddles *ready made* are always forthcoming for an "Engilitz". In a few minutes we were in sight of the temple, and use our utmost exertions to reach it. My obstinate animal has been there often enough, and now runs into a cornfield, where I leave him and trust to my own legs. . . . On a flat plain of beautiful verdure rises a small dark mound, covered with ruins, in the centre of which appears the celebrated temple of Dendera. On nearer approach, the surrounding fragments, which had given the principal features of the picturesque, vanish into the mud walls of an Arab village.

Dendera has been so often described in the large square books, that to repeat what has already been said would be wearisome to us both . . . arrived at the Portico; I am lost in admiration, even though the concomitant filthy hill is nearly on a level to the top of the portal—. . . the peculiar and characteristic beauties of Egyptian architecture are here in full perfection.

The French archaeologist Maspero approached the temple in the early evening, meeting the sugarcane reapers returning from their labor. The great Champollion visited at night.

Approaching Dendera, 1902
Sir Gaston Maspero
We have already left them far behind when we still hear the women's laugh and the shrill tones of the children. The ground soon rises, and the sebakh diggers have dug into it so terribly, that it is necessary to be very careful not to fall into some hole.

Rows of ruined walls show the position of the ancient streets and mark on the ground the grouping of the buildings: here the ruins of a vaulted house, there a half-overturned basilica, its pillars of grey stone, its architraves broken, its mortar in black basalt, the whole submerged in incredible masses of broken glass and reddish potsherds. On the top of the eminence is a thick, heavy gate, the sides cut about

and covered with mediocre hieroglyphics in praise of the Emperor Domitian and
of the Antonines. We enter, and suddenly at the end of a kind of dusty avenue
see a dozen yards above us in the air an army of large, calm, smiling faces sheltered by a stiff, hard cornice. It is as if the temple was starting from the ground to
go to meet the visitor.

Coming upon Dendera by Night, 1829
Jean François Champollion
The moonlight was magnificent, and we were only at a distance of one hour from
the temples; could we resist the temptation? I ask this of the coldest of mortals!
To eat and to leave immediately was the work of a moment: alone without
guides, but armed to the teeth, we set off across the fields, presuming that the
temples were in a direct line with our boat. We walked like this, singing the most
recent opera marches, for an hour and a half, without finding anything. Finally a
man was discovered; we called to him, and he bolted, taking us for Bedouin, for,
dressed in the eastern manner and covered with a great white hooded cape, we
resembled to the Egyptian man a tribe of Bedouins, whilst a European might have
taken us without hesitation for a guerrilla force of Carthusian monks armed with
guns, sabres and pistols. The runaway was brought to me—I ordered him to lead
us to the temples. This poor devil, barely reassured at first, took us along a good
route and finished by walking with good grace; thin, dry, black, covered with old
rags, this was a *walking mummy*, but he guided us rather well and we treated him
in the same way.

The temples finally appeared to us. I will not try to describe the impression
which the great propylon and especially the portico of the great temple made on
us. One can measure it easily, but to give an idea of it is impossible. It is grace and
majesty brought together in the highest degree.

Ikhmim: A Wondrous Thing, 1183
Ibn Jubayr
The most remarkable of the temples of the world talked of for their wonder is the
great temple east of the city and below its walls. Its length is two hundred and
twenty cubits, and its breadth one hundred and sixty. The people of these parts
know it as *birba*, and thus too are known all their temples and ancient constructions.
This great temple is supported by forty columns, beside its walls, the circumference of each column being forty spans and the distance between them thirty
spans. Their capitals are of great size and perfection, cut in an unwonted fashion
and angulated in ornate style as if done by turners. The whole is embellished with
many colours, lapis lazuli and others. The columns are carved in low relief from
top to bottom. Over the capital of each column and stretching to its neighbour is
a great slab of carved stone, the biggest of which we measured and found to be
fifty-six spans in length, ten in width, and eight in depth.

The ceiling of this temple is wholly formed of slabs of stone so wonderfully joined as to seem to be one single piece, and over it all are disposed rare paintings and uncommon colours, so that the beholder conceives the roof to be of carved wood. Each slab has a different painting. Some are adorned with comely pictures of birds with outstretched wings making the beholder believe they are about to fly away; others are embellished with images of men, very beautiful to look upon and of elegant form, each having a distinctive shape, for example holding a statuette or a weapon, or a bird, or a chalice, or making a sign to another with the hand, together with other forms it would take too long to describe and which words are not adequate to express.

Within and without this great temple, both in its upper and lower parts, are pictures all of varied form and description. Some are of dreadful, inhuman forms that terrify the beholder and fill him with wonder and amazement. There was hardly the space of an awl or needle-hole which did not have an image or engraving or some hieroglyphic writing that I did not understand. This remarkable decoration which can be wrought from hard stone where it cannot be worked in soft wood, covers the whole of this vast and splendid temple, in wonder at which the beholder might conceive that all time spent in its adornment, embellishment, and beautifying would be too short. Glory to the Creator of wondrous things. There is no God but He.

9
Luxor
Both Sides of the Nile

 Many travelers had translated Homer's words on Thebes in the schoolroom, and coming to Luxor was a high point of their travels. Pierre Loti found tourism had spoiled it for him; the magnificence of Karnak silenced Amelia Edwards; across the Nile, the isolated Valley of the Kings and its tombs awed the travelers.

Luxor—Ancient Thebes, 1846
Cuthbert Young
Thebes—old Egyptian Thebes—what strange ideas does the word conjure up! It was very different from any of my conceptions, and its real character is best told by saying that it is strangely old and strangely interesting. I had most reluctantly passed it on our upward voyage, and now it was with feelings of an intense kind that I put my foot for the first time on Theban soil.

A Hundred Gated Thebes, 1817
Captains Charles Irby and James Mangles
We now returned to Luxor, and having seen every thing we began to think of returning. I cannot quit Thebes, however, without a few observations most

travellers, when speaking of this ancient capital, make mention of the lines of
Homer, wherein he alludes to Thebes in such glowing characters. I shall give you
Alexander Pope's translation of the passage, and then add a few observations
which occurred to me on the spot.

Plain of Thebes

Not all proud Thebes' unrivalled walls contain
The world's great Empress on th' Egyptian plain;
That spreads her conquest o'er a thousand states,
And pours her heroes through a hundred gates,
Two hundred horsemen, and two hundred cars,
From each wide portal issuing to the wars.

In our researches throughout the whole of the Theban ruins we could not
meet within any remains of either walls or gates, unless the term is applied to the
pylons and other buildings which constitute the approach to the sacred edifices.

**Captain Frederick Norden and his company were not wel-
comed on their arrival in Luxor. Matters were very different
a century and a half later.**

The Struggle to Visit Thebes, 1737
Captain Frederick Norden
14 December

It was four o'clock in the afternoon, when I began to perceive, on the eastern side, an obelisk: little after I discovered a great number of peristils, some portals and antique structure, confusedly scattered up and down the plain.

From these signs I immediately concluded that I saw the ruins of ancient Thebes; but I could not prevail upon our reys to put me ashore, by fair words, promises or menace. He did not here plead his fear of the Arabians; his only excuse was the impossibility of landing, on account of the islands and sandbanks that obstructed. He swore, moreover, by his beard, that there was no going thither, without making a great round of land.

[The next day they crossed the Nile to the west side. Norden landed and] . . . did not go far before [he] met two great colossuses. Encouraged by this first discovery, I returned for my arms, and the company of those whom curiosity might incite to be of the party. The reys perceiving our design, spared no pains to thwart it, nay employed all his eloquence to intimidate us. But when he found his representations had no weight with us, he had recourse to another stratagem, which he thought would prove more effectual to deter us, which was to swear, that if we went ashore, he would go homeward with his bark, and not wait for our return. But he was made to understand our fixed determination, and that if he dared to sail off, as he threatened, that we would certainly overtake him and make him pay dearly for his insolence. This threat had the desired effect upon him; and he changed his note, humbly conjuring us not to land, for the sake of him; [saying that if misfortune befell the party, he would be blamed].

Good Morning, Luxor! 1873
Amelia Edwards

Coming on deck the third morning after leaving Denderah, we found the dahabeeyah decorated with palm-branches, our sailors in their holiday turbans, and Reis Hassan *en grande tenue;* that is to say in shoes and stockings, which he only wore on very great occasions.

"Nehârak-sa'id—good morning—Luxor!" said he all in one breath.

It was a hot, hazy morning, with dim ghosts of mountains glowing through the mist, and a warm wind blowing.

We ran to the side; looked eagerly; but could see nothing. Still the Captain smiled and nodded; and the sailors ran hither and thither, sweeping and garnishing; and Egendi, to whom his worst enemy could not have imputed the charge of bashfulness, said 'Luxor—kharûf—all right!' every time he came near us.

We had read and dreamed so much about Thebes, and it had always seemed so far away, that but for this delicate allusion to the promised sheep, we could

---

1. Arabic. "kharûf ", pronounced "hanoof",—*English* Sheep.

hardly have believed we were really drawing nigh unto those famous shores. About ten, however, the mist was lifted away like a curtain, and we saw to the left a rich plain studded with palm-groves; to the right a broad margin of culti-vated lands bounded by a bold range of limestone mountains; and on the farthest horizon another range, all grey and shadowy.

'Karnak—Gournah—Luxor!' says Reïs Hassan triumphantly, pointing in every direction at once. Talhamy tries to show us Medinet Habu and the Memnonium. The Painter vows he can see the heads of the sitting Colossi and the entrance to the Valley of the Tombs of the Kings.

We, meanwhile, stare bewildered, incredulous; seeing none of these things; finding it difficult, indeed, to believe that any one else sees them. The river widens away before us; the flats are green on either side; the mountains are pierced with terraces of rock-cut tombs; while far away inland, apparently on the verge of the desert, we see here a clump of sycamores—yonder a dark hillock—midway between both a confused heap of something that may be either fallen rock or fallen masonry; but nothing that looks like a Temple, nothing to indicate that we are already within recognisable distance of the grandest ruins in the world.

Presently, however, as the boat goes on, a massive, windowless structure which looks (Heaven preserve us!) just like a brand-new fort or prison, towers up above the palm-groves to the left. This, we are told, is one of the propylons of Karnak; while a few whitewashed huts and a little crowd of masts now coming into sight a mile or so higher up, mark the position of Luxor. Then up capers Egendi with his never-fail-ing 'Luxor—kharûf—all right!' to fetch down the tar and darabukkeh. The captain claps his hands. A circle is formed on the lower deck. The men, all smiles, strike up their liveliest chorus, and so, with barbaric music and well-filled sails, and flags flying, and green boughs waving overhead, we make our triumphal entry into Luxor.

The top of another pylon; the slender peak of an obelisk; a colonnade of giant pillars half-buried in the soil; the white houses of the English, American, and Prussian Consuls, each with its flagstaff and ensign; a steep slope of sandy shore; a background of mud walls and pigeon-towers; a foreground of native boats and gaily-painted dahabeeyahs lying at anchor—such, as we sweep by, is our first panoramic view of this famous village. A group of turbaned officials sitting in the shade of an arched doorway rise and salute us as we pass. The assembled dahabeeyahs dozing with folded sails, like sea-birds asleep, are roused to spasmodic activity. Flags are lowered; guns are fired; all Luxor is startled from its midday siesta. Then, before the smoke has had time to clear off, up comes the Bagstones in gallant form, whereupon the dahabeeyahs blaze away again as before.

Luxor Temple: Grandeur and Craft, 1844
Prince Puckler-Muskau
The first observation that forced itself upon me, was one that has occurred to many others: viz. how much better the Egyptians understood architecture than we do, and how little we have been able to learn from them. The removal of the

Obelisk and Propylon, Luxor

second obelisk from here, in order to place it in the centre of the great square of
Louis Quinze, at Paris, which was attended with an enormous expense, is no slight
proof of this latter assertion. The entrance of the temple at Luxor, is formed by
two imposing Pylones of a hundred feet in height; close to the sides of the gate
are placed two colosses of forty feet in height, and a few steps from it, and at about
double the distance from the colosses to the Pylones, stood the two obelisks, of
from eighty to ninety feet in height, one of which has been carried off. This close
assemblage of monuments produces a most imposing effect, whilst the same
objects dispersed and spread over a large surface, would be completely lost.

The Egyptians never erected an obelisk without a companion, any more than
an isolated pillar; but least of all, would they have placed a single obelisk like this
in the midst of a large square, where it would only resemble an unmeaning pole,
and spoil the appearance of the square, whilst the size of the latter would take
away all its importance as a mass, and thus make the great appear artificially small.
It is really the greatest pity, that for such an object the noble appearance of the
temple entrance was so much weakened, for to destroy it entirely was impossible.
The remaining obelisk, formed of the finest pink granite, is in an excellent state
of preservation, excepting a trifling damage near the base, on two sides, and the
hieroglyphics cut into it two inches deep, are acknowledged to be the most perfect of the kind executed even by the Egyptians. It would, in fact, be impossible

to surpass this work, and in the present day it cannot be conceived how they man-
aged to cut into this rocky granite, the most delicate and chastely executed figures
with the same precision and facility, as our best sculptors cut into stone. A boy of
eleven years of age offered, for the sum of one karie (an Egyptian coin of the value
of two and a-half francs) to climb the obelisk by means of these hieroglyphics, and
in fact performed this hazardous feat as far as two-thirds of the height, without
experiencing the least difficulty; but when he got thus far, he was blown about so
violently by the wind, that we promised him two karie, if he would immediately
descend.

In order to obtain a distinct idea of the disposition and the plan of the temple,
one ought to ascend to the top of the Pylones, although this is rather a trouble-
some task, on the dilapidated, narrow staircase, and afterwards on open blocks,
where the visitor is obliged to jump from one stone to another. The view is, in
every respect, worth the trouble, and the original constructor of this palace,
Amenepht the Third (Memnon) could, from its turrets, behold the two colossal
statues of himself, which stand on the opposite side of the river.

It is very interesting to try and trace the shape and extent of the ruins, in the
labyrinth of the village, the houses of which, (very decent ones, by the bye, for
Egypt) have singularly enough imitated the forms of the Pylones on a Lilliputian
scale, in the dust of their mud bricks. More than a hundred of the old pillars still
rear their heads amongst them, and one of the principal courts of the temple continues in a state of almost perfect preservation. I found several sculptures here of
indescribable grandeur and beauty; several of the faces were of a delicacy and
depth of expression which would have done credit to any European artist. These
paintings date from the most flourishing period of Egyptian art. The decline of the
arts begins to show itself about the time of the reign of the later Pharaohs; at that
of the Ptolomies, it was already far advanced, and in the time of the Romans a
caricature of it only remained.

> Many travelers spent weeks, even months, on both banks of
> the Nile at Luxor. Florence Nightingale enjoyed it; Pierre
> Loti, French naval officer, was critical of much that he saw
> in Egypt—both the local people and other travelers and the
> very hotel that is now seen to be redolent of the past.

Life at Thebes, 1850
Florence Nightingale
11 February
Dear People,
Do you want to know how we pass our days? We rise up early in the morning,
and are breakfasted perhaps by eight o'clock. Then we cross the water in the "sandal",
which is a small "dingee", to western Thebes; the asses rush into the water to meet

us, or the crew carry us ashore: we mount the asses, and with a great multitude—for in Egypt every attendant has his ass, and every ass his attendant—we repair (preceded by a tall man with a spear, his wild turban coming undone in the wind), like a small army, to a tomb; the tomb instantly fills—we suffocate for two or three hours, the guides having, besides, lighted fires and torches therein. When nature can sustain no more, we rush out, and goollehs, bread and dates are laid upon a stone. Those who have strength then begin again, till dark; those who have not, lie on stones in the valley.

Then begins the delightful ride home, the quiet, the silence (except that no Arab is ever silent—the donkey men and the guides talk without one moment's interruption, if it is ten miles or if it is one, the whole way home), the sunset tints, the goats coming home, the women spinning at the head, the gamous (the great Nile buffalo) crossing the little branches of the Nile in large herds on their way home, two little children perhaps riding on the neck of the largest, a stray jackal coming out, and the Pair looking golden in the western sunlight; the evening picture is all beautiful. Our asses enter the river and slide us into the sandal, and home we come to the little fleet of European boats moored under the colonnades of Luxor, which really from the river are almost beautiful.

We dine, and after dinner, when we are all hung up by the tails, like the chameleons, pretending to be dead, and waiting for half-past seven, or at latest eight, to bury us, lo! a dreadful plash of oars, or Paolo puts in his head, with an abominable grin at our mute misery, and says "the Hungarian count!" or "the German professor!" and so on. Mr. B—— immediately retires to his own room, whence he is generally heard to snore. We unwillingly, but nobly, sacrifice ourselves to our duty, sit up (in brown Holland dressing gowns we are sure to have on, having been much too tired to dress), and talk; but we never give one drop of tea, which has greatly limited these visitations, for, in our street, the doors stand always open, and the people have nothing to do but to spend their evenings on board each other's boat. One night, and one night only, we were got out. Capt. ——, good-natured man, came himself in his sandal, and positively carried us off; and one day the ——'s dined with us, and with all the devotion of Arab hospitality which distinguished us, we killed—was it not beautiful of us?—no, not our horse, we had none, but our dog, for dinner. I think I told you of our dog—a turkey, "as big as donkey", as Paolo said. Oh what a loss was there, how he used to walk majestically up and down the beach in front of the boat, which he believed it his duty to guard, bastinadoing the chickens when they made a noise. He killed two cocks the day he died. No man could get him into a coop (the crew were afraid to go near him), yet he never strayed. No dog ever ventured near our boat while he lived; the moment he was dead, the hungry Luxor dogs used to come on board every night, till Mustafa, like Cuddie's lady, greeted them with boiling water; and after his death, we never could keep a quail a single night, though our numerous acquaintances kept us well in quails, for our four cats had parties every night, and bared the larder: and we killed him!

As soon as our guests were gone, sometimes before, we went to bed. Don't think us grown quite savage and uncivilised. It is very hard to be all day by the deathbed of the greatest of your race, and to come home and talk about quails of London.

Modern Life Overshadows the Past, 1910
Pierre Loti

The thing that dominates the whole town, and may be seen five or six miles away, is the Winter Palace, a hasty modern production which has grown on the border of the Nile over the last year: a colossal hotel, obviously sham, made of plaster and mud, on a framework of iron. Twice or three times as high as the Pharaonic temple, its impudent façade rises there, painted a dirty yellow. One such thing, it will readily be understood, is sufficient to disfigure pitiably the whole of the surroundings. The old Arab town, with its little white houses, its minarets and its palm-trees, might as well not exist. The famous temple and the forest of heavy Osiridean columns admire themselves in vain in the waters of the river. It is the end of Luxor. And what a crowd of people is here! While, on the contrary, the opposite bank seems so absolutely desert like, with its stretches of golden sand and, on the horizon, its mountains of the colour of glowing embers, which, as we know, are full of mummies.

Poor Luxor! Along the banks is a row of tourist boats, a sort of two or three storeyed barracks, which nowadays infest the Nile from Cairo to the Cataracts. Their whistlings and the vibration of their dynamos make an intolerable noise. How shall I find a quiet place for my dahabiya, where the functionaries of Messrs. Cook will not come to disturb me?

We can now see nothing of the palaces of Thebes, whither I am to repair in the evening. We are farther from them than we were last night. The apparition during our morning's journey had slowly receded in the plains flooded by sunlight. And then the Winter Palace and the new boats shut out the View. . . . In a line with the Winter Palace a number of stalls follow one another. All those things with which our tourists are wont to array themselves are on sale there; fans, fly traps, helmets and blue spectacles. And, in thousands, photographs of the ruins. And there too are the toys, the souvenirs of the Soudan: old Negro knives, panther-skins and gazelle horns. Numbers of Indians even are come to this improvised fair, bringing their stuffs from Rajputana and Cashmere. And, above all, there are dealers in mummies, offering for sale mysteriously shaped coffins, mummy-cloths, dead hands, gods, scarabæ—and the thousand and one things that this old soil has yielded for centuries like an inexhaustible mine.

Along the stalls, keeping in the shade of the houses and the scattered palms, pass representatives of the plutocracy of the world. Dressed by the same costumiers, bedecked in the same plumes, and with faces reddened by the same sun, the millionaire daughters of the Chicago merchants elbow their sisters of the old nobility. Pressing amongst them impudent young Bedouins pester the fair travellers to mount their saddled donkeys. And as if they were charged to add to this babel a note of beauty, the battalions of Mr. Cook, of both sexes, and always in a hurry, pass by with long strides.

.Beyond the shops, following the lines of the quay, there are other hotels. Less aggressive, all of them, than the Winter Palace, they have had the discretion not to raise themselves too high, and to cover their fronts with white chalk in the Arab fashion, even to conceal themselves in clusters of palm-trees.

And finally there is the colossal temple of Luxor, looking as out of place now as the poor obelisk which Egypt gave us as a present, and which stands today in the Place de la Concorde.

> The site of Karnak Temple still overpowers and astounds today. It was once much more derelict, with columns fallen or broken and the dust of ages clogging up the ruins. Yet, even in that state, it vied with the Pyramids for its impact upon visitors. Vivant Denon and the French army halted here in 1798. Amelia Edwards stood in silent awe in the First Court, and her excerpt is wonderful to read in that very place. Howard Hopley tried to describe the parts of the temple and realized that it is the whole that overwhelms one. Princess Bibescu dined high in the propylon with a sense of magic.

Karnak at Last, 1799
Vivant Denon

Unable, by myself, to take the plan of Karnac temple, or make large views of this mass of ruins, which, at first sight resembles the saw-yard of a quarry, or rather piled mountains, my design was to employ the two hours there in making draughts of the historical low-reliefs. . . .

. . . The day advanced, and the soldiers had not yet obtained anything to eat: travellers are not like Roman heroes, they sometimes feel the want of refreshment: the sun gained upon them, and it was resolved to sleep at Karnac. . . .

[Even so, Denon decided that he would need eight days to make a plan, 'in the least degree satisfactory.'] I was unable to measure the surface of this group of edifices; but, in encompassing it several times on horseback, at a full trot, I always performed the ride in twenty-five minutes.

[Denon worked on the next day until heat overcame him.] It was so hot that the sun had burned my feet, through my boots; I could remain in one place only by caus-ing my servant to walk between the sun and myself, that the rays might be interrupt-ed, and a little shade thrown upon me by his body; the stones had acquired so much heat, that, in picking up some cornelean agates which are found in great number even within the enclosure of the town, I was so burnt by them, that, in order to carry them, I was obliged to throw them on my handkerchief, as I would have touched hot coals.

Worn out with fatigue, I threw myself down in a little Arabian tomb, which had been prepared for me for the night, and which appeared a delicious chamber, till I was told that, at the time of our passing Karnac before, the throat had there been cut of a Frenchman who had lagged behind the column: the marks of this assassination, still imprinted on the walls filled me with horror; but I was laid down, I was sleepy, and so weary that I believe I should not have risen off the dead body itself of the unfortunate victim.

Karnak, 1813
Captain Henry Light

My visit to Karnak, the ancient Diopolis, a ruined temple farther from the banks of the river, on the same side as Luxor, was equally gratifying. It was impossible to look on such an extent of building without being lost in admiration; no description will be able to give an adequate idea of the enormous masses still defying the ravages of time. Enclosure within enclosure, propylae in front of propylae; to these, avenues of sphinxes, each of fourteen or fifteen feet in length, lead from a distance of several hundred yards. The common Egyptian sphinx is found in the avenue to the south; but, to the west; the crio sphinx, with the ram's head, from one or two that have been uncovered, seems to have composed its corresponding avenue. Those of the south and east are still buried. Headless statues of grey and blue granite, of gigantic size, lay prostrate in different parts of the ruins. In the western court, in front of the great portico, and at the entrance to this portico, is an upright headless statue of one block of granite, whose size may be imagined from finding that a man of six foot just reaches the patella of the knee.

The entrance to the great portico is through a mass of masonry, partly in ruins; through which the eye rests on an avenue of fourteen columns, whose diameter is more than eleven feet, and whose height is upwards of sixty. On each side of this are seven rows, of seven columns in each, whose diameter is eight feet, and about forty feet high, of an architecture which wants the elegance of Greek models, yet suits the immense majesty of the Egyptian temple.

Though it does not enter into my plan to continue a description which has been ably done by others before me, yet, when I say, that the whole extent of this temple cannot be less than a mile and a half in circumference, and that the smallest blocks of masonry are five feet by four feet in depth and breadth, that there are obelisks of eighty feet high on a base of eighteen feet, of one block of granite; it can be easily imagined that Thebes was the vast city history describes it to be.

Karnak in Silence, 1873
Amelia Edwards

An immense perspective of pillars and pylons leading up to a very distant obelisk opened out before us. We went in, the great walls towering up like cliffs above

Karnak, retrospective view of the Grand Hall

our heads, and entered the First Court. Here, in the midst of a large quadrangle open to the sky stands a solitary column, the last of a central avenue of twelve, some of which, disjointed by the shock, lie just as they fell, like skeletons of vertebrate monsters left stranded by the Flood.

Crossing this Court in the flowing sunlight, we came to a mighty doorway between two more propylons—the doorway splendid with coloured bas-reliefs; the propylons mere cataracts of fallen blocks piled up to the right and left in grand confusion. The cornice of the doorway is gone. Only a jutting fragment of the lintel stone remains. That stone, when perfect, measured forty feet and ten inches across. The doorway must have been a full hundred feet in height.

We went on. Leaving to the right a mutilated colossus engraven on arm and breast with the cartouche of Rameses II, we crossed the shade upon the threshold, and passed into the famous Hypostyle Hall of Seti the First.

It is a place that has been much written about and often painted; but of which no writing and no art can convey more than a dwarfed and pallid impression. To describe it, in the sense of building up a recognisable image by means of words, is impossible. The scale is too vast; the effect too tremendous; the sense of one's own dumbness, and littleness, and incapacity, too complete and crushing. It is a place that strikes you into silence; that empties you, as it were, not only of words but

of ideas. Nor is this a first effect only. Later in the year, when we came back down
the river and moored close by, and spent long days among the ruins, I found I
never had a word to say in the Great Hall. Others might measure the girth of those
tremendous columns; others might climb hither and thither, and find out points
of view, and test the accuracy of Wilkinson and Mariette; but I could only look,
and be silent.

Dining at Karnak, 1930
Princess Marta Bibescu
Arab musicians sing:
> Gardener, give me a rose,
> If you give me no rose,
> Then a kiss—
> A kiss and a bite.

It is light music, but it lasts.

We follow in the night the sandy avenue of sacred rams, that series of 'pater-
nosters'. The perfume of mimosa from the abandoned house of Legrain, a little
French dwelling shadowed by the great pylons, comes to us on the Nile breeze.

Prince I.D. points out certain lights which move on the pylons up near the
stars.

"Your dinner awaits you there," he said.

We went up to the lofty terrace by a half-ruined spiral staircase, like the ones
in cathedrals. The handsome serving-men, black shadows against the sky, stood
mute and motionless around a small laden table. They must have been jinn out of
the air to have carried such a large meal to this place.

At my right, the Nile and mountain Assasif with its strawberry and cream tint.
At my left, the prodigious ruin of the eighth wonder of the world. The moon
hangs high above the table exactly in the center of the four candles enclosed in
glass globes. . . .

The Prince has brought a phonograph.

Some American tourists, attracted by the familiar sounds of *Old Man River* in
that great solitude, appear, like jacks-in-the-box, at the head of the stairway. The
jinn have to drive them away with great flappings of napkins.

When our meal is finished, a jinni who comes to carry out the coffee cups
brings me the moon on a silver salver.

> In the back streets of Luxor there are many craftsmen, as
> there have been since the days of the pharaohs. With the
> advent of modern tourism, some of them turned their skills
> to the making of 'antiques.' Others, responding to the taste
> of travelers for souvenirs from the past, discovered and sold
> real ancient artifacts.

Antique Makers, 1855
William C. Prime

I left the *Phantom* and walked around the village [Luxor], my footsteps dogged by twenty donkey-boys, and as many donkeys, each of the former hoping that I would grow tired and patronize one of them. At every corner and turn a Coptic scoundrel would produce a lot of antiques for sale, and I amused myself by asking prices. At Luxor rates, Dr. Abbott's collection is worth a million.

Oh! confident Howajji [foreign traveller], beware in Luxor of Ibrahim the Copt, and on the western shore of Achmet-el-Kamouri, the Mussulman. Skilful manufacturers of every form of antique are plenty in the neighbourhood, and these men have them in their employ, and sell to unwary travelers the productions of the modern Arabs as veritable specimens of the antique. Achmet is the chief manufacturer himself, and has a ready hand at the chisel.

The manufacture of antiques is a large business in Egypt, and very profitable. Scarabi are moulded from clay or cut from stone, with close imitation of the ancient, and sold readily at prices varying from one to five dollars. At Thebes is the head-quarters of this business. Still, no antiquarian will be deceived; and it requires very little practice to be able in an instant to determine whether an article is ancient or modern. When the Copt finds that you do know the distinction, he becomes communicative, and readily lets you into the secret of his business; and while he is confidentially informing you of the way in which the Arabs do it, and how this is modern and that is not, beware lest you become too trusting, and he sells you in selling a ring, or a vase, or a seal. He is a wily fellow and sharp, and he knows well how to manage a Howajji.

There were two Thebes, just as there are two Luxors. On the east bank, from where the sun rises, is the city of the living with the temples and places of worship and now studded with hotels, bazaars, and all the life of a busy urban area; on the west bank is the 'Other Side' with its mortuary temples and the tombs of people long dead. But the 'Other Side' also has life, particularly in the village of Gurna, whose residents have guarded and overseen the tombs for centuries.

Protectors of the Tombs, 1792
W.G. Browne

On landing with my Greek servant at Kourna no male inhabitant appeared; but two or three women were standing at the entrance of their dens. As we passed, in quest of the sheck-el-bellad, to request a guide, one of the women said, in Arabic, 'Are you not afraid of crocodiles?' I replied in the negative. She said, emphatically, 'We are crocodiles,' and proceeded to depict her own people as thieves and murderers. They are indeed a ferocious clan, differing in person from other Egyptians. Spears twelve or fourteen feet in length are deadly weapons in their hands.

In the temple at Medinet-Abu we observed a large quantity of blood, and were told by the peasants of Beirat that the Kournese had there murdered a Muggrebin and a Greek, travellers passing from Assuan to Kahira, who had strayed thither from mere curiosity, or perhaps with a view to finding treasure, in which the Muggrebins pretend to superior skill.

Temples on the Other Side, 1819
John Fuller

We reached the plain at a spot several miles to the southward of Gournou and proceeded to the Medinet Abou, which is about equidistant from the mountains and the river. The vast mass of buildings known by that name is so choked up with the ruins of more modern brick structures, that it is difficult to discover its original design. It is supposed to have composed a royal palace and two temples, the largest of which is the most magnificent to be found in the western division of Thebes. It was approached by two gateways connected by a colonnade on each side, together forming a quadrangle. Within the inner gate is the portico of the temple, on the walls of which is a series of bas-reliefs, representing battles, sieges, and triumphal processions, frightful from the barbarities which they exhibit as practised on the vanquished, but remarkable for the spirit and freedom with which they are executed. They stamp the temple of Medinet Abou as being among the most ancient Egyptian monuments, and as having been constructed while Egypt was still a warlike and conquering nation.

Medinet Habu and the Tombs, 1799
Vivant Denon

I galloped forward to catch some features of the ruins of the temples of Medinet Abu, where the troop would take me up in passing. I arrived an hour before it. I saw that on the right of the temple which adjoins the village there was a square edifice which had been a palace, very small indeed, but to which the neighbouring porticoes would have served for additions, in a climate where galleries of columns and terraces are apartments. This little palace has a character which differs very much from that of all other edifices, both in its plan, in its double storey of square windows, and in a sort of balconies, each of which are sustained by four heads, in the attitude of cary-atides. It is to be regretted that this private edifice is in so great a state of destruc-tion, especially in its interior, and that that which remains of its exterior decoration has been so much injured: the sculptures which decorate the exterior walls, as in that part of the temple of Karnak which I suspect to have been a palace, represent the figures of kings, threatening groups of prostrate captives.

Still going before the troop, and pressed onward by its march, I hastened to the two colossuses, and saw them with the effect of the rising sun, at the hour in which it is customary to go and hear that of Memnon speak: after this, I went to the insulated palace called the *memnonium*.

Medeénet Habou, on the edge of the inundated land

While I had forgotten to observe, my companions had forgotten to warn me, and I perceived that the detachment had left me half a league in its rear: I galloped to rejoin it. The troop was fatigued, and it has again become a question whether the expedition to the tombs should take place. I swallowed in silence the anger I felt; and I believe that this silence gained more than any words my discontent could have dictated, for, in the end, the route was proceeded on without further discussion. We first crossed the village of Kûrnû, the ancient Necropolis: on approaching these subterraneous abodes, the inhabitants, for the third time, saluted us with several discharges of musketry. This was the only spot in upper Egypt in which it was refused to acknowledge our government; secure in their sepulchral retreats, like larves, they left them only to terrify mankind: guilty of many other crimes, they hid their remorse, and fortified their disobedience, in the obscurity of these excavations, which are so numerous that they alone attest the immense population of ancient Thebes. It was through these humble tombs that the kings were carried two leagues from their palace, into the silent valley that was to become their final dwelling-place: this valley, to the north-east of Thebes, straitens insensibly; flanked by steep mountains, time can have effected but trivial changes in its antique forms, since, toward its extremity, the opening of the rock still scarcely affords space for a passage to the tombs, especially for the sumptuous trains which

doubtlessly accompanied ceremonies like these, and which must have produced a striking-contrast with the austere asperity of these wild rocks: nevertheless, it is to be believed that this road was taken only for the sake of grander
display, for the valley, from its entrance to its end, tending wholly to the
south, the point at which are the tombs, can be but a very short distance from
the memnonium and yet it was not till after three quarters of an hour's march
in this desert that, in the midst of the rocks, we suddenly found the openings,
even with the ground. These openings at first present no other architectural
ornament than a door, with plain chambranles, of a square form, decorated on
the superior part with a flattened oval, on which are inscribed in hieroglyphics a *scarabæus*, a figure of a man having the head of a sparrow-hawk, and, out
of the oval, two figures on their knees, in the attitude of adoration: as soon as
the sill of the first door is passed, there are found long galleries of twelve feet
in width, by twenty in height, lined with stucco, sculptured and painted; the
roofs of the vaults, formed in elegant elliptic arches, are covered with hieroglyphics, disposed with so much taste, that, in spite of the uncouthness of their
forms, and though there be neither middle-tint nor aerial perspective in these
paintings, the ceilings present an agreeable whole, and an assortment of colours
of which the effect is rich and grateful.

It would require a stay of some weeks in order to seek and establish a system
on the subjects of pictures so numerous, and moreover so mysterious, and I was
allowed only a few minutes, and these with a bad grace.

It had been sounded to horse, when I discovered some little chambers, on the
walls of which were painted the representations of all sorts of arms, such as
maces, coats of mail, tiger-skins, bows, arrows, quivers, pikes, darts, sabres, helmets, goads, and whips; in another, a collection of household utensils, such as
cabinets, commodes, chairs, elbow-chairs, stools, and folding mattresses, of an
exquisite form, and such as we have these many years admired as the productions
of our cabinet-makers, when they have been guided by skilful designers: as
painting only copies that which exists, we must suffer ourselves to be convinced
that the Egyptians employed indian wood, sculptured and gilt, for their furniture, and brocaded silks for the coverings; to these were added various vessels,
as vases, coffee-pots, a ewer, with its salver, a tea-pot, and a basket. Another
chamber was devoted to agriculture, and decorated with its implements and
labours; as, a plough similar to that used at present, a man sowing grain on the
brink of a canal, from the banks of which the inundation has retired, a reaping,
performed with the sickle, and rice-fields, in the act of being tilled. In a fourth
is a figure in white clothing, playing on a harp of eleven strings; the harp sculptured with ornaments of the same tint and the same wood as those at this
moment used by ourselves.

How could I, thus hastily, leave these precious curiosities? I begged with
earnestness for a quarter of an hour; and, watch in hand, I was allowed twenty
minutes: one person lit the way, while another held a torch to each particular
object to which I directed my attention.

The Italian excavator Giovanni Belzoni first came to Luxor
to take down the Nile the huge bust of Ramesses II, known
as the 'Young Memnon,' which now stands in the British
Museum. Dean Stanley writes of his admiration for the
immense, fallen statue of the pharaoh.

Preparing to Collect the 'Young Memnon,' 1817
Giovanni Belzoni

After having taken a cursory view of Luxor and Karnak, to which my curiosity
led me on my landing, I crossed the Nile to the west, and proceeding straight to
the Memnonium, I had to pass before the two colossal figures in the plain. I need
not say, that I was struck with wonder. They are mutilated indeed, but their enormous size strikes the mind with admiration. The next object that met my view
was the Memnonium. It stands elevated above the plain, which is annually inundated by the Nile. The water reaches quite to the propylon; and, though this is
considerably lower than the temple, I beg leave to observe, that it may be considered as one of the proofs, that the bed of the Nile has risen considerably higher since the Memnonium was erected; for it is not to be supposed that the
Egyptians built the propylon, which is the entrance to the temple, so low as not
to be able to enter it when the water was at its height. There are other proofs of
this opinion, which I shall have an opportunity of introducing in this volume. The
groups of columns of that temple, and the views of the numerous tombs excavated in the high rock behind it, present a strange appearance to the eye. On my
approaching these ruins, I was surprised at the sight of the great colossus of
Memnon, or Sesostris, or Osymandias, or Phamenoph, or perhaps some other
king of Egypt; for such are the various opinions of its origin, and so many names
have been given to it, that at last it has no name at all. I can but say, that it must
have been one of the most venerated statues of the Egyptians; for it would have
required more labour to convey such a mass of granite from Assouan to Thebes,
than to transport the obelisk, commonly known under the appellation of
Pompey's Pillar, to Alexandria.

As I entered these ruins, my first thought was to examine the colossal bust I
had to take away. I found it near the remains of its body and chair, with its face
upwards, and apparently smiling on me, at the thought of being taken to England.
I must say, that my expectations were exceeded by its beauty, but not by its size.
I observed, that it must have been absolutely the same statue as is mentioned by
Norden, lying in his time with its face downwards, which must have been the
cause of its preservation. I will not venture to assert who separated the bust from
the rest of the body by an explosion, or by whom the bust has been turned face
upwards. The place where it lay was nearly in a line with the side of the main
gateway into the temple; and, as there is another colossal head near it, there may
have been one on each side of the doorway, as they are to be seen at Luxor and
Karnak.

All the implements brought from Cairo to the Memnonium consisted of four-teen poles, eight of which were employed in making a sort of car to lay the bust on, four ropes of palm leaves, and four rollers, without tackle of any sort. I select-ed a place in the porticoes; and, as our boat was too far off to go to sleep in it every night, I had all our things brought on shore, and made a dwelling house of the Memnonium. A small hut was formed of stones, and we were handsomely lodged. Mrs. Belzoni had by this time accustomed herself to travel, and was equal-ly indifferent with myself about accommodations.

The Great Statue of the Ramesseum, 1852
Dean Arthur Penrhyn Stanley

By some extraordinary catastrophe this statue has been thrown down, and the Arabs have scooped their millstones out of his face; but you can see what he was,—the largest statue in the world. Far and wide his enormous head must have seen,—eyes, nose and ears. Far and wide you must have seen his hands resting on his elephantine knees. You sit on his breast and look at the Ostride statues which support the porticos of the temple, and they seem pigmies before him. Nothing that now exists in the world can give any notion of what the effect must have been when he was erect . . . Rameses was resting in awful majesty after the conquest of the whole known world.

> From the temples of the plain, the traveler moves on into Biban al-Muluk—the Valley of the Kings.

To the Valley of the Kings, 1904
William Jarvie

28 January

We rode through a valley which wound about hills and giant rocks for about four miles up to the place known as the 'Tombs of the Kings'. You cannot imagine a more appropriate way to these tombs, for it is truly a way of the dead. Not a tree, not a shrub, not a blade of grass, not even a human being lives in this valley. Yet it is marvellously beautiful in its impressiveness, and the grand tombs at the end are a fitting termination and a most fitting place for the burial of these great men.

We went into the tombs of Sethos I, Rameses I, VI and IX, and afterwards had lunch in a tomb, which had been prepared for that purpose.

To the Valley of the Kings, 1938
H.V. Morton

It is a pity that the donkeys that once took you there have almost disappeared, because the slow ride into the Valley of the Dead, the gradual approach to that

Valley of the Tombs of the Kings

fiery cleft in the hills, every yard becoming more grim and more desolate, was, I think, a better approach than the rush in a car over a bumpy road.

'Belzoni's Tomb,' 1819
John Fuller

From Gournu a road leads up a ravine in the mountains to an open space surrounded on all sides by steep rocks, in which are excavated the tombs of the Egyptian kings. All of them that have hitherto been discovered are nearly on the same plan. A broad passage leads into one or more lofty saloons which are flanked by smaller chambers, and the walls are richly ornamented with paintings, alluding to the mysterious doctrines and ceremonies of the Egyptian religion, and showing at how early a period the human mind had begun to indulge in speculation as to its future state and destiny.

By far the most interesting of these sepulchres is that called the Tomb of Psammis [now known to be the tomb of Seti I], which had been recently opened by Belzoni, and is fully described in his work. Never having been disposed to the air or wanton injury, the paintings are in perfect preservation, and their colours are as brilliant as the first day they were put on. One apartment appears never to have been finished, as the figures all remain in outline; but this is so fresh, that it seems as if the artist had just quitted his work and was about to return to complete it.

The passage that leads into the tomb slopes downwards, and on the sides there are various groups of figures, among which is distinguished the deceased prince, who appears to be going through various initiatory ceremonies previous to being admitted into the society of the Gods. The passage opens into a vestibule supported by six massive square pillars, where the deities are represented welcoming the hero to their abodes, and Isis is presenting him with the *crux ansata*, the emblem of sovereignty. Within the vestibule is the apartment where the sarcophagus was deposited; a lofty oblong hall with a vaulted ceiling, on which are painted some uncouth figures, supposed to have reference to astronomy.

Entering a Tomb, 1888
E.W. Merrick

We were told of a tomb in which, when first opened, the footprints of the slaves who carried the corpse in thousands of years before could plainly be seen on the sand.

Through their reading of classical texts by such writers as Herodotus, travelers knew of mummified people and creatures. They knew, too, of the tombs in the Valley of the Kings. Now the tourists' presence encouraged the local people to seek, display, and sell the harvest of the mummy pits—often to the dismay of the travelers. They were also led to reenter and wonder at tombs that no human being had seen for centuries, and often found them in a state of almost unbelievable preservation. Yet the mere presence of people who wanted to uncover antiquity carried an inevitable threat to that very past. In fact, some of these travelers used the tombs themselves as their temporary homes in Egypt.

Making a Mummy, c. 450 B.C.
Herodotus

Mummification is a distinct profession. The embalmers, when a body is brought to them, produce specimen models in wood, painted to resemble nature, and graded in quality; the best and most expensive kind is supposed to represent a being whose name I shrink from mentioning in this connexion; the next best is somewhat inferior and cheaper, while the third sort is cheapest of all. After pointing out these differences in quality, they ask which of the three is required, and the kinsmen of the dead man, having agreed upon a price, go away and leave the embalmers to their work.

The most perfect process is as follows: as much as possible of the brain is extracted through the nostrils with an iron hook, and what the hook cannot reach is rinsed out with drugs; next the flank is open with a flint knife and the whole contents of the abdomen removed; the cavity is then thoroughly cleansed and washed out, first with palm wine and again with an infusion of pounded spices. After that it is filled with pure bruised myrrh, cassia, and every aromatic substance with the exception of frankincense, and sewn up again, after which the body is placed in natrum, covered entirely over, for seventy days—never longer. When this period, which must not be exceeded, is over, the body is washed and then wrapped from head to foot in linen cut into strips and smeared on the under side with gum, which is commonly used by the Egyptians instead of glue. In this condition the body is given back to the family, who have a wooden case made, shaped like the human figure, into which it is put. The case is then sealed up and stored in a sepulchral chamber, upright against the wall.

When, for reasons of expense, the second quality is called for, the treatment is different: no incision is made and the intestines are not removed, but oil of cedar is injected with a syringe into the body through the anus which is afterwards stopped up to prevent the liquid escaping. The body is then pickled in natrum for the prescribed number of days, on the last of which the oil is drained off. The effect of it is so powerful that as it leaves the body it brings with it the stomach and intestines in a liquid state, and as the flesh, too, is dissolved by the natrum, nothing of the body is left but the bones and skin. After this treatment it is returned to the family without further fuss.

The third method, used for embalming the bodies of the poor, is simply to clear out the intestines with a purge and keep the body seventy days in natrum. It is then given back to the family to be taken away.

> The tombs of the workmen at Deir al-Medina—the tombs of men who created the kings' tombs—can be reached by walking along the same path that the workmen took thousands of years ago.

The Tombs of the Private Thebans, 1836
Lord Lindsay

But why should the king's tombs engross all my praise? Gorgeous as they are, and interesting for the study of ancient mythology, those of the private Thebans are yet more so for the history of manners and daily life among the old Egyptians. Every light and shadow, indeed, of human life, is portrayed in them, from the laughter of the feast to the tears of the funeral—ointments poured on the head at one, dust heaped on it at the other. You see on one side the arrival of the guest in his chariot, white horses and a train of running footmen betokening his consequence; the other guests, already assembled and seated, the men apart from the women, wait for their dinner, and beguile the intervening moments with smelling the lotus-flower, and listening to the music of the dancing-girls. The master of the house and his wife, richly dressed, and lovingly seated side by side, preside at the entertainment. But the tableau would be incomplete without side-views of the shambles [meat stall] and the kitchen, and a beggar at the gate receiving a bull's head and a draught of water from one of the menials. Facing this, on the opposite wall, the mourning women, with wailing cries and dishevelled hair, precede the coffin that bears the hospitable Egyptian to his long home; the wife or the sister walks beside it, silent in her sorrow; a scribe takes account of the dead man's riches, his cattle, his horses, his household chattels; Death—and then the Judgement:—the deceased is ushered into Amenti; Horus and Aroeres weigh his merits against the ostrich feather, the symbol of Truth; Thoth, the god of letters, presents a scroll, the record of his thoughts, words, and works, to the judge Osiris, into whose presence he is at length admitted on the favourable result of the scrutiny. Sad presumption for man thus to usurp his Creator's prerogative of reading and judging the heart!

And amidst all these varied scenes, as if to show how narrowly joy may be partitioned off from sorrow, how the merry-hearted and the broken-hearted may unconsciously pillow within an inch of each other, and how the world jogs on in daily routine, indifferent to the feelings of either—the occupations of every-day life are pictured in their minutest detail around you,—the scenes of industry, scenes of frolic, parties pledging each other's healths, young folks dancing to the music of the harp, husbandmen in the fields, artificers of every trade at their work, (many of them with tools precisely like those now in use), carpenters, smiths, glass-blowers, shoemakers, wheelwrights, statuaries, idol-makers—I saw a god under a graver's hand, and I thought of Isaiah's noble apostrophe, which Sir Frederick P. you may remember read so beautifully that delightful evening . . . last summer. The illustration was perfect.

Mummies Unearthed, 1819
John Fuller
Of the forty tombs which were reported to exist when Strabo wrote, about ten or twelve are now open. They are in different states of preservation, but they are all curious from the infinite variety of the representations on their walls.

From the Bab el Maluk, or "Gate of the Kings" (as this valley of sepulchres is called), a steep path leads to the ridge of the mountains, from whence there is a view of the whole plain of Thebes with its various antiquities, and a fine reach of the Nile. The eastern face of the mountains is one vast cemetery, and in descending into the plain we continually passed the openings of mummy pits, and almost stumbled over the bodies which had been extracted from them. Some of them still remained in their original grave-clothes; some were stripped of all their cerements and yet remained entire; and others had been broken into fragments and scattered about, exhibiting altogether a most disgusting spectacle. The resinous substance with which the cavities of the head and trunk were filled in the process of embalming is used for various purposes, and the profits arising from the sale of it are sufficient to induce the natives thus to violate the repose of the tomb. Their labours are sometimes better rewarded, by the discovery of more curious mummies which are sought for by travellers and collectors.

Resurrection Men, 1825
Anne Katherine Elwood

It is said, the Egyptians had a tradition that they were to rise again at the end of three thousand years, but it may be assumed they anticipated a more glorious resurrection from the grave than being thus ignominiously torn from their tombs, and exposed and examined in a manner so revolting to humanity, to satisfy the curiosity of the traveller. For my part I see little difference between the resurrection-men in London, who steal the bodies of the dead for the purposes of science, and the mummy-seekers in Egypt, who exhume for curiosity. Why are not the corporeal frames of ancient Egyptians to be considered as sacred as those of Europeans? And why should not those who disinter the Egyptians expect to be haunted by the ghosts of Amenophis or Rameses of Thebes, as soon as those of Mr. Smith and Mr. Johnson of London?

Most of these mummies were wrapped in cloth of a saffron hue, and a quantity of it, their former habiliments, was scattered about, but we were so pressed for time that we could spare but little for the investigation of objects so curious and so interesting: and, oh! how did we wish for some of those hours of frivolity and ennui, which, from the conventional forms of society, are necessarily often spent in civilised company, to devote to the wonders that surround us; but we saw so much in so short a period, that neither my physical nor my mental powers were competent to appreciate properly all I beheld. In comparison with what we had just viewed, Pompeii appeared modern, and bread out of the Tomb of King Sesostris made that in Italian ovens no curiosity.

Lodging in the Valley, 1829
Jean François Champollion

Our caravan, composed of donkeys and *savants*, therefore set itself up here on the same day, and we are occupying the best and most magnificent lodging that it is possible to find in Egypt. It is King Rameses (the fourth of the 19th dynasty) who gives us hospitality, for we are all living in his magnificent tomb, the second that one meets on the right when entering the Valley of Biban-el-Malouk. This rock-cut tomb, admirably preserved, receives enough air and enough light that we lodge there marvellously. We occupy the first three rooms, which form a length of sixty-five paces; the walls, from fifteen to twenty feet in height, and the ceilings are all covered in painted sculptures, whose colours preserve almost all their brilliance. It is a true habitation of a prince. . . . Such is our establishment in the Valley of the Kings, a true resting place of the dead, because you find here neither a blade of grass, nor living beings, with the exception of the jackals and hyenas, who—the night before last—devoured at a hundred paces from our *palace* the donkey which had carried my servant Mohammed.

Treating with the Mummy-snatchers, 1873
Amelia Edwards

There were whispers about this time of a tomb that had been discovered on the western side—a wonderful tomb, rich in all kinds of treasures. No one, of course, had seen such things. No one knew who had found them. No one knew where they were hidden. But there was a solemn secrecy about certain of the Arabs, and a conscious look about some of the visitors, and an air of awakened vigilance about the government officials, which savoured of mystery. These rumours by and by assumed more definite proportions. Dark hints were dropped of a possible papyrus. . . .

In a fatal hour we expressed a wish to see it. From that moment every mummy-snatcher in the place regarded us as his lawful prey. Beguiled into one den after another, we were shown all the stolen goods in Thebes. Some of the things were very curious and interesting. In one house we were offered two bronze vases, each with a band of delicately engraved hieroglyphics running round the lip; also a square stand of basket-work in two colours, precisely like that engraved in Sir Gardner Wilkinson's first volume, after the original of the Berlin Museum. Pieces of mummy case and wall sculpture and sepulchral tablets abounded; and on one occasion we were introduced into the presence of—a mummy!

All these houses were tombs, and in this one the mummy was stowed away in a kind of recess at the end of a long rock-cut passage; probably the very place once occupied by its original tenant. . . . I shall never forget that curious scene—the dark and dusty vault; the Arabs with their lanterns; the mummy in its gaudy cerements lying on an old mat at our feet.

Meanwhile we tried in vain to get sight of the coveted papyrus. A grave Arab dropped in once or twice after nightfall, and talked it over vaguely with the dragoman; but never came to the point. He offered it first, with a mummy, for £100. Finding, however, that we would neither buy his papyrus unseen nor his mummy at any price, he haggled and hesitated for a day or two, evidently trying to play us off against some rival or rivals unknown, and then finally disappeared. These rivals, we afterwards found, were the M.B.'s. They bought both mummy and papyrus at an enormous price; and then, unable to endure the perfume of their ancient Egyptian, drowned the dear departed at the end of the week.

The Mummy's Hand, 1938
H.V. Morton

When I came out of the tombs at Qurna, and before my eyes had become used to the light, I was aware that people were running towards me. One of the first to arrive thrust something into my hand. I looked down and saw that I was holding the hand of a mummy. I did not wonder to whom it had belonged, or whether it had been a beautiful hand or an ugly one; I was only anxious to get rid of it. It was dry, black and claw-like, and was even more hideous than it need have been by the loss of one finger.

The man to whom it belonged refused to take it back, believing that as long as I held it there was a chance I might give him the shilling he was asking in preference to all the other things that old and young were thrusting on me. While I was wondering what to do, I saw a man who looked as old, as brown, as dried up, and as horrible as any mummy, coming slowly in my direction, leaning on a staff.

Although his eyes were closed and he seemed to be blind, he found his way nimbly over the stone-scattered ground, and when he came near he cleared a way for himself by making savage swings with his staff at the legs of the crowd. Several children ran away howling, but I noticed that not one of those who received the blows showed any resentment, for such is the respect for age in the East.

The old man evidently had something important to say to me. When a few yards away, he slowly opened his eyes; and they were white. A desire to get away from this terrible old man came over me, but I waited to see what he wanted. Slowly he thrust his hand into the body of his shirt and drew forth a piece of coffin. It was horrible to see this old man, himself a walking mummy, trying to sell me a bit of coffin, and a nausea for this disgusting trade in tomb relics swept over me until I was ready to put distinguished archaeologist and all others who have dug up Egypt's dead on the same level with this dreadful apparition.

I looked down at the mummy's hand, which I was still holding, and decided to buy it for a shilling and bury it, or get rid of it somehow to put it out of its misery. My purchase seemed to astonish the crowd, and especially the man who had sold it, and they all disappeared shouting into the sandhills, leaving only the terrible old man standing in a bewildered, half-witted way, holding a piece of yellow coffin-wood.

I had no newspaper in which to wrap the mummy's hand, and when I tried to put it in my pocket it clawed at the edge of the cloth and refused to go in. I began to feel sorry that I had bought it. To have buried it where I stood, or to have slipped it behind a rock, would have been futile, for it would have been rediscovered in a few hours and offered to some other visitor. There was nothing to do but to walk hand in hand with it until I could find a safe place to bury it.

Walking above the Valley, 1927
Annie Quibell

Most of us feel the need of quietness in the Valley, above all other places, and when often it is very difficult to get it. If one goes with a large party and must stick to them, it is hopeless, but more independent travellers can do better. I would make earnest counsel to make a day of the royal tombs and not to go back for lunch either to Luxor, or over the hill to the rest house at Der el Bahri. People will probably remonstrate and think me mad to stay on after the electric light [in the tombs] is taken off at one o'clock, but by that time we have seen the tombs and want to see the Valley. When the carriages have all clattered down the road and the last of the donkeys has jingled up the slope to Der el Bahri, let us seek out a place under the shadow of a great rock and settle down for an hour or two of peace among the solemn cliffs. There is shade at midday and in the afternoon at the head of the Valley.

After we have rested and filled our souls with the great scene around, there is a choice of ways to return. Down the Valley is the dullest; over the cliff to Der el Bahri is fine and lets us have a beautiful view from the top, but there is a better to be done. There are few good walks in Egypt, but there are some, and perhaps the best of them is the path from Biban el Muluk to Der el Medineh. . . .

At the top of the pass are the remains of the shelters where the sentinels of old used to be posted to guard the royal cemetery. From this point onwards the view is glorious. All the line of temples lies below us: Seti's the farthest south, in a clump of palms, Der el Bahri, lying right under the precipice, the Ramesseum, and the big bulk of Medinet Habu to the north. On a desert, in a valley to the right of Medinet Habu are the Tombs of the Queens. On a low desert over the hill of the Sheikh Abd el Gurneh and in the surrounding cliffs, is the cemetery of Thebes, of the nobles and the commonality.

Beyond Medinet Habu, lines on the desert surface show us the palace of Amenhotep III, and the big oblong, just on the edge of the cultivated land, enclosed by high mounds, was once a lake, where he took his pleasure boating. Across the Nile are the temples of Luxor and Karnak and the green country, with three distant peaks closing the prospect.

It is too obvious, perhaps, to say that the more often we can cross to the West Bank the better we shall like it. There is more to see than anywhere else in Egypt and the beauty of the surroundings is so remarkable that every day we spend among them leaves a memory that does not fade in the years.

On the Other Side, 1927
Constance Sitwell

We lingered a little where the Colossi stonily sit, gazing out over the land with strange battered calm, their shadows stretching far over the corn that grows thickly to the very base of their thrones. Not far beyond them is the limit of the irrigated ground, and here we found a camel and an ox yoked together ploughing up the caked soil along the last line of living green. Arid and dusty, the earth flew up behind them. In front of us now was a scorched strip of desert, a stone-strewn waste backed by the tawny precipices of the Libyan mountains, and in that mountain face are the Tombs of the Kings.

It was too hot to hurry the donkeys and slowly we rode us towards the ravine which leads to the tomb where Amenhotep still lies. In the ravine itself the heat and glare grew even more intense. The sun beat down with gathering strength upon the crags of yellow and orange limestone, whose jagged edges quivered above us against the blazing sky. Our narrow path was walled in by ribs of rock which threw out all the heat. At last, in the bare face of the cliff we came to a small door. I thanked heaven, saying to myself that we should find darkness inside; surely, too, inside it would be cool? But I was wrong, for after jumping off our donkeys and leaving the guide behind, we plunged into a yet heavier heat. Deeper we went and deeper into an oven of stone,—down long sloping corridors and down steps, past an empty painted chamber and past a well, then down another stretch of stifling dark until right in the heart of the rock we reached the crypt where the king lies.

The tomb has been lit by electricity, and a harsh light now strikes down on the long-dead face. I looked at it with astonishment; it is wonderful that the mummied flesh, the withered tendons, the brittle bones, should have kept so royal an air. Yes, in spite of time and our desecrations, Amenhotep reposes with kingly calm in his ponderous sarcophagus of sandstone. The silent centuries have come and gone and he has lain alone in the sweltering darkness, suffering no change that seems of any account. How noisily the years have passed by outside, how peacefully for him! No change! Only his stained wrappings have become rags, and some one has put in his folded hands a tiny bunch of flowers that have become skeletons. 'Well,' they made me think, 'flowers were the same, I suppose, in Thebes and Babylon. Poppies in Ninevah and jonquils in Tyre! Solomon saw the bright anemones of Judea growing scarlet and purple amongst the stones; and here are Amenhotep and I each with our little bunch.' I looked at the flagging handful which I still held; the dying fragrance of the clover hung heavily in that stagnant air. Maybe, I thought, as we walked back along the soundless passage, this king liked the honey smell of warm clover too when he was outside in the sun.

10
Toward and at Aswan

Nile boats now ply this 220-kilometer stretch of the river more than any other, so it is well known to latter-day travelers with its two important towns of Esna and Edfu. The temple at Esna was for centuries buried beneath the houses of the town and used as a storehouse, seen only by local people and a few adventurous travelers. In 1842 Muhammad 'Ali ordered that the hall of columns be dug out, but it was many years before the temple was fully excavated. Calmer and more easily accessible is the temple at Edfu, which Michael Haag describes as "pure theatre" at which the visitor might cry out, "Cecil B. de Mille, they have outdone you!" At Kom Ombo the temple of Sobek and Horus stands prominently on high ground over-looking the Nile.

At the end of this stretch of a Nile journey is Aswan—a smiling, lively city. It has a sense of being less concerned with the distant past, more concerned with government and commerce, and the to-ing and fro-ing of peoples. The Nile here seems more sparkling as it flows in a narrower bed created by the islands of the First Cataract—and all day long the white-winged sails of the feluccas speed along its surface.

Upper Egypt in January, 1836
William Ramsay

Edfou, Jan. 9: The fields were looking very beautiful; the system of irrigation is carried on at an immense extent here; it is everything; at every short distance, one sees the water raised from the Nile, by men who hand it up in buckets one to another, into little tanks, till it reaches the top, when it runs down the channels formed for it. There is one great channel which branches off into smaller ones, and these into smaller, till at last it enters the small fields or plots, generally about ten feet square, where it spreads and remains, each little plot being enclosed by raised banks, on which the channels run; when one plot is watered, the entrance for the water is closed with a lump of earth, and the water passes onto the next; when the whole of one division has received its share, the connection with the grand passage is stopped, and so on. The squares are all very carefully kept, and, in fact, in this irrigation consists the whole system of husbandry. A plough, I suppose, is never used; all the land requires is a rough breaking up with a hoe for wheat—for clover not even that. Indian corn is now ripe, and the harvest is going on. It is sown before the rise of the Nile, and is ripe soon after its fall; and it is thus calculated that it must have been the corn which was *not* smitten in the Plagues of Egypt by the hail, as it was sprouting above ground when the other corn, which is sown on the waters retiring, was ripe and fit for the harvest.

The same system seems to be persuaded now as in the early and palmy days of this country. The drawings on the walls of some of the tombs display all the processes of husbandry and other daily occupations—and allusions to the Bible might have been made as to what happens at the present day, so much the same has everything remained. It is called "the country that thou waterest with thy foot" and it is so now—the people use their naked feet for stopping the water channels, when required.

A very beautiful plant, which we saw a good deal of today in the fields, is the castor-oil tree—I never saw such a diversity of appearances on one plant at the same time: two totally different flowers on the same stalk, one red, the other white, berries, buds and fruit, something like horse-chestnuts, but more delicate—the young leaves also were of a deep purple, the old ones bright green.

Edfou, 2 Feb. Since we were here last, the appearance of the country is very much altered. The forests of Indian corn are cut down, and the stubble is a poor substitute, especially when the sun is so hot as today; the wheat has grown to eight inches or a foot, in three weeks; the cotton plants have withered, and the irrigation has altered its character.

Raising the Water from the Nile, 1844
Edward Lane

The most important of the occupations which employ the modern Egyptians, and that which engages all but a very small proportion of them, is agriculture.

The great proportion of the cultivable soil is fertilised by the natural annual inundation; but the fields in the vicinity of the river and of the large canals, and some others, in which pits are dug for water, are irrigated by means of machines of different kinds. The most common of these machines is the *shadoof*, which consists of two posts or pillars of wood, or of mud or cane or rushes, about five feet in height, and less than three feet apart, with a horizontal piece of wood extending from top to top, to which is suspended a slender lever, formed by a branch of a tree, having at one end a weight chiefly composed of mud, and at the other, suspended to two long palm-sticks, a vessel in the form of a bowl, made of basket-work, or of a hoop and a piece of woollen stuff or leather; with this vessel the water is thrown up to the height of about eight feet, into a trough hollowed out for its reception. In the southern parts of Upper Egypt, four or five shadoofs are required, when the river is at its lowest, to raise the water to the level of the fields. There are many shadoofs with two levers, etc, which are worked by two men. The operation is extremely laborious.

Another machine much used for the same purpose, and almost the only one employed for the irrigation of gardens in Egypt, is the *sakiyeh*. This mainly consists of a vertical wheel, which raises the water in earthen pots attached by cords, and forming a continuous series; a second vertical wheel, fixed to the same axis, with cogs; and a large, horizontal cogged wheel, which, being turned by a pair of cows or bulls, or a single beast, puts in motion the two former wheels and the pots. The construction of this machine is of a very rude kind; and its motion produces a disagreeable creaking noise.

> Armant is less than ten miles from Luxor, and even by 1873 *Murray's Guide* dismissed its ruins as "hardly worth a visit, except for the purpose of seeing what is supposed to be an authentic portrait of Cleopatra." Yet the remains are in themselves a record of past importance, and Young was fascinated by the carvings.

Armant: Ancient Hermonthis, 1846
Cuthbert Young

At half-past six in the morning, we visited the remains of the ancient city. The present village is large, and situated among a profusion of palms. Rounding a hill, you come suddenly upon the ruins of four ancient temples. Granite columns lie scattered on the site of one; a truncated pillar of great diameter, with a few sculptures, are all that remain, with the foundation stones to mark the second. A fox was startled by our entrance. Of the third there is but the site; of the fourth seven columns remain perfect, and have a graceful effect—the capitals representing the palm leaf under different forms. The porch and the two sanctuaries of this temple are also perfect, though houses are built upon them, and people live inside. A fire was lighted and mats laid for sleeping, in the larger sanctuary. No wonder that the walls are much blackened with smoke.

This temple, small as it is, has most extraordinary sculptures, and it might be called the Pantheon, or caricature-shop of Egypt. On the left as we entered the large sanctuary, is represented a procession of hippopotami in two rows, standing erect on their hind legs; and above them two others, one of which presents offerings to Horus, who is seated upon lotus flowers; two crocodiles with heads defaced, a group of seven cats, seven snakes, and seven dogs, appear in rows of four and three, above each other; a huge hippopotamus stands by himself, while two individuals, marshals perhaps, hand over his offering to the god.

On the opposite wall, a human figure with the ibis head, presents offerings to a monstrous cat; two animals with the hawk's head and alligator's body, stand on shrines or sarcophagi, under one of which is a human head, and under the other a snake;—a human face with the body of a hippopotamus, looks grotesque in the extreme, like an ancient gentleman with the fall of his periwig hanging down to his heels, and well muffled up in ermine. Twelve human heads in four rows of three each, peep over, as their twenty-four feet peep under, an oblong chest, which may represent a sarcophagus carried by them. It is elegantly and profusely ornamented with flowers.

Above the entrance door is the hawk-headed Horus, perched on a bull's horns. On the ceiling I distinguished two rams with wings, also the scorpion and the bull of which Irby and Mangles [earlier travelers] speak, but the head of the latter seemed defaced. Three large groups of figures on the left wall of the entrance, above the animals, represent a little boy on a large raised box, his mother, perhaps Cleopatra (for she founded this mammeisi) behind him, and a man, perhaps Julius Caesar, before.

In the inner and smaller sanctuary are pictured two cows, and a child sucking each, the animals having their heads turned towards the infants,—they are meant perhaps for Isis and Horus. On the opposite wall are several females suckling infants. Worshippers on bended knees are adoring the scarabaeus, and two sets of birds with human heads are in the act of flying.

We had torches to see this chamber, but the smoke soon forced us out.

The Sailors Enjoy Esna, 1842
W.H. Bartlett

Esneh, which we reached next day, detained us for some hours. The Reis and sailors went into town to obtain provisions, and we had great difficulty in getting them together. There were, in fact, potent attractions on shore, Esneh being the head quarters of the banished dancing-girls, who flaunt about the bazaars with loose, immodest dresses, and dusky cheeks thickly covered with paint. The portico of the temple struck us as the most magnificent specimen of the Ptolemaic style in Egypt. The earth has almost covered the exterior, although Mehemet Ali has cleared out the inside, into which you, accordingly, have to descend. The columns are unusually tall and slender, and the exquisite variety and graceful designs of the capitals, all formed upon the type of different plants and flowers of the country, is no where surpassed, if equalled.

Esneh is a town of some little consequence, but, like Nile towns in general, presents nothing to interest the traveller beyond this splendid portico, and as soon as we could drive on board our reluctant sailors, we spread our sails and hastened up the river.

The Barrage at Esna, 1907
Douglas Sladen

Esna, as we approached it in 1907, was all in a ferment; it was beside itself with importance. A fourth of the great Nile barrages was in the full swing of construction. Already a monster viaduct, long and high, was advancing upon the river from the eastern bank; and scores of huge *gyassas,* the Nile merchant-men, laden with earth, were running upstream with their vast wings of sails blown out stiff, to dump their cargoes on the advancing dam. The presence of all these native craft, of an army of fellahin navvies, and a posse of English engineers made business in the little town brisk. It reminded the Esnites of the palmy days when Esna had a governor, and was the chief town of a province, which was quietly cut in two and handed over to Kena and Assuan in 1889. Its government offices were moved to Assuan; the staff at any rate must have been pleased, since Assuan in winter is the most fashionable place in Egypt.

Most of the 13,500 inhabitants of Esna, who were not earning wages at barrage-building, were assembled on the shore for the arrival of our streamer. A barber was doing a thriving trade by the water's edge, and you could have any number you wanted of leather water-bottles, decorated with shells. But the principal feature of the al fresco market which was accommodating itself to the steep slopes of the bank, was the display of baskets, about four feet high, shaped like oil-jars, and woven of purple, green and white cane splints, arranged in rows.

Until the barrage was commenced travellers only regarded Esna from one point of view—as a place with a temple; and until the time of Mohammed Ali this was buried up to the capitals of its façade, and over head and ears and everywhere else. He had one chamber of it—the hypostyle hall, cleared out in 1842; the rest of the temple, which is said to be complete, was underground when I was there, and half the city of Esna was built on top of it. As it had formally stood at the top of the town, this was naturally the airiest situation.

Edfu, the Ancient Apollinopolis Magna, 1827
The Modern Traveller

At the north-western corner of the village, and on the highest ground, stands a magnificent temple, which, though seen after Dendera, and inferior in size to that of Karnak, is said to yield in effect to neither, the mole and entrance being particularly noble. Numerous brick huts have been erected upon the top of the temple, in the peristyle, and in front of the propylon, so as to render access to it difficult every way. The propylon is in the form of a truncated pyramid, and

Edfou, entrance court

is at once the most imposing and one of the best proportioned in Egypt. From a base 90 feet in length by 30 feet in width, it rises up on each side of the gateway, 'like two square towers without embrasures', gradually narrowing till, at the height of 100 feet, it measures on the flattened top only 75 feet by 18. Handsome stairs lead from the gateway on either hand to the different chambers and to the summit. Over the entrance is the globe with the serpent and wings, and on each side is sculptured on the wall a colossal figure of Isis, attended by the hawk-headed deity and another colossal figure armed with a hatchet.

Within the propylon is an open court, or *dromos,* enclosed with high walls covered with sculpture, and adorned with a peristyle of eleven columns, besides five on each side of the doorway, all covered with sculpture. The pronaus, at the northern end of the court, has six columns in front, with varied capitals, resembling the leafs of the *doum,* or Thebaic palm, the leaf of the date-tree and the budding lotus. The winged globe and serpent occur again over the door, and are frequently repeated on each side, with other strange devices of beetles, long-tailed monkeys, etc. A moulding passes down the corners of the temple, the same as at Dendera and Esneh, so as to include the whole in a frame. Within the pronaus are two rows of columns, three in each row, loaded with hieroglyphics and devices; the globe with wings are painted along the centre of the ceiling, and each intercolumniation has its peculiar ornament; but there is no zodiac. On the walls, Osiris, Isis and Horus are receiving offerings. The entrance to the cella is quite blocked up with sand and rubbish.

Edfu Seen with Clarity, 1927
Constance Sitwell

The massive outer walls of the temple are still whole at Edfu; one can look right down the open passages that run all the length of the building; one can walk unseen along those mighty corridors between calm golden walls incised with histories of gods and warriors and kings. There is no painting here, no colour but the scorched bright amber of the stone, and the pure cobalt of the sky above. I wandered about by myself without the fear of being alone, which haunts one beneath the monstrous columns of Karnac. This building is neither stupendous nor strange, and centuries of quiet burial beneath the drifting sand have kept it from falling into ruin. It stands now as it stood then, its beauty, unchanged, its shadow clear-cut and distinct under the fierce insistent sunlight as they were of old.

As I passed between the towers of the gateway which lift their splendid sloping sides high into the blue, I tried to imagine the scene on a feast day when decorated poles were fixed to the walls, and the coloured banners streamed fluttering against the sky. In the court, the arrogant painted priests assembled in their brightly fringed robes of fine linen. I suppose they had the same proud mouths and delicate oval faces that one still sees here and there among the living as well as in the sculptured dead. Did they stand in solemn order, their shadows sharp upon the ground, with the vivid walls behind, all fresh with tints of daffodil, turquoise, and pale vermilion? And the King, would he be there with the leopard-skin thrown over his shoulder and the sun striking dazzling on the golden cobra, with lifted head that made his royal headdress? Yes, and his arms are heavy with bracelets and ornaments set with lapis lazuli and emeralds.

The stones of the stairs leading to the roof are worn by the feet of men who walked there thousands of years ago. I climbed them now, going in the steps of those who carried offerings to the sun-god, and stood looking down on the wide empty view. There is no town here now; nothing moves at this somnolent hour, only down a path through the doura and maize a man in a yellow-striped bournous walks slowly along, carrying a squawking turkey blue with rage.

Go to the Other Side, 1847
John Gardner Wilkinson

Silsileh is remarkable for the immense quarries of sandstone from which the blocks used in the greater part of the Egyptian temples were taken. They extend on both sides of the river, those on the East bank being the most remarkable for their extent, and those on the West for their curious grottoes and inscriptions. The dahabiyeh is usually moored to the West bank, but it is easy to row over the other side in a felucca, and no one should omit to do so.

Kom Ombo Observed, 1817
Dr. Robert Richardson

There is no propylon or *dromos* in front of the temple, but the portico is very magnificent, and presents an imposing façade 83 feet in length towards the river. It has consisted of fifteen massy columns, five in front and three in depth. They are about 30 feet high, and nearly 20 feet in circumference at the base, and are covered with sculptured figures or hieroglyphics, with capitals modelled after the palm-branch, the *doum* and the lotus. The remains of the whole building are about 120 feet in length. The interior is quite different from that of any other temple in the country. It is entered from the portico by three doors, which have the globe and serpent with wings sculptured over each. The middle door leads into a large chamber, which seems to have no communication with any other part; but it is so much filled up with sand and stones, that this cannot be ascertained. The other two doors lead to passages passing on through the whole suite of four chambers, almost all of which have doors communicating with the outside, but not with each other, through the partition-wall in the centre of the edifice. . . . The whole of the interior is very much filled with sand, and the walls have partly fallen down. . . . The sculpture on this temple does not appear ever to have been finished: the best executed is on the pronaus. Osiris is frequently depicted with a crocodile's head, with the sceptre and sacred *tau* in his hand, and receiving offerings.

Observed at Kom Ombo, 1848
Harriet Martineau

One curious architectural device of the Egyptians, which we found almost everywhere by looking for it, is here apparent at a glance, when one stands on the great circuit wall which encloses the whole group of edifices:—their plan of regularly diminishing the size of the inner chambers, so as to give, from the entrance, an appearance of a longer perspective than exists. They evidently liked an ascending ground, the ascent of which was disguised as much as possible by the use of extremely shallow steps. The roof was made to ascend in a great degree, the descent being concealed inside by the large cornices and deep architraves they employed. The sides were made to draw in; and thus the Holy Place was always small; while to those who looked towards it from the outer chambers, (and it was entered by priests alone) it appeared, not small, but distant. I had observed this in some of the Nubian temples, when looking at them sideways from a distance; but here it was particularly evident; the roof descending in deep steps from the portico to the pronaus; from the naos to the corridors; and from the corridors to the adyta, which last were level with the sand.

When I was in the portico, looking up at the architraves, I saw into another ancient secret, which I should have been very sorry to have overlooked. Some of the paintings were half-finished; and their ground was still covered with the intersecting red lines by which the artists secured their proportions. These guiding lines were meant to be effaced as soon as the outlines were completed; yet here they are at the end of at least, two thousand years! No hand, however light, has touched them, through all the intervening generations of men;—no rains have washed them out, during all the changing seasons that have passed over them;—no damp has moulded them; no curiosity meddled with them. It is as if the artist had lain down for his siesta, his tools beside his hand, and would be up presently to resume his work; yet that artist had been a mummy, lying somewhere in the heart of the neighbouring hills, ever since the time when our island was bristling with forests, and its inhabitants were dressed in skins, and dyed their bodies blue with woad, to look terrible in battle. In another part of the temple, the stone is diced in small squares, to receive the hieroglyphic figures.

Approach to Aswan: The Country Changes, 1817
Dr. Robert Richardson
. . . We came in sight of the mountain range that bounds the extremity of Egypt towards the south. On the west of the river, the mountain range that had accompanied us all the way from Cairo, destitute of vegetation throughout the whole extent, began to assume a bolder aspect, rising into a round bluff point, overlooking the plain, the town, the ruins of Assuan, the island of Elephantina, the rugged cataract, and the branching Nile. It is called Djibl Howa, or mountain of the wind. Its summit is crowned with the tomb of Sheikh Bass, an honoured Maraboot; halfway down its side are the extensive ruins of the convent of St George, with numerous vaults and excavations, soliciting the attention of the enquiring traveller.

On the east bank of the river the mountain is low, the valley more extended, cultivated and covered with the picturesque palm tree. The aspect gradually ascends in a rocky inclination, and, winding towards the west, terminates at the river, in a precipitous granite cliff, on which stand the ruined walls and houses of the ancient Syene.

Passing the eye along the river as we advance, it was impossible not to be impressed with the singular majesty of its appearance, parted at the bottom of the cataract by the granite base of the green and beautiful island of Elephantina, it poured along its sides as if from an invisible source, and, having joined its divided waters at the low northern end of the island, held on its noble and rapid course to the ocean.

Nearly Five Hundred Miles up the Nile, 1843
Countess Hahn-Hahn
We arrived here yesterday afternoon, having left Fostat on 19th December, and spent 24 hours at Denderah. This is no inconsiderable time for a distance of 480 miles. Such dilatoriness would drive one to despair in Europe—but here the journey is considered a very fair one; and had the wind been contrary we should have been a week or fortnight longer.

The wind was favourable nearly the whole time, and but rarely fails altogether, and then the excessively tedious process of pulling the vessel along the shore, or

pushing it with poles among the innumerable sandbanks, did not advance us much.
We reached Assuan in full sail, with a favourable wind and the jubilant cries
of our crew. Assuan presents a highly picturesque appearance, rising upon the
eastern bank; it consists of the modern town, which is advantageously concealed
behind a grove of palms, and the old Arab town, which is built upon the ruins of
the Roman, as that probably was erected on the yet more ancient Egyptian. It is
situated upon a high, rugged hill, close to the river, and is now a complete ruin.
The unburnt bricks used by the ancient Arabs, and still employed by their descen-
dants, form very remarkable ruins, and heaps of rubbish as those of burnt bricks,
or of stones; but they are more jagged and stand out in rising, isolated, perpendicular masses of cliffs, which look as if they had been dashed to pieces by some
giant's hand. They have a very good effect at a distance, with the transparent background of the beautifully tinted sky; but, on a nearer approach, the materials are
too mean for effect; in this respect we are spoiled in Egypt, not indeed by the
present, but by the past.

Not far from Assuan are the granite quarries, which produce the magnificent
red granite, so admired by the ancients, and called syenite after its locale; the small
island of Bidsha, opposite to Philæ, produces the infinitely more beautiful rose
granite, of which a gateway still continues to adorn Elephantina, as a remnant of
its former magnificence. This latter island lies opposite Assuan, on this side of the
cataracts; the two other cataracts are about a league beyond it, and the Nile
whirling and foaming, rushes between them.

Life on the Nile, c. 960
Ebn Haukal

The Nile produces *crocodiles,* and the fish *sekenkour;* and there is also a species of
fish, called *raadah,* which if any person take it in hand while it is alive, that person will be affected by a trembling of his body; when dead, this fish resembles
other fish. The crocodile's head is very long, so long as to be one half of his whole
form, and he has such teeth, that, if a lion were to come within their hold, he
would be destroyed. It sometimes happens that the crocodile comes out of the
water on dry ground; but he has not then the same powers as when in the water.
His skin is so hard that it resists the blows of all weapons when stricken on the
back; they then wound him where the forelegs join the body, and between the
thighs. The *sekenkour* is a species of the crocodile, but the crocodile has *hands and
feet;* and they use the *sekenkour* in medical and culinary preparations. This creature is not found anywhere but in the River Nile.

Doing Business at Aswan, 1879
Villiers Stuart

On awaking, and taking a bird's eye view from our cabin window of the outer
world, a very amusing scene occupied the foreground. A number of Nubian men,

women and children were squatting on the sandy shore with their wares arranged on mats before them, patiently awaiting our appearance, smoking and chatting with our crew the while; but no sooner did we step forth, than the greatest excitement prevailed, they started up with one accord and took to brandishing their merchandize over their heads, advertising them by power of lung, and deafening us with a perfect Babel of sounds.

They held out towards us: ostrich eggs, Nubian spears, armlets, necklaces, bracelets, porcupine quills, bows and arrows, ebony clubs, daggers, ostrich feathers, leopard skins, hippopotamus-hide whips, cunningly made baskets, and Egyptian antiquities. Our dragoman took very good care not to let them come on board. Their wares were handed in for our inspection; they themselves were made to keep their distance; and when we went on shore, we landed under escort of a body-guard of our crew, who kept the Nubian merchants off with their sticks.

A little higher up the beach were the goods of a caravan, bound for Khartoum; boxes and bales arranged in a circle formed a sort of camp; their saloon, reception-room, and dining-room was the home of the travellers by day, and their dormitory by night. We visited them at the hour of breakfast; their wants were being ministered to by a number of Nubian girls, some having milk to sell, others cheese, butter, new-baked cakes, cucumbers, buttermilk, and other delicacies. Some were smoking, some were cooking, some were bargaining with the vendors of the eatables; in the middle was a sort of trophy supported on three poles, and consisting of water skins; jars covered with goats' hide with the shaggy hair still on, lanterns, pots, and other camp equipage. Outside the magic circle squatted some camels; it was a very picturesque and amusing scene.

When the Cataract Hotel, high above the pool of the Nile that lay below the First Cataract, was officially opened in 1900, it brought a surge of tourists to Aswan—a new kind of traveler in Egypt.

The Cataract Hotel and the Invalid, 1899
W.E. Kingsford

In the construction of this hotel great attention has been given to the requirements of invalids—most of the rooms have verandas, and a warm, sunny aspect; many are fitted with fireplaces, and the position and form of the building has been chosen to provide shelter from the prevailing winds. The sanitary arrangements have been carefully studied, Moule's earth closet system being adopted, and the water being filtered through Reeves' gravity, and Berkefeld filters.

Every modern convenience is provided in the form of electric light, hot and cold water baths etc, and a reference to the plan will show that there are a number of private sitting rooms to meet the requirements of invalids. There is an English physician and nurse in Assuan, and an English housekeeper is in charge of the domestic arrangements of the Hotel.

The Tourists Make Their Mark, 1902
Sir Gaston Maspero

. . . now from the middle of December to the middle of March Assuan never sleeps. It has become a winter resort, like Nice or Sorrento, and has had to transform itself to satisfy the demands of passing visitors. The embankment, formerly so picturesque, though rough and dirty, has been replaced by a regular quay, with decorations in black, adorned with palms already high and with lebakhs which will grow if Heaven pleases. The whole front is almost European in appearance, with its banks, post office, hospital, fountain, chapel, cafes, hotels, taverns, shops with glass windows and covered with advertisements. A Dalmatian photographer invites you in composite French not to buy your films anywhere except at his shop. His neighbour, a Greek tobacconist, offers you the best to be had in cigarettes and silks, all English, but if you need eau de Cologne you must go further to the Italian bookseller, who will supply you. As you pass obliging Parsees cry their cloths, printed in loud colours, and their coarse Indian silver-work. At the southern end two or three cabs of the most correct pattern await custom with resignation, at the head of a rank of numbered donkeys, and then the railway station, with its level entrance marks at the end of the esplanade.

Here, then, the quay ends, and the shore reappears, capricious, scattered over with all kinds of breakneck objects, bristling with heaps of broken stones, piles of wood, of barrels or of sacks, but also with booths and tents that betray a fair in which toys and popular cakes are offered for sale, where there is cooking in the open air, and even an itinerant circus under a French flag, whence a newly shorn ass's foal and a superb white camel come forth to the tune of a polka to drink at the river.

> The seventh-century monastery of St. Simeon, on the west bank of the Nile, is thought of as the finest example of an early Christian monastery in Egypt—though it was later used as a fortress.

The Monastery of St. Simeon, 1799
Vivant Denon

I took the opportunity offered by the reconnoitring which was pushed into the desert on the right bank, to seek for the quarries spoken of by Pococke, and an ancient convent of Cenobites. After half an hour's march, I discovered this building, in a little valley, surrounded by rugged rocks, and by sands which their decomposition produced. The detachment, in pursuit of its route, left me to my researches in this place.

Scarcely was this gone, when I was alarmed by my solitude. Lost in long corridors the re-echoed noise of my steps under their melancholy vaults, was perhaps the only one which, for many ages, had troubled their silence. The cells of the monks resembled the cages of animals in a menagerie; a square of seven feet was illumined only by a dormer-window at the height of six feet; this refinement of austerity, however, robbed the recluse only of a view of a vast extent of sky, an equally vast horizon of sand, an immensity of light as melancholy and more painful than night, and which would have but increased, perhaps, the afflicting sentiment of his solitude. In this dungeon, a couch of brick, and a recess serving for a press, was all that art had added to the bareness of the four walls; a turning box, placed beside the door, still proves that these solitaries took their repasts apart. A few mutilated sentences written on the walls, were the only testimonies that men had inhabited these abodes. I thought I saw in these inscriptions their last sentiments, a last communication with the beings who were to survive them, a hope which time, that effaces all, had still frustrated. . . .

Oppressed by the feelings with which these series of melancholy objects had inspired me, I went into the court, in search of space: surrounded by lofty and embattled walls, covered ways, and the embrasures of cannon, all announced that, in this dismal place, the storms of war had succeeded to the horrors of silence; that this edifice . . . had at divers epochs, served for the retreat of vanquished parties, or the advance post of vanquishers. The different character of its construction may also give the history of this edifice. Begun in the first ages of Christianity, of all that was built by her has still preserved its grandeur and magnificence; that which war has added has been done in haste, and is now more ruinous than the former. In the court, a little church, built with unburnt bricks, attests that a small number of solitaries has returned at a later time, and reassumed possession; to conclude, a more recent devastation gives reason to believe that it is only a few ages since the place has been wholly restored to the abandonment and silence to which it has been condemned by nature.

I was rejoined by the detachment, and, on leaving the convent, I seemed to leave a tomb.

The Brassy Landscape of Nubia, 1927
Constance Sitwell

Some hours later we set out, Jim and I riding in front, Philip following at a little distance behind.

We were going up a mountain from which one got a distant view over the brassy landscape of Nubia. It was past noon when at last we reached our goal, a ridge on a craggy cliff facing the south. Arid was the land immediately around us, a confusion of jagged peaks and twisted ravines. It might have all been cast in some heavy metal, so hard and so massive with its surface spread out under a sky hazy with heat.

11
Beyond the Cataract and into Nubia

Above the cataract, the land we see now is a very different land from that described, for example, by the German Prince Puckler-Muskau. The Nile Valley has entirely changed its appearance; temples have been moved, or even shipped overseas in gratitude for help given with the rescue of monuments during the creation of Lake Nasser. Only by looking at old drawings and photographs, and reading past accounts can we comprehend the change wrought on the landscape by the creation of the two dams at Aswan. The cataract once barred the way to Nubia, and ascending and descending it was a hazardous undertaking. Now, only by standing on the Aswan Dam (built 1898–1902), can one gain some idea of the cataract as it once was: the water swirls round the jagged rocks, it froths but no longer roars. That dam created a reservoir during the annual inundation, and under its waters sank the island of Philae, so winter visitors drifted in boats between the temple columns. The High Dam, completed in 1970, created Lake Nasser: 510 kilometers long, stretching far into Sudan; its width ranging from five to thirty-five kilometers across; its surface about 182 meters above sea level, so one sails on it above the crags of Nubia.

Fifty countries, including some of the newly independent
African states, joined together to fund the Nubian Rescue
Campaign, and temples were moved above the flood to sites
as near to and as similar as possible to their origins. The
temples on Philae were moved to nearby Agilkia Island; the
temple of Kalabsha was moved fifty kilometers north, the
temple of Dakka, forty kilometers south; the temple of
Dendur, coveted by Prince Puckler-Muskau, traveled to the
Metropolitan Museum in New York; the temple of Derr
crossed the Nile; Qasr Ibrim, built on a towering headland,
is the one ancient site to remain where it was built—though
the headland is now an island. Not everyone knows of the
movements of these smaller temples, but the dramatic rescue
of the two rock-cut temples of Ramesses II at Abu Simbel is
rightly recognized as one of the world's greatest cooperative
efforts. As Jocelyn Gohary comments in her *Guide to the
Nubian Monuments on Lake Nasser,* "How gratified Ramesses
II must be feeling in whatever afterlife he is enjoying!"

But the ordinary Nubian people fared less well. They were
moved too, to other areas of Egypt and into Sudan, and under
the waters of Lake Nasser are their homes and farms, their villages and towns. At the Nubia Museum in Aswan and in some
villages along the Nile one catches a glimpse of the village life
and folklore that has disappeared under the water. Only an
occasional fisherman remains to remind one of the people
who once lived here. Yet so successful was the rescue of the
ancient sites that many of the observations and emotions that
the writers of another age left us continue on as vibrant and
understandable as in their day. For many of today's travelers
this is the end of the journey; once people pressed on to Wadi
Halfa, the beginnings of Sudan, the Second Cataract, and the
rock at Abusir where they often left their marks.

The Cataract Bars the Way, 1777
Claude Etienne Savary

The cataract is still in our days what is described by Strabo: the rock which bars
the middle of the river is bare for six months of the year. Then boats mount and
descend by the sides. During the inundation, the waters heaped up between the
mountains form one great sheet, and, breaking down every obstacle, . . . The
boats can no longer ascend the stream, and merchandize must be conveyed two
leagues over land, above the cataract; they descend, however, as usual, and suffer
themselves to be plunged in the gulph. They precipitate themselves into it with
the rapidity of an arrow and in an instant are out of sight. It is necessary for the

Frontier of Egypt and Nubia

boats to be moderately laden, and for the boatmen who hold by the stern, to be in exact equilibrium, otherwise they would infallibly be swallowed up in the abyss.

Geographical Outline of Nubia, 1833
Reverend Michael Russell

No sooner does the traveller pass the cataract of Es Souan, than he finds himself in Nubia, a country of which it is now impossible to fix the precise extent. Indeed we cannot otherwise define it than by saying, that it occupies the valley of the Nile from Philae to Dongola, and is bounded on either side by formidable deserts, which can only be crossed by large bodies of men assisted by that useful animal the camel. The first section which terminates at Ibrim, has been so long subject to Egypt that it is usually known as Turkish Nubia; but we are told that the natives of the upper country, who roam in comparative independence as far as the second cataract, restrict the proud name to their own land, which, till lately, spurned the dominion of every foreign sword.

For a considerable distance above Syene, the mountains press so closely on the banks of the river that there is little land on either side for the purposes of agriculture; and the small portion that is suitable for raising a crop is continually threatened by the approach of the sand which the winds of the desert carry towards the stream. From the structure of the valley, through which the Nile here forces a passage, it is obvious that there could not at any time have been an extensive population. The labour of man would have exerted its powers in vain against the sterility of nature, which, amidst rocks and shingle, occupies, by an everlasting tenure, a wide domain in the Lower Nubia. But beyond the parallel of Wady Halfa . . . there is ample space for the great nations which are said to flourish in Ethiopia. At the southern termination of the second cataract immense plains stretch out from the margin of the river, manifesting even in their present neglected state the most unequivocal symptoms of a prolific soil.

Into Nubia, 1897
Sir Arthur Conan Doyle
Between these two huge and barren expanses [of desert], Nubia writhes like a green sand-worm along the course of the river. Here and there it disappears altogether, and the Nile runs between black and sun-cracked hills, with the orange drift-sand lying like glaciers in their valleys. Everywhere one sees traces of vanished races and submerged civilisations. Grotesque graves dot the hills or stand up against the skyline,—pyramidal graves, tumulus graves, rock graves,—everywhere graves. And, occasionally, as the boats round a rocky point, one sees a deserted city up above,—houses, walls, battlements,—with the sun shifting through the empty window squares. Sometimes you learn that it has been Roman, sometimes Egyptian; sometimes all record of its name or origin has been absolutely lost. There they stand, these grim and silent cities, and up on the hills you can see the graves of their people, like the port-holes of a man-of-war. It is through this weird, dead country that the tourists smoke and gossip and flirt as they pass up to the Egyptian frontier.

> Passing through the cataract before the dams were built could be dangerous depending on the season of the year and the flow of the river. Travelers' boats were taken through the rushing waters by the age-old skills of experienced local teams. Isambard Kingdom Brunel was one of Britain's greatest engineers and ship builders, so his appreciative assessment of the management of taking boats up the cataract above Aswan is of very special significance.

An Engineer at the Cataract, 1859
Isambard Kingdom Brunel
Philae, February 13, 1859
I now write to you from a charming place; but Assouan, which I left to come here, is also beautiful, and I will speak of that first. It is strange that so little is said in the guide books of the picturesque beauty of these places. Approaching

Assouan, you glide through a reef of rocks, large boulders of granite polished by the action of the water charged with sand. You arrive at a charming bay or lake of perfectly still water and studded with those singular jet-black or red-rock islands. In the distance you see a continuation of the river, with distant islands shut in by mountains, of beautiful colours, some a lilac sandstone, some of the bright yellow of the sands of the desert. Above the promontories the water excursions are delicious. You enter at once among the islands of the Cataracts, fantastic forms of granite heaps of boulders split and worn into singular shapes.

After spending a week at Assouan, with a trip by land to Philae, I was so charmed with the appearance of the Cataracts as seen from the shore, and with the deliciously quiet repose of Philae, that I determined to get a boat, and sleep a few nights there. We succeeded in hiring a country boat laden with dates, and emptied her, and fitted up her three cabins. [Mr. Brunel's Nile boat, being of iron, could not safely go up the Cataract.] We put our cook and dragoman and provisions etc on board, and some men, and went up the Cataract.

It was a most amusing affair, and most beautiful and curious scenery all the way. It is a long rapid of three miles, and perhaps one mile wide, full of rocky islands and isolated rocks. A bird's eye view hardly shows a free passage, and some of the more rapid falls are between rocks not forty feet wide—in appearance not twenty. Although they do not drag the boats up perpendicular falls, of three or four feet, as the travellers' books tell you, they really do drag the boats up rushes of water which, until I had seen it, and had then calculated the power required, I should imprudently have said could not be effected. We were dragged up at one place a gush of water, what might fairly be called a fall of about three feet, the water rushing past very formidably, and between rocks seemingly not more than wide enough to let our boat pass, and this only by some thirty-five men at three or four ropes, the men standing in the water and on the rocks in all directions, shouting, plunging into the water, swimming across the top or bottom of the fall, just as they wanted, then getting under the boat to push it off rocks, all with an immense expenditure of noise and apparent confusion and want of plan, yet on the whole properly and successfully.

We were probably twenty or thirty minutes getting up this one, sometimes bumping hard on one rock, sometimes on another, and jammed hard first on one side and then on the other, the boat all the time on the fall with ropes all strained, sometimes going up a foot or two, sometimes losing it, til at least we crept to the top, and sailed quietly on in a perfectly smooth lake. These efforts up the different falls had been going on for nearly eight hours and the relief from noise was delicious. We selected a quiet spot under the temples of Philae. . . .

The Rush of the Cataract, 1836
Lord Lindsay

. . . the cry arose that we were going down the stream again! I sprung out, the vessel was edging away from the rock—I leapt and caught by my hands, my feet in the water; the Arabs pulled me up, and I was safe, thank God! Twice did the boat nearly escape us, the current was so violent; at last we got her safely lashed to the rock with all the ropes we had, and for an hour, or more, the men were occupied in landing everything portable: first our things, then the oars, planks, etc, of the boat, lastly their own stores of dates and biscuits, which they could not touch (honest fellows!) till ours were safe. We expected every minute to see the ropes break and the boat topple over, lying sideways as she did, the deck half under water.

Here we were then, and a most extraordinary scene it was to be in! Wild and picturesque at all times, doubly so now, dark purple clouds lowering around us, rain pouring (a wonder of itself in Upper Egypt), lightning flashing, and thunder outroaring the rapids that were dashing past on either side of our islet, covered as it was with boxes, books, pipes, guns, crockery, pigeons, fowls, lambs, goats, and last but not least, two chameleons, poor things!

Delayed, 1817
Dr. Robert Richardson
It was our intention to have sailed at an early hour next morning; but on giving directions for that purpose, it was discovered that the colours had been left behind at Assouan, and it was impossible to sail without them; they were our national banners, the badge and ensign of our country, which we were deter-mined to display wherever wind or wave would carry us. . . . A trusty British tar [a sailor] was despatched with a guide back to the vessels [which they had left below the cataract, transferring to smaller local boats to sail into Nubia], to bring the flag which he had often defended. . . . The next day we spread our sails and banner to the wind, and with a favourable breeze began to stem the current of the north.

Whose Flag is This? 1855
John Gadsby
We met a boat with a flag flying aft something like the Union Jack with a goose in the centre. As I did not know to what country it belonged, I took out a chart which I had, 'Flags of all Nations', to satisfy myself. The crew all came round me, to look at the chart, and were highly amused; and I was surprised to see that they knew so many of the flags as they did. Pointing to the Stars and Stripes, they exclaimed, "American! American!" To the Tricolour, "Fransowee!" (French); To the Union Jack, "Inglees, tyeeb!" (English, good!); To the Double-Headed Eagle, "Moscow!" (Russian); "Whoo! whoo! whoo!" (holding out their arms as if firing a gun). This was during the war [in the Crimea]. I could not, however, find the looked-for flag anywhere upon the chart; so I concluded it was some goose or other who had stuck itself in the middle of the English flag to make itself look sin-gular, and attract attention.

In Nubia more than elsewhere in Egypt, the travelers wrote
of the animal life: large mammals, reptiles, and small but
destructive insects.

Animal Life, 1792
W.G. Browne

The wild and ferocious animals are, principally, the lion, the leopard and the
hyena, the wolf, the jackal, the wild buffalo, but they are not commonly seen
within the more cultivated parts of the [Ottoman] empire, except the hyena and
the jackal.

The former comes in herds of six, eight and often more, into all the villages
at night, even within the enclosure of the houses, and fail not to assemble wherever a dead camel or other animal is thrown, which, acting in concert, they sometimes drag a prodigious distance. . . . The people of the country dig pits for them,
and lying in ambuscade, when one is entrapped, stun him with clubs, or pierce
him with their spears.

The jackal is harmless, but his uncouth cry is heard far off, and wherever there
are rocks to shelter them, their howling community dwells undisturbed.

The Chameleon as a Pet, 1836
William Ramsay

Jan 22. Gave half a piastre for a couple of chameleons, which we have been trying
unsuccessfully, to tame. Their natural colour appears to be a fine green, which is
changed into a deep brown or black, and varies between the two. It is a very curious animal, like a lizard in general appearance, but much slower in its motions, and
differently organised. The body is about four inches long and tapering, about double
that length. It has a large and enormous mouth; the eyes are covered with a skin the
same as its body, with a small hole in the centre, which they have the power of
directing to any point they choose, so that they can see in all possible directions,
without moving the head; each eye is moved quite independently of the other, so that
one is often pointed forward while the other looks backward. The feet are divided
into two parts, of the same size and form, with three sharp claws on each part, and
they have the power of grasping with the two divisions, as well as hanging by the tail;
the division and action of the feet are on much the same principle as those of our
hands and thumb, only as if they were two hands thus united, with three fingers each.

Locusts, 1827
Robert Hay

This morning the cries of the people were heard on both sides of the river
lamenting the certain loss of their crops and calling on God and the Prophet to
spare them. Last night's (southerly) wind had brought down a large flight of

locusts which now darkened the air and was settling on every green spot they could find. The whole morning they were very numerous but not as they were at first, as a great proportion of them had settled.

About one o'clock I went out of the boat and my surprise was indescribable when I witnessed the scene of devastation that lay before me. A field of young dura was eaten level with the ground, so that there existed scarcely part of a stalk! Yet notwithstanding the clearance they made, the ground was literally yellow with them, and I think without any exaggeration, and even perhaps I am within bounds when I say they were 40 to each square foot! How frightful then must have been their numbers when we consider the distance they spread themselves? As we walked through [a field] they rose like a swarm of bees, at this time the air was so filled with them that it had perfectly the appearance of a heavy fall of snow which appearance was increased by the thickness of the atmosphere.

Hay moved on up the river.

The water wheels had ceased to work and everything wore so sad an aspect that we could not feel too thankful that our own country is not visited by such a dreadful and appalling scourge! Labour lost, and money that can be ill afforded spent. All to begin again! and perhaps it may be again the fate of the second crop to be devoured in a few hours after weeks of labour!!!

Along the banks every tree and bush was yellow with the *crop* of locusts that it bore; all verdure was fast disappearing and in a great many instances, perfectly gone. Sunt trees and doums. Palm-trees with their fruit. The cotton plant. The dura and even the coarse grass all shared the same fate!

I believe it almost impossible for any one to conceive such a scene without having witnessed it. For though they may give credit to what has been related by so many, they cannot form an idea of the scene of rapid desolation that follows the appearance of this destructive insect.

Philae, 1825
Dr. R.R. Madden
There are four recollections of a traveller, which might tempt him to live forever: the sea view of Constantinople, the sight of the Coliseum by moonlight, the prospect from the summit of Vesuvius by dawn, and the first glimpse of Philae at sunset.

Philae, 1852
Dean Arthur Penrhyn Stanley
And now, it is immediately above the roar of these rapids—but still in the very

Approach to Philæ

centre of these colossal rockeries—that emerges into sight an island lying in the river—fringed with palms, and crowned with a long line of temples and colonnades. This is Philae.

The Island of Philae, 1833
Robert Curzon

Excepting the Pyramids, nothing in Egypt struck me so much as when on a bright moonlit night I first entered the court of the great temple of Philae. The colours of the paintings on the walls are as vivid in many places as they were the day they were finished: the silence and the solemn grandeur of the immense buildings around me were most imposing; and on emerging from the lofty gateway between the two towers of the propylon, as I wandered about the island, the tufts of palms, which are here of great height, with their weeping branches, seemed to be mourning over the desolation of the stately palaces and temples to which in ancient times all the illustrious of Egypt were wont to resort, and into whose inner recesses none might penetrate; for the secret and awful mysteries of the worship of Osiris were not to be revealed, nor were they even to be spoken of by those who were not initiated into the highest orders of the priesthood. Now all may wander where they choose, and speculate on the uses of the dark chambers hidden in the thickness of the walls, and trace out the plans of the courts and temples with the long lines of columns which formed the avenue of approach from the principal landing-place to the front of the great temple.

I have been three times at Philae, and indeed I had so great an admiration of the place, that on my last visit, thinking it probable that I should never again behold its wonderful ruins and extraordinary scenery, I determined to spend the day there alone, that I might meditate at my leisure, and wander as I chose from one well-remembered spot to another, without the incumbrance of half a dozen people staring at whatever I looked at, and following me about out of pure idleness. Greatly did I enjoy my solitary day, and whilst leaning over the parapet on the top of the great Propylon, or seated on one of the terraces which overhung the Nile, I in imagination repeopled the scene with the forms of the priests and worshippers of other days, restored the fallen temples to their former glory, and could almost think I saw the processions winding round their walls, and heard the trumpets, and the harps, and the sacred hymns in honour of the great Osiris. In the evening a native came over with a little boat to take me off the island, and I quitted with regret this strange and interesting region.

To Philae after the Dam, 1908
Sir Gaston Maspero

We must take half an hour's journey by train, first through one of the native suburbs of Assouân, then in sight of a horde of Bicharis encamped on the outskirts of the suburb so as to give the tourists an impression of life in the desert, and lastly along a monotonous slope of rocks and reddish sand. The train is a real Paris suburban train, with its carriages too old for the service of the long-distance lines, with an old-fashioned locomotive, a great boiler stuck on wheels, which will resolutely do its fifteen miles an hour if the driver will let it. It goes painfully panting over the slope until at last straight in front of it, above the line of sandstone that just now bounded the horizon, there slowly come into view mounds of blackish granite and a blue-grey plain flooded with light in which the currents thread their way and cross each other. Groups of dying palms or withered acacias are set in the water in front of the embankment itself, marking the outline of the ancient banks, and a mass of submerged buildings of different heights seem as if fallen into the middle of the basin—pylons, colonnades, kiosks, tops of temples—exactly what is to be seen of Philæ between December 15th of one year and May 15th of the following year. We get out of the train and embark, and coast successively the sanctuary of Isis, the propylæa of Hadrian, the Quay Wall on the east, and doubling at the spot where the obelisk of Nectanebo formerly marked the landing-stage of the ancient place of disembarkation, we arrive between the two porticoes of Augustus and Tiberius. We go through the monumental door, almost at the level of the inscription engraved by the French soldiers of Desaix, and passing through the courtyard reach the top step of the grand staircase. The water flows noisily from the house of the priests of Isis to the chapel of Hathor, then it runs to the right of the pronaos through the postern that opened on to the propylæa of Trajan and Hadrian. We seem to be transported unawares into one of the fantastic havens bordered with watch-towers and palaces that the Romans of the Imperial epoch were fond of painting on the walls.

Tourists may still go dryshod over the place of disembarkation, the hypostyle, the Holy of Holies, the courtyard and Chamber of the New Year, the portions of buildings grouped in front or on the sides of the naos, and the corridors that form communications between them. At least the Nile only wets them exceptionally when the north wind, stirring the water, raises waves which flow through the halls. But if the water only seldom flows over the pavements, its presence is felt everywhere in the veinings and under the outer layer of the stone. Without possibility of preventing its progress, it has silently filtered through from bottom to top, by rills as fine as hairs, and between two inundations has impregnated the entire fabric. The walls look damp to the eye and are damp to the fingers if they are touched. The sandstone has shed the grey granulated covering, the dryness of which had clothed it for centuries, and it slowly resumes the yellowish colour it had in the quarry. The faded and dirty colours which here and there clothe the figures of the gods or the architectural ornaments are strengthened and revived by the damp. Even the celebrated capitals of the pronaos have less dry and inharmonious tones than formerly. The reds, blues, yellows, and greens have insensibly run into each other at the edges under the persistent influence of the dampness acting behind them in the stone: and while this interior work softens and shades them, the reflections of the ever-moving water which light them from below through the bay of the pylon make the colours vibrate delightfully.

Their beauty should be enjoyed while it remains entire, for work is still going on at the barrage on that side. The granite causeway is being enlarged, since it no longer offers a sufficiently firm base for new courses of masonry, and the rocks of the Cataract, blasted every day, provide the material which will allow the engineers to raise the present plan of the reservoir six or seven yards. And in five or six years nearly all that was spared in 1902 will be delivered up to the flood. It will flow over the threshold of the doors, it will invade without hindrance the parts provisionally guarded from it, it will deliberately attack the walls, and will not desist until it has reached the prescribed level. The figures of divinities and kings who meet or pursue one another from the plinth to the frieze, presenting and accepting the offering, prostrated, bowed, ranged in ceremonious rows, will be gradually drowned—the feet one day, then the knees, the loins, the bust, the head—so that nothing of them more will be seen, and the mystery of the worship of Isis will be for ever hidden. A sort of rectangular balustrade will mark the site of the kiosk of Trajan.

View from Philæ

The Temple of Kalabsha, 1848
Harriet Martineau

I was glad to go over it, and admire its magnificence, and the elegance of many parts; and be amazed at its vastness: but it is too modern to interest us much here. It was founded and carried on,—(not quite to completion)—by one after another of the Cæsars: and it is therefore not truly Egyptian. The most interesting circumstance to me was that here we could form some judgment of the effect of the Egyptian colour-decoration: for here there were two chambers in fine preservation, except where water had poured down from the massive lion-head spouts (Roman) and had washed away the colours. The relief to the eye of these strips of pure sculpture was very striking. My conclusion certainly was, from the impression given by these two chambers, that, however valuable colour may be for bringing out the details, and even the perspective, of sculptured designs, any large aggregate of it has a very barbaric appearance.—Still, we must not judge of the old Egyptian painting by this Roman specimen. The disk of Isis is here painted deep red,—the colour of the ordinary complexion. The pale green and brilliant blue of the ancient times are present; and I was here, and here only, a violet or plum-colour.

As for the rest, this temple is a heap of magnificent ruin; magnificent for vastness and richness; but not for taste. One pillar standing among many overthrown,— rich capitals toppled down among rough stones; and such mounds of fragments as make us wonder what force could have been used to cause such destruction,—these are the interests of this temple. It may be observed too, that the adytum has no figure at the end, and that it appears never to have been finished. It is a singular spectacle,—the most sacred part unfinished, while the capitals of the outer columns, with their delicate carvings of vine-leaves and tendrils twining among the leaves of the doum palm, are overthrown and broken!

Graffiti of the Romans, 1819
John Fuller
In the afternoon we landed at Dakki. The temple here is differently situated from that at Sibouah, being placed parallel with instead of facing the river, and the approach is from the north. The propylon is lofty, and almost covered with the 'proscunemata' of Roman officers, who came from the stations of Philae and Elephantine to pay their homage to Mercury, the tutelary deity. Their dates are chiefly in the reigns of Tiberias and Adrian. The temple itself, which is united to the propylon not by a peristyle, as is usually the case, but merely by low walls, appears to have been originally very small, and to have been enlarged afterwards. It is in very fine preservation; and from the elegance of its proportions and its detached and solitary situation, is perhaps one of the most striking of the Nubian antiquities. [Moved to New Sebua in 1961–65.] In place of the usual winged globe over the entrance, is a Greek inscription, in which the name of Ptolemy occurs. It is accompanied by a translation in hieroglyphics, and afforded one of the earliest keys to the study of the ancient writings of the Egyptians, which has since been successfully prosecuted by the literati of Europe.

Weather on the River, 1817
Giovanni Belzoni
A few miles above this place the Nile turns towards the north-west, and as the wind blew mostly from that quarter, we had it right against us, besides a very strong current, for the Nile was nearly at its height. Though the day was very hot, the night was exceedingly cold, considering the climate we were in. At this place we found it very difficult to advance, for the wind still continued strong ahead, and the sailors could not track the boat by ropes on the shore, as the bank was covered with thorns and acacia trees, so that it took us two days to reach the territory of Derr, where the river resumes its course again to the south. From the trees I have mentioned we gathered a little gum-arabic; and the reis of the boat caught some chameleons, which we intended to keep alive.

At Derr, 1840
Mrs. M. Carey
Derr is quite a comfortable-looking town. It is the capital of Nubia, and is worthy the distinction, for the houses are much larger and better built than in any

other of the towns. They all have doors and at least the appearance of cleanliness. The streets, though three or four inches thick in unavoidable dust, are also very clean. There are large open spaces, 'squares' we might call them, planted round with date-trees, which Mohammed said were used for the meetings of the 'Parliament', by which grand title he designated any meeting of any kind, in village or town. The date-trees are all protected by little mud walls to the height of four or five feet, and in the centre of one of the squares is a large 'Egyptian fig-tree' (a species of sycamore).

Close on the river's bank is a Roman ruin, over-shadowed by one of these large trees, and now inhabited by some of the grandees of Derr. It is a picturesque object, and is backed by a large grove of beautiful palm-trees, all equally protected with walls like those in the square. Under one of them we observed a small mud trough with three circular holes in it, quite black with castor-oil mixture [used as a cosmetic for the hair] which had been manufactured in it by the 'belles' of Derr.

The People of the Country, 1836
William Ramsay

Jan 17, beyond Derr. The country grows wilder and more picturesque. The varieties of inhabitants are remarkable; each village appears to have a different race— at one point, a group of thoroughbred Negroes—at another, that race we call (whether rightly or no) *Nubians,* a handsome interesting people, not black, though nearly approaching to it—at another, the Berbers (I suppose), a peculiarly fine set, with the free independent air of the desert, and simple elegant dress. They are considered as having the best character of any people in every respect. The Arabs also here and there appear, the same as in Egypt.

The women's dress in some places is peculiarly elegant, consisting of wide trousers, drawn tight to the ankle, and apparently continued as a sort of boots over the shoes. These reach to the waist; the upper robe is very elegantly formed, apparently of a double cloth, square, with a hole for the head, which is passed through it, and then falls gracefully over the whole body. The hair is always in layers of curls, with something black on the top. The whole dress is of coarse unbleached linen cloth, and has a thoroughly different appearance from that of the Arab women, which is always deep blue or black. But I have seen none of them near; they never show themselves, nor ever appear in company with the men, who come in troops down to the bank.

I Fell in with . . . , 22nd March, 1813
John Lewis Burckhardt

At one hour and a half, ascended a steep sandy mountain . . . on the west side the mountain bears the name Ebsambal, probably a Greek word. . . . When we reached the top of the mountain I left my guide, with the camels, and descended an almost perpendicular cleft, choked with sand, to view the temple of which I had heard many magnificent descriptions. . . . It stands about twenty feet above the surface of the water, entirely cut out of the perpendicular, rocky side of the mountain and in complete preservation. . . .

Having, as I supposed, seen all the antiquity of Ebsambal, I was about to ascend the sandy side of the mountain by the same way I had descended, when, having luckily turned more to the southward, I fell in with what is yet visible of four immense colossal statues cut out of the rock, at a distance of about two hundred yards from the temple, they stand in a deep recess, excavated in the mountain, but it is deeply to be regretted, that they are now almost entirely buried beneath the sands, which are blown down here in torrents. The entire head, and part of the breasts and arms of one of the statues are yet above the surface; and of the one next to it scarcely any part is visible, the head being broken off, and the body covered with sand to above the shoulders; of the other two, the bonnets only appear.

It is difficult to determine whether these statues are in a sitting or standing posture; their backs adhere to a portion of the rock, which projects from the main body, and which may represent part of a chair, or it may be merely a column for support. They do not front the river, like those of the temple just described, but are turned with their faces due north, towards the more fertile lands of Egypt, so that the line on which they stand forms an angle with the course of the stream. The head which is above the surface has a most expressive, youthful countenance, approaching nearer to the Grecian model of beauty, than any one Egyptian figure I have seen. . . .

The statue measures seven yards across the shoulders, and cannot, therefore, if in upright posture, be less than from 65 to 70 feet in height; the ear is one yard and four inches in length. On the wall of the rock in the centre of the four statues, is the figure of a hawk-headed Osiris, surmounted by a globe; beneath which, I suspect, could it be cleared away, a vast temple would be discovered. . . .

On First Entering the Temple at Abu Simbel, August 1, 1817
Giovanni Finati

We availed ourselves of such implements and contrivances as seemed adapted to facilitate the labour, and as soon as some appearance of the great architrave of a portal came to light, trunks of the palm-trees were driven down as piles, at the distance of two or three yards from it, which bore the loose mass from behind, and enabled us to scoop out a sort of well in front of them, which we consolidated, from time to time, by the pouring of water.

After three weeks . . . a corner of the doorway itself became visible. . . . At that very moment, while the fresh clamours and new disputes were going on with our crew , and the attention of all distracted, I, being one of the slenderest of the party, without a word, crept through into the interior, and was thus the first that entered it, perhaps for a thousand years.

Unlike all the other grottoes in Egypt and Nubia, its atmosphere, instead of presenting a refreshing coolness, was a hot and moist vapour, not unlike that of a Turkish bath, and so penetrating that paper, carried within, soon became as saturated as if it had been dropped in the river. It was, however, a consoling and almost an unexpected circumstance, that the run of sand extended but a little way within the aperture, and the remainder of the chambers were all unencumbered.

Abu Simbal

The Great Temple at Abu Simbel, 1817
Captains Charles Irby and James Mangles

We now entered the temple, and thus ended all our labours, doubts and anxiety. This morning we built a wall to barricade the door; it was made of stones and mud, with a foundation of date trees driven in to prevent the sand from giving way. A toad crept out of the temple while we were thus employed, and hid himself in the rubbish at the entrance. We now bought down to the boat some statues of calcarious stone which we found in the temple.

At three we went to work again; two of the Ebsambul peasants came, and appeared astonished that we succeeded. They said the country people had no idea we should have accomplished our undertaking. They appeared to think the temple would make a good hiding place for their cattle, etc, whenever the Bedouins came to rob them.

> Each party of travelers employed the local people to remove the sand from the temple site. As soon as they left, the sand began to drift down again, and later the local people were once again employed to clear it . . .

Digging at Abu Simbel, 1836
David Roberts, RA
Mr. Hay (the archaeologist) had the sand so far removed as to disclose entirely the two columns on the south side of the door, together with the doorway to its base, and now nine or ten Nubians can remove the sand in a few hours which may fall in, and can give ready access to the temple.

Night in the Temple, 1862
Reverend John William Burgon
At about ten o'clock in the evening of this most interesting day, a strong wish came over me to go back, and pay one more visit to Rameses the Great. Two of our party expressed their willingness to bear me company. We furnished ourselves with a slender pole, to the extremity of which we secured a candle: left our shoes behind us—(the sand was so warm and soft to the feet, and walking with shoes was so very inconvenient)—and after the most noiseless fashion imaginable, took our starlight way towards the Temple.

Having entered, we made a complete survey over again of every part; leisurely exploring the walls in every direction with our solitary candle, so as to obtain a notion of what was anywhere incised upon them. The silence was intense: the whirring of the wings of a nervous little bat, who made the circuit of the Temple with us, the only thing audible. We found our way into the remotest chamber of all,—the shrine, where four gloomy gods face you, in a sitting posture. Quite awful was it to find them still sitting there in the dark, as twelve hours before we had left them motionless, in grim majesty. "And there they will sit," we said to ourselves, "unconscious of change, until the ages shall have run out, and the end shall be!"

The last thing I did on entering the great gall of the Temple was the first thing I had done on entering it,—namely, to obtain a careful survey of the features of the colossus on the right, by lifting up the candle above the head of the figure. I cannot express how striking was the result. In that vast, mysterious cavern–like chamber the only object in bright relief was the countenance of the monarch who, 3,200 years ago, had caused this mighty fabric to be wrought out of the solid rock. The serene majesty of those features was ever affecting. It was the deep repose, the profound calm, of death. Making the boatman who waited on us hold the light for me, I drew for a few minutes—minutes which seemed like hours; so many solemn thoughts crowded themselves in, unbidden. None of us spoke. The silence was so intense that one might have heard the ticking of one's watch. What is strange,—at last, on looking up from my papers, I thought I saw the beginning of a smile on the lips of Rameses. Intently I gazed and of course recognised the sufficiently obvious fact that the supposed smile was merely the effect of my own imagination. But it is just as certain that I gazed on until,—I am half ashamed to write it, but it is true—until the features seemed to me to smile again. Then they grew graver than ever: but at last I felt sure that they relaxed—just a little bit— again. One's nerves were getting over-strung. I invented a sentiment for the lips to utter, and felt sure that I was interpreting their most expressive outline rightly. I daresay, if I had been alone, and had stopped long enough, I should have heard Rameses speak. It would have been somewhat to this effect:

"You seem astonished, Sir, at what you are beholding in this remote corner of my dominions. No wonder; for with all your boasted civilisation and progress, you could not match this edifice in the far-away land to which (as I gather from your uncouth dress and manners) you and your friends belong. I have been reposing here in effigy for upwards of 3000 years. I have seen generation after generation of ancient Greeks, and generation after generation of ancient Romans, enter this hall; peep and pry,—as you have done this evening; and then vanish at yonder portal,— as you will yourself do a few minutes hence. If I smiled for an instant just now—(it is not my wont to smile)—it was only because you really looked alarmed as well as awed at my presence. But I shall not smile again. So now, go home, Sir,—go and write a book, like the rest, about the little you have seen in Egypt; but let it humble you to remember that Rameses will be standing here, unchangeable, long after you, and your book, and all that belongs to you is utterly forgotten. You may go, Sir. It is getting late—for you. You had better go, Sir. Good night!"

We lingered: retiring a few steps, and then turning again to look; profoundly conscious that we were looking our last; that we should never fasten our eyes on those glorious forms again. I fancy that we were, all three, impressed with an uneasy suspicion that it was not mere lifeless stone that we had been visiting, and were now leaving the profoundest silence and utter gloom. . . . It was a relief to emerge into the fresh evening air; to survey the starry heavens overhead, Orion, and the rest; and to recognise our two boats, bright with lights, beneath us, moored to the banks of the bright shining river.

Celebrating at Abu Simbel, 1855
William C. Prime

Mindful of the brilliant illumination of the boat the previous evening, at Wady Halfeh, it occurred to us that we might realize somewhat of the ancient glory of Abou Simbel by lighting it with our coloured lanterns.

Abd–el–Atti entered into the idea with his accustomed alacrity, and I went up into the temple to advise and assist in the desposition of candles and lanterns, while the ladies, who did not go into the temple on our passage up, waited on board until the illumination was complete.

The sand hill was almost impassable. It was like climbing a snow bank fifty feet high, the feet going in deep and slipping far back at every step, so that we had to lie down and breathe several times before we reached the top and descended into the doorway of the temple.

When our arrangements were complete we returned and brought the ladies up. The procession was picturesque. Two blazing torches led the way, and four more brought up the rear.

Never since the days of Rameses has his great temple shone so brilliantly. Every statue held bright lanterns, and for two hundred feet through the long rooms we placed them—rows of every colour, shining on painted walls and lofty statues. The altar was in shadow—for so we arranged it—hiding the lights behind it that they might shine on the faces of the gods, and not on the altar front. When all was ready we called in the ladies, and, as they entered, the sailors who had busied themselves about the lamps, suddenly disappeared, and the temple was apparently empty. But at the moment of our re-entering, in place of the chorus of priests and attendants that was wont to arise in the hall, deep, sepulchral voices, from unknown recesses, uttered in loud and terrible unison, the well-known cry, "Bucksheesh, Hawajji!"

It was vain to resist such an appeal, and we answered it instantly; whereat the voices changed, and the men emerged from their hiding-places with shouts of thanks.

Creatures Come down to Drink, 1817
Captains Charles Irby and James Mangles

Wednesday, July 23. It was curious to observe in the morning, on the smooth surface of the sand, drifted by the night breeze, the tracks of the snakes, lizards, animals, etc, etc which had come down to the water's side during the night to drink; and we could plainly discern the traces of their return to their solitary haunts in the desert. Sometimes their track indicated the presence of reptiles of considerable size; and with these proofs of their nocturnal movements, we easily accounted for the dread our guides expressed of walking near the water's side the night we returned from the second cataract.

Climbing the Colossi, 1848
Harriet Martineau

I was impatient to get to the Colossi of the large temple, which looked magnificent from our deck. So, after breakfast, I set forth alone, to see what height I could attain in the examination of the statues.

The southernmost is the only complete one. The next to it is terribly shattered: and the other two have lost the top of the helmet. They are much sanded up, though, thanks to Mr. Hay, much less than they were. The sand slopes up from the half-cleared entrance to the chin of the northernmost colossus: and this slope of sand it was my purpose to climb. It was so steep, loose, and hot to the feet, that it was no easy matter to make my way up. The beetles, which tread lightly and seem to like having warm feet, got on very well; and they covered the sand with a net work of tracks: but heavier climbers, shod in leather, are worsted in the race with them. But one cannot reach the chin of a colossus every day: and it was worth an effort. And when I had reached the chin, I made a little discovery about it which may be worth recording, and which surprised me a good deal at the time. I found that a part of the lower jaw, reaching half way up the lower lip, was composed of the mud and straw of which crude bricks are made. There had been evidently a fault in the stone, which was supplied by this material. It was most beautifully moulded. The beauty of the curves of these great faces is surprising in the stone:—the fidelity of the rounding of the muscles, and the grace of the flowing lines of the cheek and jaw: but it was yet more wonderful in such a material as mud and straw. I cannot doubt that this chin and lip were moulded when the material was in a soft state:—a difficult task in the case of a statue seventy feet high, standing up against the face of a rock. I called the gentlemen up, to bear witness to the fact: and it set us looking for more instances. Mr. E. soon found one. Part of the dress of the Second Osiride on the right hand, entering the temple, is composed of this same material, as smoothly curved and nicely wrought as the chin overhead. On examining closely, we found that this layer of mud and straw covered some chiselling within. The artist had been carving the folds of the dress, when he came upon a fault in the stone which stopped his work till he supplied a surface of material which he could mould.

The small figures which stand beside the colossi and between their ankles, and which look like dolls, are not, as is sometimes said, of human size. The hat of a man of five feet ten inches does not reach their chins by two inches. The small figures are, to my eye, the one blemish of this temple. They do not make the great Ramses look greater, but only look dollish themselves.

On the legs of the shattered colossus are the Greek letters, scrawled as by a Greek clown, composing the inscription of the soldiers sent by Psammitichus in pursuit of the Egyptian deserters whom I mentioned as going up the country from Elephantine, when weary of the neglect in which they were left there. We are much obliged to 'Damearchon, the son of Ambichus, and Pelephus, the son of Udamus,' for leaving, in any kind of scrawl, a record of an event so curious. One of the strangest sensations to the traveller in Egypt, is finding such traces as these of persons who were in their day modern travellers seeing the antiquities of the country, but who take their place now among the ancients, and have become subjects of Egyptian history. These rude soldiers, carving their names and errand on the legs of an ancient statue as they went by, passed the spot a century and a half before Cambyses entered the country. One wonders what they thought of Thebes, which they had just seen in all its glory.

Days at Abu Simbel, 1873
Amelia Edwards

We came to Abou Simbel on the night of the 31st January, and we left at sunset on the 18th February. Of these eighteen clear days, we spent fourteen at the foot of the rock of the Great Temple, called in the old Egyptian tongue the Rock of Abshek. The remaining four (taken at the end of the first week and the beginning of the second) we passed in the excursion to Wady-Halfeh and back. By thus dividing the time, our long sojourn was made less monotonous for those who had no especial work to do.

Meanwhile, it was wonderful to wake every morning close under the steep bank, and, without lifting one's head from the pillow, to see that row of giant faces so close against the sky. They showed unearthly enough by moonlight; but not half so unearthly as in the grey of dawn. At that hour, the most solemn of the twenty-four, they wore a fixed and fatal look that was little less than appalling. As the sky warmed, this awful look was succeeded by a flush that mounted and deepened like the rising flush of life. For a moment they seemed to glow—to smile—to be transfigured. Then came a flash, as of thought itself. It was the first instantaneous flash of the risen sun. It lasted less than a second. It was gone almost before one could say that it was there. The next moment, mountain, river, and sky, were distinct in the steady light of day; and the colossi—mere colossi now—sat serene and stony in the open sunshine.

Every morning I waked in time to witness that daily miracle. Every morning I saw those awful brethren pass from death to life, from life to sculptured stone. I brought myself almost to believe at last that there must sooner or later come some one sunrise when the ancient charm would snap asunder, and the giants must arise and speak.

Stupendous as they are, nothing is more difficult than to see the colossi properly. Standing between the rock and the river, one is too near; stationed on the island opposite, one is too far off; while from the sand-slope only a side-view is obtainable. Hence, for want of a fitting standpoint, many travellers have seen nothing but deformity in the most perfect face handed down to us by Egyptian art.

Viewed from below, this beautiful portrait is foreshortened out of all proportion. It looks unduly wide from ear to ear, while the lips and the lower part of the nose show relatively larger than the rest of the features. The same may be said of the great cast in the British Museum. Cooped up at the end of a narrow corridor and lifted not more than fifteen feet above the ground, it is carefully placed so as to be wrong from every point of view and shown to the greatest possible disadvantage.

The artists who wrought the original statues were, however, embarrassed by no difficulties of focus, daunted by no difficulties of scale. Giants themselves, they summoned these giants from out the solid rock, and endowed them with super-human strength and beauty. They sought no quarried blocks of syenite or granite for their work. They fashioned no models of clay. They took a mountain, and fell upon it like Titans, and hollowed and carved it as though it were a cherry-stone, and left it for the feebler men of after-ages to marvel at for ever. One great hall and fifteen spacious chambers they hewed out from the heart of it; then smoothed the rugged precipice towards the river, and cut four huge statues with their faces to the sunrise, two to the right and two to the left of the doorway, there to keep watch to the end of time.

These tremendous warders sit sixty-six feet high, without the platform under their feet. They measure across the chest twenty-five feet and four inches; from the shoulder to the elbow, fifteen feet and six inches; from the inner side of the elbow joint to the tip of the middle finger, fifteen feet; and so on in relative proportion. If they stood up, they would tower to a height of at least eighty-three feet, from the soles of their feet to the tops of their enormous double-crowns.

There is but one hour in the twenty-four at which it is possible to form any idea of the general effect of this vast subject; and that is at sunrise. Then only does the pure day stream in through the doorway, and temper the gloom of the side-aisles with light reflected from the sunlit floor. The broad divisions of the picture and the distribution of the masses may then be dimly seen. The details, however, require candle-light, and can only be studied a few inches at a time. Even so, it is difficult to make out the upper groups without the help of a ladder. Salame, mounted on a chair and provided with two long sticks lashed together, could barely hold his little torch high enough to enable the Writer to copy the inscription on the middle tower of the fortress of Kadesh.

It is fine to see the sunrise on the front of the Great Temple; but something still finer takes place on certain mornings of the year, in the very heart of the mountain. As the sun comes up above the eastern hill-tops, one long level beam strikes through the doorway, pierces the inner darkness like an arrow, penetrates to the sanctuary, and falls like fire from heaven upon the altar at the feet of the Gods.

No one who has watched for the coming of that shaft of sunlight can doubt that it was a calculated effect, and that the excavation was directed at one especial angle in order to produce it. In this way Ra, to whom the temple was dedicated, may be said to have entered in daily, and by a direct manifestation of his presence to have approved the sacrifices of his worshippers.

To come out from these black holes into the twilight of the Great Hall and see the landscape set, as it were, in the ebon frame of the doorway, was alone worth the journey to Abou Simbel. The sun being at such times in the west, the river, the yellow sand-island, the palms and tamarisks opposite, and the mountains of the eastern desert, were all flooded with a glory of light and colour to which no pen or pencil could possibly do justice. At this juncture, seeing that the men's time hung heavy on their hands, our Painter conceived the idea of setting them to clean the face of the northernmost Colossus, still disfigured by the plaster left on it when the great cast was taken by Mr. Hay more than half a century before. This happy thought was promptly carried into effect. A scaffolding of spars and oars was at once improvised, and the men, delighted as children at play, were soon swarming all over the huge head, just as the carvers may have swarmed over it in the days when Rameses was king.

Words from the United Nations, 1960–63

> At Abu Simbel, now lifted high above the Nile, today's travelers will read these words:

These monuments do not belong solely to the countries who hold them in trust. The whole world has the right to see them endure.

Dr. Vittorini Veronese, former Director-General of UNESCO, 1960

Through this restoration of the past, we have indeed helped to build the future of mankind.

René Maheu, former Director-General of UNESCO, 1963

At the Second Cataract, 1927
Constance Sitwell

The naked black boys run panting across the sand and up the slope toward us. They have been swimming and shooting the rapids of the second cataract, and now, having each been given a coin, they fling themselves down for a rest.

I, too, lie outstretched in a patch of shade on the top of a great rock that stands high above the surrounding country. Jim and Philip, their eyes shut, are resting in the shadow of another ledge. We made our start many hours ago, at break of dawn, to avoid the heat of the day. For part of the way our boatman rowed, and sometimes they had to tow the boat along, but there were spells when they could sit and sing while the boat beat its way up the river under sail. At last we reached these curious rocks sticking up out of the broad flood that swirls around them— black rocks, rounded and glistening like gigantic lumps of coal.

From my place here I can see our boat tied up to the bank far below; it is gaily bedecked with flags, and at the top of the mast one long pennon with the star and crescent hangs limp in the lifeless air. On deck lies a dog, asleep, with lolling tongue. As far as I can see the Nubian crew, squatting on the shore, are still as busy as ever talking. Their voices do not reach me, but I can see their gesticulations. So dead black is their skin that they look as if they had been rubbed over with blacklead and then polished like a grate; their hair is glistening with castor oil. They talk and talk, but here there is silence except for the far-off sound of the water rushing, leaping and dashing amongst the rocks.

I have to shut my eyes at last because of the glare, and when I open them again it is to watch a beetle crawling over the glittering flakes of stone. It is a shiny and fantastic creature with glassy wings and a silver body spotted with bronze. It moves slowly among a host of ants that are hurrying in and out between the hot boulders. Idly I look at them and their settlement full of stirs; ant jostles ant in the narrow ways, and they are all black—as black as those Nubian boatmen down below. Here is a city of Ethiopians—a miniature city that with one brush of my hand I could sweep way. Ethiopia! How rich and hot the name sounds; but it tells of a glory which is fled. . . .

Ethiopia lies there before me; on one side of the Nile its sand is ashen grey, on the other a tawny gold. And this terrible waterless desert stretches away eastward to the coast; beyond there heaves the Red Sea. Southward and eastward it shimmers in the heat-haze, and somewhere beyond the horizon there roam dapple giraffes—fairy-tale creatures with velvety skins and liquid eyes. I wonder, are they frightened of the lions? The Kings of Ethiopia used to hunt with lions. . . . Kings with lions at their side! Ethiopia, once great, your glory has indeed been swept away! Where are the emeralds and the gold, where are the gums, and resins, and fragrant woods that once you poured forth? How long ago is it since travelling companies of tall merchantmen brought their riches to Egypt over these blazing sands—their white ivory, white wool and white ostrich plumes, their ebony and slaves like ebony. Bunched feathers of bright colours, and small bewildered Negro boys were offered to the great ladies of Thebes and Heliopolis.

The Great Rock at Abu Sir, 1836
Lord Lindsay

. . . our sailors, full of fun and merriment, punted and rowed us up the river, as far as the boat could ascend, and then, landing on the western bank, we proceeded on foot, alternately over sand and rock, to Abousir, a lofty cliff that overhangs the rapids, conspicuous from afar, and covered, we found, with the names of former travellers.

Climbing the rock, the Nile lay before us like the map of an Archipelago—so it seemed to me at first, till the eye presently discovered the main stream of the river winding between myriads of little black islets, tufted with Egyptian acacia, and glistening in the sunbeams like those at Philæ—themselves washed by hundreds of collateral streamlets that glitter, foam and roar in emulation of their parent. Ten miles in length, and two in breadth, are these rapids. It is the lower cataract (that above Assuan) on an infinitely larger scale, but the impressions excited are widely different; there you feel an interest in every rock as you pass it, you admire their savage grandeur individually, and the rapids the while are dashing away under your feet—there you thread a labyrinth—here you look down on one, quite bewildered.

The prospect, miles to the eastward, is bounded by the prolongation of Gobel Mokkatam—to the south, by the mountains of Dongola—it was something to have seen them! It was a sad thought that I had reached the limits of my southern excursion; sad, though now every step I took would bring me nearer to my happy family homes in England and Scotland! From one of the western crags I had a partial view over the Libyan desert—a dreary sight. While William carved our names in the rock, where many a future traveller will read them in association with those of Belzoni, Burckhardt, Irby and Mangles, etc. I enjoyed half an hour's delightful rumination, on a most commodious natural seat that overhangs the Nile beyond the rock Abousir, and on which before departure, I cut my cipher by way of claiming it as my own. . . . Nowhere else have we attempted to immortalize ourselves in this way.

Hub of the Universe, 1913
Rudyard Kipling

At Halfa one feels the first breath of a frontier. Here the Egyptian Government retire into the background, and even the Cook steamer does not draw up in the exact centre of the postcard. At the telegraph-office, too, there are traces, diluted but quite recognisable, of military administration. Nor does the town, in any place whatever, smell—which is proof that it is not looked after on popular lines. There is nothing to see in it any more than there is in Hulk C. 60, late of her Majesty's troopship *Himalaya*, now a coal-hulk in the Hamoaze at Plymouth. A river front, a narrow terraced river-walk of semi-oriental houses, barracks, a mosque, and half-a-dozen streets at right angles, the Desert racing up to the end of each, make all the town. A mile or so up stream under palm trees are bungalows of what must have been cantonments, some machinery repair shops, and odds and ends of railway track. It is all as paltry a collection of whitewashed houses, pitiful gardens, dead walls, and trodden waste spaces as one would wish to find anywhere; and every bit of it quivers with the remembered life of armies and river-fleets, as the finger-bowl rings when the rubbing finger is lifted. The most unlikely men have done time there; stores by the thousand ton have been rolled and pushed and hauled up the banks by tens of thousand of scattered hands; hospitals have pitched themselves there, expanded enormously, shrivelled up and drifted away with the drifting regiments; railway sidings by the mile have been laid down and ripped up again, as need changed, and utterly wiped out by the sands.

Halfa has been the rail-head, Army Headquarters, and hub of the universe—the one place where a man could make sure of buying tobacco and sardines, or could hope for letters for himself and medical attendance for his friend. Now she is a little shrunken shell of a town without a proper hotel, where tourists hurry up from the river to buy complete sets of Soudan stamps at the Post Office.

12
To Suez and Sinai

Going east from Egypt to the Red Sea and thence to Sinai or to Mecca was one route through these lands. The journey northward up the Red Sea to enter Egypt from the east was made by travelers from India, until the Suez Canal opened in 1869. Many traveled on pilgrimage to Sinai with the Old Testament in their heads, making the country seem strangely familiar—as it was to Egeria in 383 A.D.

Through the City of Qolzom (Suez), c. 1050
Naser-e Khosraw
Going east from Egypt, you reach the Red Sea. The city of Qolzom is located on the shore of this sea, and is thirty parasangs from Cairo. This sea is a gulf of the ocean that splits off at Aden to the north and ends at Qolzom. The width of this gulf is said to be two hundred parasangs. Between Cairo and the Gulf is mountain and desert where there is neither water nor growth. Whoever wants to go to Mecca from Egypt must go east. From Qolzom there are two ways, one by land and one by sea. The land route can be transversed in fifteen days, but it is all desert and three hundred parasangs long. Most of the caravans from Egypt take that way.

Music and Sail from Luxor to the Red Sea, 1843
Dr. Richard Lepsius

On the Red Sea, between Gebel Zeit and Tor, Good Friday, 21st March 1843.

On 20th of February we changed our abode in Thebes from the western to the eastern bank, from Qurna to Karnak. We settled ourselves here in some chambers of the great royal temple; but as I was desirous of setting out on my journey to the Peninsula of Sinai as soon as possible, I limited myself for the time, to merely taking such a survey of the monuments as was absolutely necessary, in order to enable me to appoint the work that was to be done during my absence.

On 3rd March I set out on my journey. . . . We first went down the Nile as far a Qeneh. After it became dark and the stars had risen, the conversation, which had hitherto been animated, ceased and, lying on the deck, I watched the star of Isis, the sparkling Sothis (Sirius), this Polar star of Egyptian chronology, as it gradually ascended over our heads. Our two oarsmen were only too musically inclined, and went through their whole stock of songs, quivering them with innumerable repetitions, sometimes interrupted by the short cry of *Scherk, Gharb* (East, West), which was softly answered by the feeble and obedient boy's voice of our little steersman. Half waking, half dreaming, we then glided down the river till about midnight, when the Arab quivering also ceased; the strokes of the oar became fainter, and at length the boat was left entirely to the waves. The rising of the moon in her last quarter, and dawning day, first aroused them to renewed activity. . . .

After spending a couple of days at Qeneh, we quitted it, on 6th March, with fifteen camels. The first day we only rode three hours, as far as the copious spring of Bir Amrar, charmingly situated between palms and nebek-trees and provided by Ibrahim Pascha with a dome-shaped building for the caravans. We also reached early on the following day the second night-encampment, at the station of Leqeta. . . . Five wells furnish here a supply of tolerably good water; two buildings, with domes half fallen down, are destined for the reception of travellers.

> **Richard Lepsius and his party traveled across the mountain chain to Gebel Zeit from where a boat took them to Tor. They faced various problems: guides with insufficient knowledge, shortage of water, missing the track, but eventually they reached their destination.**

Yesterday evening it was perfect calm. It was only during the night that a light wind rose from the north, which we immediately availed ourselves of, for setting sail. With the wind in our favour we might have accomplished the passage across in one night; but now the day is again drawing to a close, and we have not yet reached the port. The ship of burden scarcely stirs, though the long oars have been at length set in motion.

The sailors of this sea are very different from those on the Nile. Their deportment is more reserved, less sly and subservient. Their songs, which commence at the first stroke of the oar, consist of fragmentary short lines, which are sung first by one, and are taken up by another, while the remainder utter short and deep grunting sounds, as an accompaniment, at equal intervals.

Travelers to Sinai always wanted to decide where the Children of Israel had crossed the Red Sea followed by the army of Pharaoh. Each one had a theory or supported the theory of another.

Across the Red Sea, 1908
Elbert Farman

We were taken across the shallow waters and the Suez Canal in a small native boat, and thence by donkeys. After crossing the Canal, we were in Asia and on the border of a vast desert. East and south, there was an extended view of plains, hills and mountains of sand, gravel, earth and rock, without vegetation, and of a dull monotonous yellow tint. It was the last of November. The long, dry, hot summer parched and burned up all vegetation, and a brisk north wind enveloped us in a continuous cloud of dust.

On our right was the Red Sea, or more correctly speaking that arm of it which is known as the Gulf of Suez. It is only a few miles in width at this point, but deep, and as blue as the sky it reflects. Beyond it, rising from near the water line, are the mountains of Atâka, nearly three thousand feet in height, and wholly destitute of vegetation. On our left was only the desert, bordered by the mountains in the distance. . . .

There were several mud huts occupied by Arabs who irrigated and cultivated a small plot of ground. Most of the mounds with their basins of water were but little above the desert. One of them was remarkable for its size and altitude, rising, according to our estimate, to a height of thirty feet. It was very regular in form and had on its top a basin of shallow water, five or six feet in diameter, whence a very little water ran over the rim and down the sides. Standing on the top, I looked about the country to discover a high point that might be the source of the water that fed the spring, ten to twenty miles to the east. The desert gradually descended westward to the sea, distant one or two miles.

Where Was the Crossing? 1846
Lord Castlereagh

Our tents were pitched about an hour's distance from Adjerout, where we found the fires lighted, and the baggage piled up. The fort of Adjerout was a faint object in the distance, and before us rose the range of Gebel Ataka. These were the mountains which the children of Israel looked upon in the hour of their fear and the day of their deliverance. Those brown summits, frowning upon the sandy plains below, saw Judah saved, and the mighty host of Pharaoh, with his chariots and horses, his men of war, and his captains, overwhelmed by the breath of the Lord. At this spot, was continued that series of miracles by which the Almighty proved his own might and power, as well as his affection to his chosen people, and though they had rebelled, and through their long trials never ceased to rebel against him, He led them to the land He had promised, and established them as a mighty people. Writers and travellers are divided in their opinions as to the exact place where the sea was dried up for the passage of the children of Israel, and their various theories are obstinately discussed and maintained. My own opinion coincides with that of Dr. Robinson, that the flying multitudes arrived from Goshen, or what we should now designate as the banks of the Nile, opposite the delta. As the Scriptures declare their flight to have lasted three days, the nearest point they could have attained within that period, was the plain below Gebel Ataka, and this stopped their further progress south,—with its precipitous rocks, rising like a barrier near the sea,—while on the ground below it they were hemmed in, between the mountains and the waters, by the pursuing Egyptians. The question as to whether they crossed at Ras Ataka, the promontory, or actually at Suez, over the shoals, laid bare by the action of a sudden wind, cannot alter the engrossing interest of this region, for all the land must have borne the traces of their footsteps, when the mighty multitude filled the plain.

May 16th—We left our tents at sunrise to find a good point for sketching Gebel Ataka; and when the caravan had moved off, followed slowly on our dromedaries, having the blue sea stretched out before us, washing the base of Gebel Ataka, and the opposite shores of Sinai. Early in the day we passed the fort of Adjerout, which is merely a pile of low ruined walls. Our track shows that death has not confined his visits to the poor animals of the caravan. The tired Hadji, who sinks on this way from Mecca, is covered with a few stones to distinguish him from the carcase of the abandoned camel that lies by him. The hyena, probably, feeds on both.

Water, Flora, and Fragments, 1871
Samuel Manning

The route southward from Ayun Mousa [the well of Moses near the Red Sea] leads along the shore over gravely plains many miles broad, which slope upward from the sea to the mountains of the Tih. After heavy rains the tenacious marl is pitted with numerous pools of water, and is sprinkled with the aromatic shrubs which constitute the flora of the desert, but the scorching sun soon dries up the pools, and the short-lived plants wither into dust. Several wells of bitter water are passed, each of which has been fixed upon as Marah, according to the view taken of the place of passage [of the Israelites across the Red Sea]. About fifty miles south of Ayun Mousa the Wady Gjarandel is reached. The entrance into the valley, or wady, is not much over eighty feet wide, and on either side grey-looking cliffs of gritstone rise with ragged faces to a considerable height. But that which adds so great a charm to the scene is an actual stream of water, rippling along, silvery and bright, garnished on each bank with luxuriant plants that thrive and flourish in the wet sand. Forget-me-nots peep out from amidst the sedgy grass reeds and mint that tower above the water; while some kind of brook plant, like a tangled mat, spreads itself over the sandy edges of the rivulet, and sends its long arms, tufted with rootlets at every joint, out into the running water.

Here the vegetation takes quite a different character. The spiny acacia, the 'sumt' of the Arabs, probably the tree of the 'burning bush' and the shittim wood of the tabernacle, grows plentifully; but, spiny though it be, it has to bear its burden of climbing plants, being generally quite hidden beneath their twisting, rope-like branches. Conspicuous amongst the larger plants is the *rete,* or wild broom, handsome alike in growth and foliage. It is probably the shrub beneath which Elijah slept in his wanderings.

Date-palms of strangely stunted stature are scattered along the sandy banks; one might readily mistake them for giant yuccas at a hasty glance, so much do they resemble those plants in their mode of growth. These may truly be called 'wild palms': dwarfed and unaltered by man's hand. Was this memorable place where "there were twelve wells of water and threescore and ten palm trees"— the veritable Elim of the Exodus? Many travellers believe this wady to be the place.

Striking eastward up the Wady we soon reach the traces of mines worked by the ancient Egyptians. Hieroglyphic tablets are found in considerable numbers, one of which contains the name of Cheops, the builder of the Great Pyramid, and some are said to be even earlier. At Sarabet el Chadam, which seems to have been the capital of the mining district, are some remarkable ruins, consisting of a temple, the remains of houses, and perhaps a necropolis. Fragments of columns, blocks of stone, pieces of rude sculpture, and mounds of broken pottery lie scattered about in perplexing confusion.

> Many travelers tried to identify the landmarks of the Bible and to visit those places where Moses had stood. On this journey, the Monastery of St. Catherine is often an important destination.

Walking through the Valley of the Cataract, 1836
Lord Lindsay

In this black chain of mountains is an extraordinary ravine, called Wady Shellal, or the Valley of the Cataract. Hussein took us through it, while the caravan went on by the usual route; the valley is not a stone's jerk wide, but the scenery is awfully grand; not a sound was heard except the *sigh* of the wind among the rocks, and the solitary chirp of a bird. Hussein and I walked on quicker than William, who was looking out for partridges and quails; as we ascended the Wady, enormous rocks, fallen from the heights, of every shape, and in several instances inscribed with the same unknown characters that I shall have to mention presently, lay on either side of the way, becoming gradually more numerous, till, at last, they formed a little valley of themselves within the large one, which, gradually diminishing into a narrow winding passage, brought us to a perpendicular rock, beyond which there seemed to be no passage. It is impossible to describe the extraordinary appearance of this cul-de-sac.

Hussein and I now sat down in the shadow, and talked after our fashion, till William and his attendant Arab overtook us; Hussein then started up, and, climbing up the rocks, led the way to an upper valley, of which I had not suspected the existence, broader than the lower, but quite as extraordinary; the ground in some places was as smooth as a gravel walk. In the rainy season the torrents pour down it, and over the rocks into the lower valley, to form the magnificent cascade from which the Wady takes its name.

We walked on some distance to a well, which we found full of sand; Hussein scooped it out with his hands, and the water rose; all of us drank—I never tasted anything so delicious, always excepted the waters of the Nile, to which no other beverage is comparable; but then I was very thirsty, for the day was by far the hottest we had yet travelled on. Returning a few steps, we climbed over the hills, and across two or three small ravines, till we reached Wady Boodra, where we saw tracks of the camels. It was well we had drunk at the spring, for the ascent and descent of the hills was dreadfully hot work; my tongue felt in my mouth like a parrot's, the sides of my throat clove together, and I could scarcely articulate when we over took the caravan. One of the most delightful walks, however, I ever took! What a blessing water is! None can appreciate it, who has not thirsted in the desert. It is a bad policy to drink during the march, if one can possibly avoid it.

Prospects of Sinai, 1843
Dr. Richard Lepsius

The following day [28 March, 1843] we proceeded farther, and passing through Wadi e'Scheikh, we reached the Wadi Firan—this most precious jewel of the Peninsula, with its palms and groves of Tarfa on the banks of a lovely rushing stream, which, winding among shrubs and flowers, conducted us to the old convent mountain of the town of Pharan, the Firan of the present day. Everything that we had hitherto seen, and what we afterwards saw, was naked, stony, desert compared to this fertile oasis, abounding in wood and water. For the first time since we had left the Nile valley, we once more walked on soft black earth, obliged to defend ourselves with our arms from the overhanging leafy branches, and we heard singing birds warbling in the thick foliage. At the point where the broad Wadi Aleyat, descending from Serbal, enters Wadi Firan, and where the valley spreads out into a spacious level tract, there arises into the centre of it a rocky hill called Hererat, on the summit of which are the ruins of an ancient convent building. At its foot stood once a magnificent church, constructed of well-hewn rocks of sandstone, the ruins of which are built into the houses of the town situated on the slope of the opposite mountain.

The same evening I went up Wadi Aleyat, passing innumerable rock inscriptions, to a well, surrounded by palm and Nebek trees, where I enjoyed the entire prospect of the majestic mountain chain. Apart from all the other mountains, and united into one single mass, Serbal rises, at first in a slope of moderate inclination, afterwards in steep precipices, with chasms, to the height of 6000 feet (above the sea). Nothing could equal the scene when the valleys and low mountains around were already veiled in the shadows of night, and the summits of the mountains still glowed above the colourless grey, like a fiery cloud in the sinking sun.

In the same district is the Wady Mokkateb, or the Written Valley, so called for the number of rude inscriptions and sculptures with which the rocks are covered. They are not peculiar to this valley, but are found in many parts of the Sinaitic range. They always occur in the lines of route along which caravans or traders or bands of pilgrims are likely to have passed, and are inscribed in the soft sandstone rock which forms the fringe of the harder granite in the centre of the peninsula. The sculptures are grotesque representations of birds, camels, asses, horses, ibexes, and other animals. The inscriptions are sometimes in Greek, Latin, or Hebrew, but more commonly in a character unlike that of any known language.

The Convent of St. Catherine, 1871
Samuel Manning

The convent was founded by Justinian (A.D. 527), and was higher up the side of the mountain, perhaps even on the summit. It now lies at the base of Jebel Mousa, in a narrow part of the valley surrounded by gardens, which are cultivated by the monks and their Arab servants.

Until recently it resembled a beleaguered fortress rather than a convent. The only admission to it was gained by means of an aperture high up in the wall. Visitors were hoisted up by means of a crane, the windlass being worked by the monks inside. The most dignified person had thus to submit to be treated like bales of goods. Recently, the Bedouins having become friendly with the monks, and the number of visitors having increased, a gateway has been opened, though the strong iron-clamped door is still jealously guarded.

Entering the Convent, 1871
E.H. Palmer

Proceeding up the valley, you pass, on your left, the hill on which Aaron is supposed to have set up the golden calf, and which is still called after him; next by some old monastic ruins, and the now deserted barracks of Abbás Pasha's soldiery, and, then following the path which they constructed, in a few minutes reach the convent walls. As you approach, your Arabs set up a shout of *Yá Músa* (for the

Convent of St. Catherine

porter's name is Moses), a little wicket in the wall opens, and a turbaned head appears and asks your business at the convent. A rope is let down, to which you attach your letter of introduction from the branch convent at Cairo, and, as it is drawn up, other faces—white, handsome, and vacant—appear and salute you, either with pantomimic gestures, or in a language of their own composing, fondly imagined by the community to represent Arabic.

Presently there issues forth from the gate at the side an old gentleman, reverend though fuddled in mien, dignified though unsteady in gait,—with a patriarchal beard, and the most mediæval of serge costumes, who, if such attention be not dexterously avoided, will fall upon your neck and greet you with a paternal kiss.

This is Brother Jacobus, the œconomos, or bursar, of the convent, once a flourishing Smyrna merchant, but now, either because he is tired of the world, or, more probably, because the world is tired of him, brought here to end his days in the Convent of Mount Sinai. "I was an unbeliever," said he to me one day, "until I came and saw what a holy place this is. For, when the earthquake shakes the mountains round, it never moves a thing within the convent walls; and that convinced me." As an earthquake has not taken place here within the memory of man, this test of the sanctity of the establishment can hardly be called a crucial one.

It was by this worthy that the members of the Sinai Expedition were ushered into the Convent of St Catherine.

Relations between the Monastery of St. Catherine and the peoples of Sinai were not always easy, but when the whole peninsula faced a problem, the communities came together for the common good.

A Problem Shared, 1897
Agnes Lewis Smith

The inhabitants of the Sinai peninsula were at that time almost at their wits' end as to how they could obtain water for their camels and their flocks. Nothing less than a famine was threatened, for not a drop of rain had fallen since March or April of the previous year—in fact, since the flood of which our young Oxford friends, Messrs. Cowley and Stenning, were witnesses. This had been only too evident during our journey from Suez. The torf-trees at Ghurundel and the palms at Feirân had all looked miserable; there was hardly a plant alive in the Convent valley; the olives and almond-trees in the garden were drooping; and the fine old cypresses had dropped their leaves, so as to resemble scaffolding poles. The monks lamented the lowness of the water in their wells, and one morning we were surprised by the arrival of three sheikhs, who had come a long four days' journey as a deputation from the tribes of the Tih, for the purpose of requesting the monks to pray for rain. This was sufficiently remarkable as between Moslem and Christian,[1] but still more curious was it when they preferred a like request to our dragoman. "But it will be of no use," they said, "unless you put on a white dress and go to the top of Jebel Musa about midnight, and pray there." Joseph excused himself by saying that the great thing was for people to pray for themselves. "If you don't do that," he said, "my prayers won't help you much." When we spoke to the monks of the drought they always said, "It is for our sins."

It will readily be understood that in these circumstances the face of the sky was to us a never-failing source of eager interest; especially in the afternoons. Every cloud we saw sailing above the summit of the Râs Sufsafah, or gathering over our own valley towards sunset, we earnestly hoped might grow and give us the coveted blessing.

On Pilgrimage to the Holy Mountain, 383
Egeria

From Jerusalem to the holy Mount Sinai is twenty-two staging-posts. . . . Before you reach the holy Mount Sinai you come to the fort of Clysma (probably a village near Suez) on the Red Sea, the place where the children of Israel crossed the sea dry-shod. (Exodus 14.29) And the tracks of Pharaoh's chariot are permanently

---

1. The Bedawîn firmly believe that the monks possess the two Tables of the Law, written by Moses, either built into a wall of the Chapel of the Burning Bush, or concealed in the ruins of the church on the top of Jebel Musa.

marked across the sand; its wheels were a good deal further apart than the chariots that we now have in the Roman Empire, ...Pharaoh's chariot tracks reach right down to the sea-shore at the point where he entered the sea in his efforts to catch the children of Israel.

This sea has the name 'Red' not because the water is red or muddy. Indeed, it is quite as sparkling clear and cold as the Ocean. Its fish are excellent and unusually sweet, and fish of all types from this sea taste as good as the fish of the Italian Sea (Mediterranean). . . . Also there is a great deal of coral on this shore. Shur, the desert where they (the Israelites) went for three days without water is of an enormous size. No one has ever seen a bigger desert, and no one could guess the quantities of sand. Between the Desert of Shur and Marah there is one staging post next to the sea, and at Marah itself there are some palm-trees (very few), and two springs which holy Moses made sweet.

> Egeria followed the route on a three-day journey to the next oasis and then went on to Abu Zenima by sea, the halfway point of the journey.

Next, two mountains come into sight on the left, and, before you reach them, there is the place where the Lord rained manna on the children of Israel. They are lofty mountains, and very steep. On one side of the mountains the valley is perfectly flat and like a colonnade two hundred yards wide, with the steep high mountains on either side. But where the mountains open out the valley is six miles wide and a good deal longer.

All around the mountains caves have been carved out, and, if you just took the trouble to put up some curtains, they would make marvellous bedrooms. Each bedroom is inscribed with Hebrew letters. At the far end of the valley there is good water in plenty . . . it is protected by mountains both sides, but it has no fields or vineyards, and there is nothing there but the water and some palm-trees (Feiran).

> Egeria traveled on and, after a sixty-kilometer journey, reached the holy Mount Sinai.

When we arrived there our guides, the holy men who were with us, said, "It is usual for the people who come here to say a prayer when first they catch sight of the Mount of God", and we did as they suggested. . . .

So, coming from Feiran we said the prayer. Then, going on, we made our way across the head of the valley and approached the Mount of God. It looks like a single mountain when you are going round it, but when you actually go into it there are really several peaks, all of them known as 'the Mount of God', and the principal one, the summit on which the Bible tells us that "God's glory came down" (Exodus 18.20), is in the middle of them. I never thought I had seen mountains as high as those which stood around it, but the one in the middle where God's glory came down was the highest of all, so much so that, when we were on top, all the other peaks we had seen and thought so high looked like little hillocks below us.

Late on Saturday, then, we arrived at the mountain and came to some cells. The monks who lived in them received us most hospitably, showing us every kindness. There is a church there with a presbyter; that is where we spent the night, and, pretty early on Sunday, we set off with the presbyter and monks who lived there to climb each mountain.

> Fourteen centuries after Egeria stood on Mount Sinai, another renowned woman traveler climbed to the same spot.

From the Holy Mountain, 1879
Isabella Bird

I was three-quarters of an hour in climbing this peak. For how many years from early childhood upwards, have I thought and dreamed about this mountain top, and have imagined its aspect! It is like and unlike—like in absolute desolation, but unlike in its grandeur and majesty. The summit is very small and shivered into boulders, and leaves little space for aught but two rude buildings, and a mosque built out of the ruins of an earlier convent. Beneath the mosque is a cave in which Mahometan tradition says that Moses passed the forty days and forty nights. Quite near is a cleft in the rock to which my Bedaween pointed and said something in Arabic, which I have since learned is the name signifying 'cleft in the rock' in which Moses was hid when the glory of God passed by. An empty champagne bottle profaned the summit, and I threw it with indignation over the southern precipice more than a thousand feet in depth. . . . I stayed two hours on the top of Jebel Musa, and was loath to leave it, never more while the earth lasts to visit its awful solitudes again. It is worth all the desert heat and dreariness, the raging thirst, the relentless hot wind, the burning glare—the many torments of the journey here, and all the prospective misery of the journey back. Apart from all association, it is the grandest mountain view I have ever seen and of mountains of which colours run wild: red, crimson, black, green, orange, brown-grey, blue-grey, all invested with a beauty not to be described by the blue atmosphere which bathed them all, and which carried the enchanted vision over the whole sea of peaks to the south of the peninsula, over deep wadis and reddened levels, to a far distance where the blue horizon was an ocean bluer than the land. Distance meant only a tenderer blue, not outlines less definite; nearness meant depths of violet shadow of infinite coolness. Everywhere granite, syenite, gneiss, micro-schist, and their varieties of basalt and porphyry, disported themselves in audacious freaks of colour which I dare not attempt to describe, flaming and flaring it would have been but for the softening effect of atmosphere. The huge mountain masses, crowned by the massive single pile of Jebel Serbal and the imposing peaks of Jebel Katarina and Jebel Zebur, both over 8500 feet in height, naked, harsh and arid, were all glorified by this exquisite medium, and their rude rocks represented not granite of every kind, but sapphire, ruby, turquoise, aqua-marine, and a whole catalogue of precious stones.

It was completely silent, unutterably lonely, awfully solemn. Every mountain of that wilderness of peaks has the same characteristic of being shivered. In reading their brief recorded history, it did not seem a great stretch of imagination to suppose that their summits were riven when they "trembled at the presence of God".

> The Suez Canal was opened on Tuesday, November 6, 1869 by Ismail, Khedive of Egypt and Eugènie, Empress of France. Thomas Cook took a tour group to witness the great occasion. Isabel, Lady Burton, sailed toward India through the Suez Canal with her husband, Richard. Constance Sitwell too was sailing to India and stood in the bow of the ship in the evening as they went through the Canal after coaling at Port Said.

Passing through Egypt, 1783
James Capper
The voyage from Tor to Suez may easily be performed in one day with a fair wind, but at any rate in five. Immediately as a ship appears in sight of Suez, a boat is sent on board to enquire the purpose of her coming; and the officer generally brings a present from the Governor consisting of a sheep or two, some small flat cakes of bread, a jar of water, and a small quantity of fruit, particularly oranges, which are juicy and of a very delicate flavour. As the messenger is a man of some rank, it is usual to salute him with coffee, tobacco, sweetmeats, etc. When he returns on shore he will carry a letter for you to any person at Cairo, and it will be forwarded by express the same evening together with an account of your arrival to the principal Bey of Cairo. It would not be prudent to write any secrets in the letter, but you may send instructions concerning your journey, and directions to have a vessel prepared for you at Alexandria.

At the Opening of the Suez Canal, 1869
Jabez Burns and Thomas Cook
On the fifth day out, we got sight of Egypt, and in the evening of that day, cast anchor within sight of the lights of Port Said, leaving behind us the lights of the

British Mediterranean fleet of seven men-of-war. Early the following morning we sailed into the harbour of Port Said and took our position amongst about seventy steamers, men-of-war, and other ships of various nations, to which afterwards twenty were added, or thereabouts. The 'America' had scarcely dropped her anchor ere it was announced that the Emperor of Austria was following us, a fact soon verified by hundreds of guns both in and out of the harbour. On that day the firing was continued at intervals, as Princes, Ambassadors, and other celebrities followed in rapid succession. But the quickest and most general firing was reserved for the arrival of the Empress of the French, on the morning of Tuesday, the 16th of November, when enthusiasm reached its highest pitch, as the 'Aigle' steamed slowly into harbour, her Imperial Majesty most pleasantly acknowledging the universal demonstration.

The serious business of the inauguration of the Canal commenced on that day, in the three kiosques erected for the occasion. It was my good fortune to get a position in the centre of the triangle of the kiosques, where I could easily observe every motion of the royal, noble and dignified assembly that occupied the central erection; whilst on my right was the Mahomedan stand, and on my left that of the Catholic Church, to both of which inaugural duties were assigned. The Mahomedan official read a paper, which no one could hear; but the Latins were gorgeously and powerfully represented by an array of richly attired priests, and one of the most clever of their orators, whose speech and benediction constituted the greatest event of the day. That oration has doubtless been published long ere this in the English papers, and it must be read—as it was listened to—with intense interest. Some thought it a little too flowery and flattering, and I noticed a slight shake of the head, and what appeared to be a little dissent on the lips of the French Empress at one of the personal allusions made to her Majesty. The only cheer was evoked by the mention of the name of Monsieur Lesseps, who bore his honours with marvellous modesty and gentleness. The clever Catholic priest must have been heard with strange feelings of interest by the Greek, Armenian, Coptic, and other patriarchs, bishops, and priests, that were crowded together on the two sides of the Imperial and Royal kiosque. At night an immense assemblage responded to an invitation of the Viceroy to a *soirée* and ball in his Royal Highness's yacht, the story of which I leave to the pens of the newspaper correspondents and the pencils of the artists of the illustrated papers. Port Said was a-blaze with gas, oil, and candles at night; and many of the ships, to their mast heads, were covered with fantastically arranged lights and coloured fires.

On Wednesday morning, the 17th Nov., the great test of the Canal was to be commenced, and at 8–30 a.m., the 'Aigle' steamed out of the harbour, other ships following at intervals of ten to fifteen minutes, until forty vessels were afloat. Our 'America' being a very wide paddle steamer, was placed lower down in the list, being No. 36, and it was 2 p.m. ere we passed the columns at the entrance to the Canal. It was impossible for all to get into Lake Timsah, the great bay of Ismailia, that night, and we were moored to the banks of the Canal, a few miles from the lake. Early the following morning the last half-dozen miles of the first half of the voyage were accomplished, and we were stationed opposite to the new town of Ismailia—a town which owes its entire existence to the construction of the Canal. Ten years ago there was not a human habitation where this beautifully laid-out town now stands, and the great lake where hundreds of ships may now find anchorage was then a swamp, subject to the annual overflow of the Nile. Little more than a year ago, I think it was, that the Prince of Wales opened the sluice which let in the waters of the Mediterranean, and converted this fresh-water marsh into an inland sea of salt water, and to this point traffic by small steamers has since been regularly conducted. From here, too, a fresh-water canal, fed by the Nile, has been temporarily used for the navigation of small craft to the Red Sea. Ismailia is much more eligible for a great town than Port Said, and its arrangement in squares and broad streets, at right-angles, indicates the importance attached to the site by its founders. Here the Khedive has built a large palace, M. Lesseps has erected a capacious and beautiful residence, good hotels have been opened, and there is collected a considerable resident population. The town is also situated at an angle of the railways to Alexandria, Cairo and Suez. Trees and graceful foliage and flowers grow profusely, and the Desert bears a smiling appearance. The festive arrangements here were conducted on a scale of the utmost prodigality. Large temporary saloons were erected, where thousands dined and took other refreshments at the expense of the Viceroy; champagne and other costly wines flowed like water; thousands met at the palace of the Khedive to dance, talk and sup together; a wild military exhibition of Arabs and Bedouins was arranged for the gratification of the visitors; fireworks and illuminations closed the night, and thousands slept in tents specially provided for the occasion. Where the tents, the bedsteads and bedding came from, it is difficult to conceive. It took several days, and various special trains, to clear away the fittings and furniture temporarily provided.

On Friday, the 19th, the Empress's boat, the 'Aigle', again headed the steamboat procession; but amongst the early departures were one or two very large steamers, and the 'Péluce' of the Messageries Impériales ran aground at the entrance of the Canal. This caused a detention of several hours, and at least half the fleet spent another night in the Lake Timsah. It was half-past one on Saturday ere we could make a fair start, and then after a splendid run over the Lake Amers, sometimes at the rate of nine to ten knots an hour, we were again blockaded by steamers in advance; and after running aground ourselves we were again compelled to halt for the night, within sight of the lights of Suez, and it was nearly mid-day on Sunday when the line was cleared for us to enter the Red Sea. Two or three ships followed us, and by Sunday afternoon over forty ships accomplished the entire voyage from sea to sea, and the passage of the Canal was an accomplished fact—a fact of immense importance, notwithstanding all the accidents incidental to the voyage.

Before the 'America' had reached her anchorage, many of the ships had been deserted by their passengers, who had hurried off by railway to Cairo, to see the last but one of the series of popular demonstrations. For myself it was pleasant to repose in the quiet roadstead of the historical waters of the Red Sea, at a point evidently not very far from that spot where the persecuted Israelites rested from the pursuit of their oppressors. Whatever may be the inability of scepticism to grasp the simple statements of Bible truth touching that great event, here was just the physical formation of mountain and plain suggested by the perusal of the sacred narrative, and I felt a pleasant satisfaction in gazing upon a spot so famous in Bible history.

Of the Suez Canal there seems now to be but one opinion. Its practicability none can now dispute. The two seas are already united; Africa is converted into an island by a combination of Mediterranean and Red Sea waters.

Through the Suez Canal, 1875
Isabel Burton

The next morning we began to steam slowly up the long ditch called the Canal, and at last to the far east we caught a gladdening glimpse of the desert—the wild, waterless Wilderness of Sur, with its waves and pyramids of sand catching the morning rays, with its shadows of mauve, rose pink, and lightest blue with its plains and rain-sinks, bearing brown dots which were tamarisks. The sky was heavenly blue, the water a deep band of the clearest green, the air balmy and fresh. The golden sands stretched far away; an occasional troop of Bedawin with their camels and goats passed, and reminded me of those dear, dead days at Damascus. It all came back to me with a rush. Once more I was in the East. I had not enjoyed myself so much with Nature for four years and a half. With the smell of the desert air in our nostrils, with Eastern pictures before our eyes, we were even grateful for the slowness of the pace at which we travelled. They were the pleasantest two days imaginable, like a river picnic. We reached Suez, with its faded glory, at length; and there we shipped a pious pilot, who said his prayers regularly, and carefully avoided touching my dog.

Looking toward the Other Side, 1926
Constance Sitwell

. . . what I was imagining: miles of colourless sand lying pale under the moon, and sand-coloured lions moving; and fields of blue vetch by the Nile; and the black tombs of the bulls of Apis, dark and stifling under their load of sand—thick heat in there, and thick darkness, and the empty sombre passages going between the great black granite tombs, sunk deep in underground halls. And fields of beans, and fields of lupins and loose-growing sugar-cane and dense corn; and behind, the rosy wall of the Libyan mountains in the jocund morning light, honeycombed with tombs—full of mummies in hard painted cases; and painted halls and creamy passages, and roofs coloured with the young blue of Egypt—the most adorable colour in the world.

13
The Deserts of Egypt

 A map of the world's vegetation zones does not tell the whole story of Egypt's geography. Sand-colored 'desert' covers the whole of North Africa and Egypt. Yet Egypt is verdant and fertile enough to feed its large population. How is this? The Nile Valley is not marked on such a map, but as one walks above the old flood plain of the Nile, the fertile land melts into near-desert and then the desert of the map. It is only continuous labor that keeps the land so verdant. Before the internal combustion engine and the paved road, the camel gave people access to the desert, though often with great discomfort and with danger. But though the desert was "dreary and solemn," it fed the mind and spirit of the traveler in a way that the city seldom could.

The Caravan to Mecca Starts, 1836
John Lloyd Stephens

It was worth my ride to see the departure of the caravan. It consisted of more than thirty thousand pilgrims, who had come from the shores of the Caspian, the extremities of Persia, and the confines of Africa; and having assembled, according to usage for hundreds of years, at Cairo as a central point, the whole mass was getting in motion for the pilgrimage of fifty days, through dreary sands, to the tomb of the Prophet.

Accustomed as I was to associate the idea of order and decorum with observance of all rites and duties of religion, I could not but feel surprised at the noise, tumult and confusion, the strifes and battles of these pilgrim travellers. If I had met them in the desert after their line of march was formed, it would have been an imposing spectacle, and comparatively easy to describe; but here, as far as the eye could reach, they were scattered over the sandy plain, thirty thousand people, with probably twenty thousand camels and dromedaries, men, women and children, beasts and baggage, all commingled in a confused mass that seemed hopelessly inextricable. Some had not yet struck their tents, some were making coffee, some smoking, some cooking, some eating, many shouting and cursing, others on their knees praying, and others, again, hurrying on to join the long moving stream that already extended several miles into the desert.

The Camel, 1834
Hon. W.E. Fitzmaurice
There is something in the aspect of a camel that instantly puts all European ideas to flight: their patient mild endurance of fatigue and privation; the docility which they show in the most trivial matters, even if girted in the smallest degree too tight for their load, their hollow gurgling moan instantly makes the Arab guides aware of the cause of their distress; they kneel down to be laden, and rise with immense burthens on their backs; their gait is unlike that of any other animal: they have neither the sprightliness of the horse, nor the obstinacy of the mule, but seem to express, by their slow and lengthened step that they are aware of the tediousness of their journeys, which are only to be surmounted by constant and arduous perseverance; nature has happily endowed them with extraordinary powers of retaining their food for a length of time, in fact, it is impossible to picture any animal so completely formed to sustain the exhaustion and fatigue that they must undergo, from the scantiness of subsistence and water in these trackless sands.

How to Travel, 1183
Ibn Jubayr
Across this desert no one will journey save on a camel, by reason of thirst. The best and most comfortable camel litters used on them are the *shaqadif*, and the best of these are those made in the Yemen for, like the travelling *ashakin* [seats] they are covered with leather and are roomy. Two of them are bound together by stout ropes and put across the camel. They have supports at each corner and on these rests a canopy. The traveller and his companion in counterpoise will thus be veiled from the blaze of the midday heat and may sit reclining at ease

beneath its covering. With his companion he may partake of what he needs of food and the like, or read, when he wishes, the Koran or a book; and whoso deems it lawful to play chess may, if he wish, play his companion, for diversion and to relieve the spirit. To be short it eases the hardship of travel. Most travellers ride their camels on top of their baggage and so painfully endure the rigours of the burning heat.

Mrs. Elwood, en route through Egypt to India crossed the desert from the Nile to the Red Sea.

The Adventure of the Takhtrouan, 1826
Anne Katherine Elwood

The body of it is about six feet long, and three broad, composed of a curiously heavy-painted open wood-work, something like the Mameluke windows; and in this I lay as in a palanquin, which it little resembled. This was placed upon shafts, and carried by camels, one going in front, the other behind, as in a sedan-chair; the latter having its head tied down, in order that it might see where it stepped; and when they were in harness, it was raised nearly six feet from the ground.

Strange-looking creatures are camels to an English eye, and a fearful noise they do make to an English ear; they stretch out their long necks one way, and they poke them out another, and there is no knowing where one is safe from them; and I was to mount a litter conveyed by these singular productions of Nature, probably the first and only Englishwoman that ever ventured in a native Egyptian Takhtrouan! My heart failed me terribly at this instant, I cannot but confess, and I was nervously alarmed at the sight of my unwieldy vehicle. However, "Come it slow or come it fast, It is but death that comes at last." thought I, as I sallied forth to ascend my Takhtrouan. There were no steps, and we had neglected to take the precaution of bringing a ladder. What was to be done? Whilst I was hesitating, an Arab crouched down at my feet, and offered his back for my footstool. Was it not the Emperor Valerian by whom the cruel Sapor was wont to ascend his horse in a similar manner? I thought of him, as in this conquering style I entered my Takhtrouan.

The motion was very unpleasant at first, and what with my fear and fatigue, I had a sensation of sickness, almost to fainting, come over me; however, I supported it as well as I could, and you cannot conceive how very strange my sensations when I found myself enclosed in a wooden cage, surrounded by wild Arabs, about to enter the Desert! Charles rode by my side upon a camel: at first he thought its movements were rough, but he ultimately preferred them to those of a horse. . . . At his own particular request, my Arab friend, who had hitherto so gallantly devoted himself to my service, was installed as my special attendant, the Knight of the Takhtrouan; and he undertook to guard me across the Desert.

More Advice to Women Travelers, 1848
Harriet Martineau

. . . And how many miles did I walk in the Desert, during those five weeks! I found, as some others did, the motion of my camel more and more fatiguing and disagreeable, all the way; and, being at home a great walker, I had recourse, more and more, to my own feet,—little heeding even the heat and thirst in comparison with the annoyances of camel-riding. I have often walked from ten to fifteen miles in the noon hours, continuously, and of course at the pace of the caravan,—sometimes over an easy pebbly track,—sometimes over mountain passes,—sometimes cutting my boots to pieces on the sharp rocks; but always giving up when we came to deep sand. Walking in deep sand in the Arabian Desert, at noonday, is a true purgatory; but there is little deep sand. We did not believe that more than one-fifth of our Desert route was sandy.

As for the camel-riding,—I could not have conceived of any exercise so utterly exhausting. The swaying motion, causing an unintermitting pull upon one part of the spine, which can by no means be exchanged for another, becomes at last perfectly intolerable, though easy and agreeable enough at the outset.—I would never say a word to encourage any woman to travel in the Desert, if she must do it on the back of a camel. If she can walk as I do, well and good; and I am told it is easy and agreeable to go on a donkey from Cairo to Jerusalem by the El Arish route. . . . A woman who can walk far and easily, and bear the thirst which is the chief drawback on walking in the Desert, may set out for Mount Sinai without fear.

A Day in the Desert, 1871
E.H. Palmer

There is but little variety in camp-life in the desert, and a description of one day's journey may answer for all the rest.

At sunrise every one is astir; a simple toilette, a still more simple meal, and you pack up your things in preparation for the start. Then comes a repetition of the noise and clamour incident on loading, you mount your dromedary, and, when once fairly under weigh, the whole caravan trails noiselessly along the sand. Following the path marked out by the skeleton of camels which lie bleaching in the sun, you ride on until the noonday heat and glare compel you to seek a little rest beneath some friendly shade, if there is any to be had, though very frequently you must put up with such shelter as a white umbrella, or the unsavoury vicinity of a kneeling camel can afford. In England one knows nothing of the luxury of shade, and cannot appreciate what it really means. How often, when reclining, five of us, beneath a dried-up furze-bush no bigger than a good-sized geranium, have consumed our bunch of dates and biscuits, washed down with just one drink of lukewarm water beautifully flavoured with goat-skin, and envied the happy terrier that laps the cool puddle of his native land!

After lunch the march is resumed until sunset, and then commences the really enjoyable part of the day. The tents are pitched, and dinner is prepared. The Arabs settle themselves cosily round the camp-fires to prepare their evening meal, and for an hour or so before retiring for the night comfort and repose reign around.

The first night in desert was an era in my life; it seemed as if all the vague images of my early dreams were about to assume a life-long reality which they had never worn for me till then. A fresh breeze blew into the tent, causing no apprehensions of nightly chills, but infusing new vigour into body and mind. The flickering camp-fires shed a lurid glow over the little knots of swarthy Bedouin as they reposed after the fatigues of the day, and produced a wondrously picturesque and Rembrandt-like effect. The hushed tones of those who had not yet fallen asleep, the whirring of a hand-mill here and there, the half-plaintive, half-surly groaning of the camels—these were the only sounds which disturbed the stillness of the night.

I contemplated the scene around me with mingled feelings of delight and awe. I was reclining perchance upon the very spot where the Children of Israel had encamped when fleeing from their Egyptian persecutors, and I could not help comparing my situation to some extent with theirs. I had just left the noisy bustling crowd of Cairo's streets, and had escaped into the freedom of the great lone wilderness, and I too felt that sense of Divine protection which must have been present to them, for never so much as in the desert does one feel that God is nigh. He it is that enables man to pass in safety through the dreary waste, and whether it be by direct miraculous intervention, . . . or by the scarcely less wonderful agency of reason and foresight, still it is His hand alone that guides him on.

Night in the Western Desert, 1923
Ahmad Hassanein

Then, the day's work is at an end. Camp is pitched. No tents are erected, for the men are too exhausted, too careless to mind what happens to their bodies. And night falls. It may be a starlit night, or there may be a moon. Gradually, a serenity gets hold of you. Gradually, after a day of silence, conversation starts. Feeble jokes are cracked. One of the men, probably the youngest of the caravan, ventures a joke with more cheerfulness than the rest and his voice is pitched to a higher key. Unconsciously the Beduins attune their voices to that higher, louder pitch and the volume of sound increases. The desert is working her charm.

The gentle night breeze revives the spirits of the caravan. In a few minutes the empty *fantasses* are used as drums and there is song and dance. At the first sound of music men may have been tending the camels, repairing the luggage, or the camels' saddles, but that first note brings all the caravan round the embers of the dying fire. Every one looks at his comrades to make sure that all are alive and happy, and every one tries to be a little more cheerful than his neighbour, to give him more confidence. . . .

Song and dance take out of the men of the caravan the little vitality that is left after the ravages of the day. Their spirit is exhausted and they fall asleep. They sleep beneath the beautiful dome of the stars. Few people in civilization know the pleasure of just sitting down and looking at the stars. No wonder Arabs were masters of the science of astronomy! So when the day's work is done the solitary Beduin has nothing left but to sit down and watch the movements of the stars and absorb the uplifting sense of comfort that they give to the spirit.

These stars become like friends that one meets every day. And when they go, it is not abruptly as when men say farewell at a parting, but it is like watching a friend fade gradually from view, with the hope of seeing him again the following night.

"*To prayers, O ye believers—prayers are better than sleep!*" The cry comes from the first man of the caravan to awaken. A few stars are still scattered in the sky.

Englishmen and Arabs in the Desert, 1835
Alexander Kinglake

I can understand the sort of amazement of the orientals at the scantiness of the retinue with which an Englishman passes the Desert, for I was somewhat struck myself when I saw one of my countrymen making his way across the wilderness in this simple style. At first there was a mere moving speck on the horizon; my party of course became all alive with excitement, and there were many surmises. Soon it appeared that three laden camels were approaching, and that two of them carried riders. In a while I saw that one of the riders wore the European dress, and at last the travellers were pronounced to be an English gentleman and his servant; by their side were a couple of Arabs on foot; and this, if I rightly remember, was the whole party. . . . This Englishman, as I afterwards found, was a military man returning to his country from India, and crossing the Desert at this part in order to go through Palestine. As for me, I had come pretty well straight from England, and so here we met in the wilderness about half way from our respective starting-points. As we approached each other, it became with both a question whether we should speak. I thought it likely that the stranger would accost me, and in the event of his doing so, I was quite ready to be as sociable, and as chatty as I could be, according to my nature; but I still could not think of any thing particular that I had to say to him. Of course, among civilised people, the not having anything to say is no excuse at all for not speaking; but I was shy, and indolent, and I felt no great wish to stop, and talk like a morning visitor in the midst of those broad solitudes. The traveller, perhaps, felt as I did, for, except that we lifted our hands to our caps, and waved our arms in courtesy, we passed each other quite as distantly, as if we had passed in Bond Street.

Our attendants, however, were not to be cheated of the delight that they felt in speaking to new listeners, and hearing fresh voices once more. The masters, therefore, had no sooner passed each other, than their respective servants quietly stopped and entered into conversation. As soon as my camel found that her companions were not following her, she caught the social feeling and refused to go on. I felt the absurdity of the situation, and determined to accost the stranger, if only to avoid the awkwardness of remaining stuck fast in the Desert, whilst our servants were amusing themselves. When with this intent I turned round my camel, I found that the gallant officer, who had passed me about thirty or forty yards, was in exactly the same predicament as myself. I put my now willing camel in motion, and rode up towards the stranger, who seeing this, followed my example, and came forward to meet me.

He was the first to speak; he was much too courteous to address me as if he admitted the possibility of my wishing to accost him from any feeling of mere sociability, or civilian-like love of vain talk; on the contrary, he at once attributed my advances to a laudable wish of acquiring statistical information; and, accordingly, when we got within speaking distance, he said, "I dare say, you wish to know how the Plague is going on in Cairo?" and then went on to say, he regretted that his information did not enable him to give me in numbers a perfectly accurate statement of the daily deaths. He afterwards talked pleasantly enough upon other, and less ghastly, subjects.

People of the Desert, 1818
Frederic Cailliaud

The Ababdeh maintain an entire independence; from time immemorial they have held possessions in the deserts, which they consider as their property. When we compelled them to come with us to the Nile, taking away their camels, their wood, their provisions, were we not liable to reprisals? Was it to be expected that the Ababdeh, who well knew our connection with the Pacha [Muhammad 'Ali], would submit to our demands without resistance? The main defence and safeguard of these people is their poverty, their innocence and the sterility of the soil which they inhabit; these are the guarantees of that savage liberty which they enjoy. Can anyone envy their lot? A few shrubs here and there . . . a few thorny herbs or plants, a little senna and coloquintda constitute the sole riches of the soil; still, however, the Ababdeh are not without apprehensions of being deprived of this their impoverished domain. They made earnest suit to me, repeatedly, to conceal from the Viceroy of Egypt the wretched productions of their deserts.

I was desirous to learn from them the reasons of their not living near the Nile, where they might lead a life more comfortable than in the wilds of these deserts. One of their Sheiks . . . one day made me this answer: "To any other European we would tell at length the attractions that allure us to a wandering life and to these deserts; but you are fully acquainted with them, and know how to value them as we do. We see you content amidst the toils of battering rocks from morn till night; but come and live with us under our tents, amidst these mountains that are works of heaven; of these flocks, wherein our wealth consists; of these sands that secure our independence. Why will you not tarry with us? By this time you may have forgotten your country, and may prefer ours. Dwell here with your friends the Abbadeh, and send back the Turkish soldiers to their master. You are accustomed to the same fatigues as we are; you sleep on the sand; your labours in the mountains are more toilsome than ours; we will select for you a young maiden that knows only the desert wherein she was born; the gazelle cannot match her for innocence and mildness. The Desert of Zabarah belongs to us; it may contain treasures (emeralds) that we are strangers to. As you are come here in quest of them, they are yours; you shall give us directions, and we will all labour with a will for you; my sheep and my camels shall be yours."

I was sensibly touched by the kindness which accompanied the effusions of this venerable Sheik; his generous offers were accompanied with the most friendly expressions that his heart could dictate. I shared in his emotions, and, strange to tell, for a moment was half persuaded.

Visiting the Monastery of Baramous, 1833
Robert Curzon

This monastery consisted of a high stone wall, surrounding a square enclosure, of about an acre in extent. A large square tower commanded the narrow entrance, which was closed by a low and narrow iron door. Within there was a good-sized church in tolerable preservation, standing nearly in the centre of the enclosure, which contained nothing else but some ruined buildings, and a few large fig trees growing out of disjointed walls. Two or three poor-looking monks still tenanted the ruins of the abbey. They had hardly anything to offer us, and were glad to partake of some of the rice and other eatables which we had brought with us. I wandered about among the ruins with the half-starved monks following me. We went into the square tower, where, in a large vaulted room with open unglazed windows were forty or fifty Coptic manuscripts on cotton paper, lying on the floor, to which several of them adhered firmly, not having been moved for many years. I only found one leaf on vellum, which I brought away. The other manuscripts appeared to be all liturgies; most of them smelling of incense when I opened them, and well smeared with dirt and wax from the candles which had been held over them during the reading of the service. . . .

There were several curious lamps in this church formed of ancient glass, like those in the mosque of Sultan Hassan at Cairo, which are said to be of the same date as the mosque, and to be of Syrian manufacture. These, which were in the shape of large open vases, were ornamented with pious sentences in Arabic characters, in blue on a white ground. They were very handsome, and, except one of the same kind, which is now in England . . . I never saw any like them. They are probably some of the most ancient specimens of ornamental glass existing, excepting, of course, the vases and lachrymatories of the classic times.

Creatures of the Desert, c. 450 B.C.
Herodotus

There is a place in Arabia . . . (the desert to the east of the Delta) . . . where I went to try and get information about the flying snakes. On my arrival I saw their skeletons in incalculable numbers; they were piled in heaps, some of which were big, others smaller, others—the most numerous—smaller still. The place where these bones lie is a narrow mountain pass leading to a broad plain which joins on to the plain of Egypt, and it is said that when the winged snakes fly to Egypt from Arabia in the spring, the ibises meet them at the entrance to the pass and do not let them get through, but kill them. According to the Arabians, this service is the reason for the great reverence with which the ibis is regarded in Egypt, and the Egyptians themselves admit the truth of what they say. The ibis is jet-black all over; it has legs like a crane's, a markedly hooked beak, and is about the size of a landrail. That, at any rate, is what the black ibis is like—the kind namely that attacks the winged snakes. . . .

> Before the Suez Canal was built many travelers passed overland through Egypt on their way to or from India. Some sailed to Suez and crossed the desert to Cairo; others disembarked at Qusayr (also spelled Kosseir) on the Red Sea and traveled across the Eastern Desert to the Nile.

Arriving from India, 1823
Moyle Sherer

Kosseir is a very poor-looking place, but its market is well and plentifully supplied. You drink the sweet water of the Nile, and eat of vegetables from the valley through which it flows. The costume of the inhabitants is dull; they all wear the robe of capuchin brown, common to the fellahs of Egypt, and everyone carries a long pipe in his hand. A few Turks or Arabs, in the employ of the Pasha, the merchants, and *nakhodas*, who frequent the port, and a few soldiers, enliven the bazaar, contribute to the support of a respectable coffee-house, and account for the existence of a sizeable mosque, of late erection, built of stone. In our evening walk, we found a garden some forty yards square, two trees, and a few wells of brackish water; we also saw a small Arab encampment, and some sailors at play near the gate, and a game not unlike trap-ball. One of these sailors had long full thick curls, one on each side of the head, very similar to those on the ancient statues of Egypt. . . . We started the following morning about six. For two hours the land wind was cool enough; but as the sun gained power, the heat became scorching and oppressive. About eleven we halted under the shadow of a rock, and refreshed ourselves. In a northern country it is a "traveller in the day of the sun", which conveys an image of joy and content. Here it is the traveller drinking his cruse of water under the overshadowing rock; the kneeling camel and the sleeping driver.

The road through the desert is most wonderful in its features; a finer cannot be imagined. It is wide, hard, firm, winding, for at least two thirds of the way, from Kosseir to Thebes, between ranges of rocky hills, rising often perpendicularly on either side, as if they had been scarped by art; here, again, rather broken, and overhanging, as if they were the lofty banks of a mighty river, and you traversing its dry and naked bed. Now you are quite landlocked; now again you open on small valleys, and see, upon heights beyond, small square towers. . . . Who passes the desert and says all is barren , all lifeless ? In the grey morning you may see the common pigeon, and the patridge, and the pigeon on the rock , alight before your very feet , and come upon the beaten camel-paths for food. They are tame for they have not learned to fear, or to distrust the men who pass these solitudes. The camel-driver would not lift a stone to them; and the sportsman could hardly find it in his heart to kill these gentle tenants of the desert; the deer might tempt him; I saw but one; far, very far, he caught the distant camel tramp, and paused, and raised and threw back his head to listen, then away to the road instead of from it; but far ahead he crossed it, and then away up a long slope he fleetly stole, and off to some solitary spring which wells, perhaps, where no traveller, no human being ever trod.

Looking down from a Desert Monastery, 1833
Robert Curzon

To those who are not familiar with the aspect of such a region as this, it may be well to explain that a desert such as that which now surrounded me resembles more than anything else a dusty turnpike-road in England on a hot summer's day, extended interminably, both as to length and breadth. A country of low rounded hills, the surface of which is composed entirely of gravel, dust, and stones, will give a good idea of the general aspect of a desert. Yet although parched and dreary in the extreme from their vastness and openness, there is something grand and sublime in the silence and loneliness of these burning plains; and the wandering tribes of Bedouins who inhabit them are seldom content to remain long in the narrow confines of cultivated land. There is always a fresh breeze in the desert, except when the terrible hot wind blows; and the air is more elastic and pure than where vegetation produces exhalations which in all hot climates are more or less heavy and deleterious. The air of the desert is always healthy, and no race of man enjoy a greater exemption from weakness, sickness, and disease than the children of the desert, who pass their lives in wandering to and fro in search of the scanty herbage on which their flocks are fed, far from the cares and troubles of busy cities, and free from the oppression which grinds down the half-starved cultivators of the fertile soil of Egypt.

Whilst from my elevated position I looked out on my left upon the mighty desert, on my right how different was the scene! There below my feet lay the convent garden in all the fresh luxuriance of tropical; vegetation. Tufts upon tufts of waving palms over-shadowed the immense succulent leaves of the banana, which in their turn rose out of the thickets of the pomegranate rich with the bright green leaves and its blossoms of that beautiful and vivid red which is excelled by few even of the most brilliant flowers of the East. These were contrasted with the deep dark green of the caroub or locust-tree; and the yellow apples of the lotus vied with the clusters of green limes with their sweet white flowers which luxuriated in a climate too hot and sultry for the golden fruit of the orange, which is not to be met with in the valley of the Nile. Flowers and fair branches exhaling rich perfume and bearing freshness in their very aspect became more beautiful from their contrast to the dreary arid plains outside the convent walls, and this great difference was owing solely to there being a well of water in this spot, from which a horse or mule was constantly employed to draw the fertilising stream which nourished the teeming vegetation of the monastic garden.

I stood gazing and moralizing at these contrasted scenes for some time. . . .

Into the Desert to the Oasis and Beyond, 1834
Mohammed Ibn Umar

When the camels were at length laden, we struck into the desert, and on the evening of the fifth day reached Kharjeh, the Theban oasis. This place is planted with date-trees that surround it as the anklets surround the ankles, or as the two arms of a lover surround the neck of his mistress, on whom he sheds a kiss. These date-trees were laden with splendid dates, the aspect of which charmed our eyes, and which were exceedingly cheap. We remained there five days; but on the morning of the sixth preceded, and, after hard travelling, on the third day reached Abyrys. This country has been ruined by the exactions of its governors; all its population, formerly so happy, is now dispersed; the date-trees are destroyed, and all the brilliance of the scenery has been tarnished.

After two days of rest we pushed on two other days to Boulac, a country also desolated, and nearly without inhabitants. Most of its houses are ruined. What surprised me was the extreme smallness of the date-trees, under which we could lie and pick the fruit with our hands. The name of Boulac recalled to me the Boulac of Cairo, and some natural tears fell from my eyes as I thought of the place where I had been brought up.

But there is little time for regret in the desert. We pushed on hastily and arrived in the evening at Maks, to which this verse may be applied: "The country has no inhabitants except the gazelles and caravans that traverse it." It is related that Maks had formerly a large population, which perished by the hand of Him who destroyed the last eagle of Lockman; all the inhabitants have disappeared—not a man is left. Scarcely at present remain there a few trees, some tamarisks, and thorny bushes. We tarried there two days, and having filled our water skins, departed.

We now entered a desert completely arid. For five days we marched through silent solitudes, over grim plains, where here and there the wandering eye could scarcely discover some stunted plants of the same colour as the ground; there was not a tree to cast a hand's-breadth of shadow. During this part of the journey we were compelled to cook our food with the dry dung of camels, which the servants collected.

On the evening of the fifth day we reached a place called Es-Shebb, situated in the midst of mountains that seemed like vast cones of sand. An unpleasant wind blew over them; but we remained there two days to rest, and then went on again for four more, until we reached the wells of Selineh, near which are the ruins of ancient buildings. It is situated at the foot of a mountain which bears the same name. We remained there two days to rest. This place is a delightful one for the traveller; but that which astonished me chiefly was that the young men of the caravan, having ascended the mountain, struck certain blocks of stone with switches, and caused them to yield a sound exactly resembling that of a tambourine. The cause of this curious circumstance is unknown. Are there hollows in these stones, or are they placed over caverns? Glory be to God, who knows the truth! At any rate the people of the caravan told me that, on a certain night, which they specified—the night of Friday, I believe—there is heard from the mountain the playing of a tambourine, as if a marriage festival were going on. The origin of these nocturnal musical entertainments is also unknown.

On the third day we filled our water-skins, and leaving Selineh entered upon the desert, and having travelled for five whole days, during which we met a caravan of Amaim Arabs coming from the natron lakes, reached Laguyeh, where we again rested two days and departed for Zaghawy. We now met a courier, mounted on a dromedary, coming from Darfur, and announcing the death of the just and glorious prince, Sultan Abd-er-Rahman-er-Rashid, sovereign of Darfur and its dependent provinces. The courier was going to Cairo to renew the state seal, no one in that country being capable of engraving it. The caravan testified its grief at this melancholy news; all feared that some disturbance might arise in the country, for the Sultan who had just died was an equitable and generous prince, loving science and those who possessed it, and the declared enemy of ignorance.

We continued our route for five days more, when at length our camels knelt at the natron lakes of Zaghawy. From thence to the frontiers of Darfur there are still ten days of travel, making forty days in all. We remained at this place eleven days, pasturing our beasts of burthen in order to prepare them for the frightful desert before us. Some camels were slaughtered at this station, and their flesh was distributed to the caravan. There came to us some Bedawin Arabs of Darfur who offered for sale camel-milk and butter. They had come to fetch salt and natron from that place.

We now sent forward a courier mounted on a dromedary, with letters for the government, and others for the relations of the caravan folks, announcing our speedy arrival. I also wrote to my father, kissing his venerable hands, and relating how Achmet Bedawi had cared for me. Indeed I had reason to be thankful; of all the journeys I had ever performed this was the pleasantest; for so soon as we quitted Beni-Ady my protector ordered his slaves to prepare for me a kind of tent on a quiet camel, and he himself assisted me to mount, and held the bridle until I was settled in my seat. He gave me, also, a great leathern bottle, to hold water, and bade all his servitors to be at my beck and call. He had with him seven middle-aged slaves and one young one, eight hired domestics, and sixty-eight camels. With him were five concubines, and a sixth woman who was his cousin, Sitti Jamal of ravishing beauty. He had also a black Dongola horse, with a saddle of green velvet.

Achmet treated me with all the kindness of a father. When the caravan halted I used to doze away, fatigued by the swinging of the camel and the heat of the sun; he would allow me to sleep until the hour of supper arrived, when he would wake me gently and bring me water, that I might wash. At meals he guided my hand to the dish, and sometimes put the morsels into my mouth.

When we left the wells of Zaghawy we marched for ten days hastily, starting before dawn and trenching on the night. On the eleventh morning we came to Mazroob, a well situated on the confines of Darfur, and in a few hours the Arabs came down to us, bringing large skins of water and little skins full of milk. We congratulated ourselves on the happy termination of our journey, and solaced ourselves at the well during the whole of that day.

The Great Oasis of the Libyan Desert: al-Kharga, 1909
Norma Lorimer

Our last day in the desert we spent in doing the Oasis proper, . . . the "fertile spot in the desert" that we had come to see; . . . it was, in fact, from first to last an agricultural day, for the picture I saw when I opened my bedroom door was white-gowned men cutting the barley harvest. The fields lay just in front of our house a little way across the desert.

I thought of my visit to the tomb of Thi at Sakkara, and how similar this desert scene was to the ones depicted on the walls of the pleasure courts of his double. But how very long ago it seemed since I had looked at the lean figure of the over-seer superintending the various operations connected with his master's fine farms. He stood just as this *rais* stood leaning on his long staff, with that lofty air of supe-riority that any man in command loves to assume.

. . . I have now before my eyes, and always shall have, a very vivid recol-lection of its greenness and beauty, for we visited the new lake and walked under the shade of the splendid palms which surround it, and paid visits to the watery spots, which showed us that magic can be worked in a few months by drilling holes in the desert and forcing it to give its hidden waters.

How cruel nature can be, it is only possible to realise it in a country where the beasts and the birds and every living thing perish for want of water, while the great earth Mother keeps it back and hoards it up in the very bowels of her being.

Can you love a country that has no water, that has no flowers, that gives her children only buffalo's milk to drink, and whose hens lay eggs so strangely flavoured and so mysteriously coloured. . . .

But it is when Nature is most cruel that we find her spell the strongest, for we are her children, and being still savages below our cheap veneer, we have much of her cruelty in us. In the mildest mother you can see the inherent taint which raises its head when danger menaces her offspring; with the most devout lovers, who can deny that cruelty stalks hand in hand with passion? In the feeblest soul the call of the wild never dies.

Daily Routine in a Desert Town, 1923
Ahmad Hassanein

The desert demands and induces a quite different attitude of mind and spirit from the bustling of the city. As I wandered about the little town [Jaghbub in the Western Desert] and out into the oasis round it, or stood in the cool, shadowed spaces of the Mosque, or sat at times in the tower above it in conversation with learned Beduins, watching the night fall over the milk-white *kubba* and the brown mass of buildings it dominates, there dropped away from me all the worries and perplexities and problems that the sophisticated life of the crowded places brings in its train. Day after day passed, with a morning walk, midday prayers in the Mosque, a quiet meal, a little work with my instruments or cameras, afternoon prayers, another walk, a meal, followed by the distribution to my men of friendly glasses of tea according to Beduin custom, again prayers, and after quiet contemplation of the evening sky with its peaceful stars, retirement to sleep such as the harassed city dweller does not know.

Mirages and My Camel in the Nubian Desert, 1848
Dr. Richard Lepsius

At a very early hour in the day we saw the most beautiful mirages, both near us and at a distance, exhibiting a very deceptive resemblance to lakes and rivers, in which the mountains, blocks of stone, and everything around is reflected, as if in clear water. They form a strange contrast with the hard arid desert, and, as it is related, must have often bitterly deceived many a poor wanderer. When we are not aware that no water can be there, it is often totally impossible to distinguish the semblance from the reality. Only a few days ago, in the neighbourhood of El Mecheref, I felt perfectly certain that I saw either the Nile water which had overflowed, or a branch of the river, and I rode up, but only found *Bahr Scheitan*, 'The water of Satan', as it is called by the Arabs.

Even though the sand may have obliterated all traces of the caravan road, it cannot easily be missed during the day, as it is sufficiently marked by numerous skeletons of camels, several of which are always in view; yesterday I counted forty-one, which we passed the last half hour before sunset. We did not lose one of our own camels, although they had not rested long in Korosko, and had scarcely anything to eat or drink on the road. My own camel, into whose mouth I had sometimes put a piece of biscuit, used to look round in the middle of the march when it heard me biting, or twist round its long neck, till it laid its head, with its soft large eyes, on my lap, to get something more.

Mines and Ancient Greeks in the Eastern Desert, 1818
Frederic Cailliaud
. . . we mounted our dromedaries, the master-miner, my interpreter, and myself,
to make some researches in the vicinity. We proceeded in a direction to the south,
to about seven leagues from Mount Zabarah. In this track we came to some
mountains with emerald quarries and mines far more considerable than those
already mentioned. They contain, perhaps, a thousand excavations; there appears
to have been long stone causeways constructed under ground, to facilitate communications. They were so contrived that the camels could convey provisions to
the workmen, ascending to the very summit of the mountains where the apertures
commence. In fact, everywhere we discerned vestiges of very extensive labours,
evidently the works of the Ancients. With so few men, we found it impossible to
enter those galleries, which were almost innumerable.

About half a league to the south of these new mines, I discovered the ruins of a
little Greek town, now called by the Ababdeh, Sekket Bendar El Kebyr. About 500
houses of rough hewn stone yet remain; three temples have partly been cut out of
the rock, and partly constructed of stone. Great was my astonishment to find, in the
desert, at so remote a distance, a town in such good repair. It was highly amusing
for me to stroll from house to house, from chamber to chamber. In these deserted
dwellings, various instruments, utensils etc. were to be seen, with lamps of burnt
earth, and fragments of vases of a beautiful form, both of earth and glass; also stones,
hollowed and fluted, that served for mills to grind their grain. With unbounded satisfaction I greeted and hailed a town, hither to unknown to all our voyagers, which
had not been inhabited, perhaps, for 2000 years, and almost entirely standing. The
town of Sekket has been erected on the slope of two opposite mountains; a wide
road, which at times becomes the channel of a torrent, separates it in the middle.
The ruins cover a space of a quarter of a league in length; the houses are well built,
though of rough stone and talc, of the same nature as the mountain. . . .The town
was, doubtless, designed for the workmen of the emerald mines.

A little north of this town are two temples, cut out in a mass of talc, of which
the mountain chiefly consists. The largest has four exterior columns, and two others on the frontispiece that decorates the entrance. To arrive at the interior, we
first ascended a staircase, and further on are three steps to penetrate into the sanctuary; at the side are two little saloons, one of which contains an isolated altar in
the middle. In the sanctuary is another large altar. At the entrance are two
columns; the cornice over it is ornamented with a globe and two serpents. The
subject is Egyptian, but the sculpture evidently Grecian. In this temple I found a
Greek inscription traced in red characters on the wall. . . .

Coming out of the Desert, 1823
Moyle Sherer
It was soon after daybreak, on the morrow, just as the sun was beginning to give
his rich colouring of golden yellow to the white pale sand; that as I was walking

alone at some distance far ahead of my companions, my eyes bent on the ground, and lost in thought, their kind and directing shout made me stop, and raise my head, when, lo! a green vale, looking through the soft mist of morning, rather a vision, than a reality, lay stretched in its narrow length before me. *The Land of Egypt!* We hurried panting on, and gazed, and were silent.

> The caravan halted in a village with a large brimming water-trough for the thirsting camels.

We walked forth into the fields, saw luxuriant crops of green bearded wheat, waving with its lights and shadows; stood under the shade of trees, saw fluttering and chirping birds; went down to a well and a water-wheel, and stood like children listening to the sound of the abundant and bright-flashing water as it fell from the circling pots . . .

Seeing, Narrating, Feeling Egypt, 1977
William Golding
I ask myself how the traveller sees when he examines an Egyptian wall painting in a tomb rather than in a museum. The first thing to remember is that he does not see it in a tomb as the word is ordinarily used, at all. Oh yes, there are exceptions, some narrow, difficult tombs! There are tombs where the climb, chute, slide and scramble, the depth and heat add up to such difficulty that only a determined interest in what you have come to see can battle with, and sometimes ward off, claustrophobia. But generally the traveller sees a wall painting in a commodious kind of wine cellar which is reached by a tall corridor. In the more famous examples the corridor is divided down the centre for two-way traffic. The strip lighting is whitish-blue, from mercury vapour lamps I suppose. In the remoter places the lighting varies. In one, the guardian crawled down in front of us. He dragged a smoky hurricane lamp behind him. In some—and this was interesting in itself— an Egyptian sat outside the entrance to the tomb itself, caught the sunlight in a mirror and shot it down the corridor to a second Egyptian who deflected it round a corner to a third Egyptian whose duty was to catch what light was left and direct it where the traveller wished to fix his gaze. All three men tried to keep their mirrors still, but they had to breathe, their hearts had to beat, the sun himself and the earth under us were all the time changing their relative positions. The rocks expanded or contracted in the varying heat; and whatever all this amounted to was not only caught and transmitted by the mirrors but by the nature of optics, each mirror, as in an old-fashioned galvanometer, doubled the movement. Add to this the generous desire of the third Egyptian to be helpful and keep the mirror impossibly still and it is clear why the last reflection cast over the wall fluttered and quivered like a butterfly at a window. Under those widely vibrating wings appeared those

portions of the painting that the archaeologists had assured the guardian would be of most interest—appeared and disappeared, stayed for a shuddering second or so then gave flittering way to another section. Turn to the man holding the mirror, he and you dim enough figures recognizable only by the random side-effects of this elaborate system, and he will smile agreeably, bow, moving his hands and the mirror so that the butterfly dashes widely from the floor to the roof then back again, perches on your boots it may be and jazzes back up the wall to cover as much as illuminate a cow and cowherd, a handful of hieroglyphics, two women walking up in step, one hand to the forehead one to the sky, the ritual tears falling for a grief that is no longer anywhere to be felt; and the butterfly flirts over a god with a bird's head; and you are lost from all chance of feeling and perception, because the life of the light, the butterfly, you have come to understand by way of the bow and the pleasant smile is the functional end of this chain of service that leads back to open air and the sun. You become aware of nerves and blood and bone and life and men, not painted on a wall. . . .

But there *was* a vocabulary, a resource of images and these were images of power—not power in the political/social sense but acting directly on the men who behold them. How should they not? They rose up in the mind of people so like us we might as well call them ourselves. Whoever examines that vocabulary whether it be painted or graven, or made of metal or clay or faience, is looking at his own interior language at some level or other. But to allow that language to carry out its business of transmutation in the less overt, less obvious regions of the mind would require the sort of self-abandonment and long absorption that no traveller can afford to give. . . . Men are prisoners of their metaphors.

The Travelers
Brief Biographies

'Abd al-Latif al-Baghdadi, Muaffaq-al-Din Abu Mohammed (1162–1231)
'Abd al-Latif was born and raised in Baghdad. Well versed in poetry, he studied chemistry and medicine. He traveled between Damascus, Jerusalem, Aleppo, and Cairo as a scientist and teacher, visiting Egypt twice and teaching at al-Azhar.

Bartlett, William Henry (1809–54)
A topographical artist, Bartlett worked on architectural publications in England, later traveling in Europe, America, the Middle and Far East. His first books had text by others; later by himself.

Belzoni, Giovanni (1778–1823)
Born in Padua, Belzoni—showman, engineer, traveler, and archaeologist—went to England in 1803, and in 1815 to Egypt where he was employed by the British Consul General to collect and explore antiquities. He collected the statue of Ramesses II now in the British Museum, excavated the great temple at Abu Simbel, and opened the tomb of Seti I. In England in 1819, he

created a replica of Seti's fabulous tomb. He planned to cross the desert to Egypt from the west, but died at Gato in Benin.

Bevan, Samuel (fl. 1840–60)
In 1848 Bevan went to Egypt to assist in the setting up of an overland route to India: through the Mahmudiya Canal and to Cairo, then across the desert and down the Red Sea.

Bibescu, Princess Marta (1888–1973)
Daughter and wife of Romanian aristocrats, Princess Bibescu was an outstanding writer. Her rare beauty consistently led men to fall in love with her. In Egypt in 1930, she wrote brief observations of her experiences.

Bird (Bishop), Isabella (1831–1904)
Miss Bird—an archetypal Victorian lady traveler—traveled to and wrote about America, Australia, New Zealand, Hawaii, China, the Malay Peninsula, India, Tibet, Iraq, and Iran. In a little known venture, she traveled alone with local guides to St. Catherine's Monastery, Sinai.

Browne, William George (1768–1813)
In 1792 Browne set off for Egypt, journeying to Abyssinia in 1793–96. He returned to England through Syria and Constantinople. He was again in Turkey and the Levant (1800–02), and set out in 1812, for Tartary. His journeying ended with his murder near Tabriz in Persia.

Brunel, Isambard Kingdom (1806–59)
It is little known that Britain's two greatest engineers met in Cairo at Christmas in the last year of both their lives. Robert Stephenson was a frequent visitor to Egypt to supervise the building of the railway between Alexandria and Cairo; Brunel only visited once, with his family, for the sake of his health, and took great pleasure in what was for him an unusual period of leisure.

Buckingham, James Silk (1786–1855)
Buckingham went to sea as a boy, traveled widely in the Mediterranean including Egypt, left the sea to become a journalist and newspaper editor, and was elected to the reformed Parliament 1832–37. He wrote about his Levant travels, but it was not until 1855 in his *Autobiography* that he wrote of Egypt.

Burckhardt, John Lewis (1784–1817)
A Swiss, Burckhardt offered his services to the British African Association to cross the Sahara with the pilgrim caravan. He studied Arabic, and traveled and lived as an Arab. He was the first European to see Petra in Jordan, and arrived in Cairo in 1812. He made two journeys to Nubia and died in Cairo.

Burgon, Reverend John William (1813–88)
Born in Smyrna, son of a British merchant, Burgon grew up in England, and worked first in his father's counting house, but was later ordained in the Church of England. Briefly employed in charge of the English congregation in Rome, he was invited by a rich lady to become her chaplain on a tour of Egypt (1861–62).

Burns, Jabez (1805–67)
Burns was a nonconformist divine, religious writer, missionary in Britain, and preacher. In 1869, with Thomas Cook, he went to the opening of the Suez Canal and wrote his *Help-book for Travelers in the East* (1870).

Burton, Isabel (1831–96)
Married to the adventurous Richard Burton, Isabel traveled with him whenever she could. After his death she edited his writings.

Burton, Richard (1821–90)
Fluent in Oriental languages, Burton traveled incognito, gaining an intimate knowledge of peoples of the region. In 1853 he made the pilgrimage to Mecca. He served as British Consul in several countries, always exploring the region of his postings.

Cailliaud, Frederic (1787–1869)
French mineralogist who came to Egypt in 1815–18, and traveled on the Nile. He was employed by Muhammad 'Ali to find emerald mines described by Arab historians. He traveled near the Red Sea, in the Eastern Desert, and to Kharga Oasis. In 1819, he went to Siwa and Meroe.

Capper, James (1743–1825)
Capper went to India to work for the East India Company and returned through Egypt. He published an account of his journey in 1784, intending to promote the use of the 'overland route' to India.

Carey, Mrs. M. (fl. 1850)
Mrs. Carey traveled up the Nile on a four-month winter cruise in 1863–64, in the company of a disabled, elderly male cousin, his manservant, Selina—his delicate daughter, and a maid. She illustrated the resulting book on her journey with some lively pictures.

Carne, John (1789–1844)
Carne traveled in the East in 1821 and returned to be ordained as a deacon and live quietly in the west of England. There he recorded his travels, wrote a book about Syria and the Holy Land illustrated by W.H. Bartlett, and several biographies of missionaries. It must have seemed a dull life after Cairo!

Lord Castlereagh (fl. 1840–50)
Descendant of a famous family, one of Castlereagh's forebears was British Foreign Secretary and, for a short period, Prime Minister. Castlereagh traveled in Egypt and the Near East in the 1840s, writing a two-volume account of his travels.

Champollion, Jean François (1790–1832)
It was Champollion who receives credit for deciphering the hieroglyphs. Born at Figeac in France, he studied Oriental languages and taught in universities, eventually becoming professor of Egyptian language and archaeology. It was not until 1828 that he visited Egypt with a team of helpers, but he died soon after.

Charmes, Gabriel (1850–86)
The French journalist, Gabriel Charmes, suffering from tuberculosis, sought health in the Near East and North Africa. He wrote books on Egypt, Turkey, Palestine, Tunisia, as well as Morocco and Syria, and a further book on Egypt, which appeared posthumously.

Chateaubriand, François René (1768–1848)
Traveling in America at the time of the French Revolution, Chateaubriand became increasingly critical of the Napoleonic regime. In 1806 he visited Egypt and the Near East and published his account five years later.

Chubb, Mary (1903–2003)
In 1930 Mary Chubb accompanied the Egypt Exploration Society's dig at Tell al-Amarna, and two years later spent a season digging in Iraq with the Oriental Institute of the University of Chicago. She wrote two memorable books, *Nefertiti Lived Here* (1954) and *City in the Sands* (1957).

Clarke, Edward Daniel (1769–1822)
Clarke was a noted traveler and antiquarian who accompanied various notables on their journeys. In 1801 he was in the Holy Land and Egypt and was present when the Rosetta Stone was handed over to the British by one of Napoleon's generals.

Cook, John Mason (1834–99)
Son and business partner of travel agent Thomas Cook, John Cook became the agent for passenger travel on the Nile in 1870. In 1880 he signed a government contract for control of the steamboat service for ten years, and was granted the exclusive right of carrying mail and civil and military officials. He set up offices in Egypt, a hotel for tourists, and a hospital for the local people in Luxor.

Cook, Thomas (1808–92)
Travel and Thomas Cook became synonymous in the nineteenth century. A Baptist missionary in England, his first organized 'excursion' was by rail to a temperance gathering in 1841. From this grew a tourist empire with guided excur-

sions. In 1865 he opened out his activities to America, Europe, and the Middle East. He personally led tours to Egypt and the Holy Land and to the opening ceremonies of the Suez Canal.

Cooper, Elizabeth (1877–1945)

The American writer Elizabeth Cooper traveled in the East and had a particular interest in the status of women. Her *Women of Egypt* (1914) records her residence in Egypt and offers insight into Egyptian ways of life, focusing on the daily life of women.

Cottrell, Leonard (b. 1913)

A BBC producer, Leonard Cottrell for many years produced programs on subjects from aviation to Egyptology, and wrote several books on such subjects. For a period he worked with UNESCO in the Middle East.

Cox, Samuel (1824–89)

Cox and his wife, American travelers, journeyed from the Arctic Circle south to Egypt. He wrote of their travels first in *Arctic Sunbeams, or From Broadway to the Bosphorus by Way of the North Cape,* and then in *Orient Sunbeams or From the Porte to the Pyramids by Way of Palestine,* both published in New York c. 1882.

Curzon, Robert (1810–73)

Curzon became a Member of Parliament, but when his constituency was disenfranchised by the 1832 Reform Act, he traveled in the Middle East—to seek out and purchase ancient manuscripts in monastery libraries. In 1841 he became private secretary to the British Ambassador in Constantinople, and later Joint Commissioner with Russia defining the Persian-Turkish border.

Denon, Baron Dominique Vivant (1747–1825)

Denon joined the French diplomatic service, and later Napoleon's Commission to · Egypt. With General Desaix he traveled on the Nile, recording antiquities. Later, in France, he became Director of the Central Museum of Art, and in 1804, Director General of Museums. He was important in establishing the Louvre's collections.

Doyle, Sir Arthur Conan (1859–1930)

The creator of the legendary detective Sherlock Holmes trained as a doctor, but gave up practice for a full-time writing career. After his visit to Egypt he wrote the novel *The Tragedy on the Korosko* (1897), about a disastrous Nile tour.

Duff Gordon, Lady Lucie (1821–69)

In 1862, suffering from tuberculosis, and unable to live in the English climate, Lady Duff Gordon settled in Egypt, mainly in Luxor. Her vivid letters were published and brought her fame. Other travelers viewed her with as much reverence as the temples they visited, but it was the Egyptians who truly loved her: "The great lady who was just and had a heart that loved the Arabs." She died in Cairo.

Ebn Haukal, Abu al-Kasim Mohammed bin Ali al-Museli (tenth century)
Trader, adventurer, and geographer, Ebn Haukal was born in Baghdad and traveled for thirty years in the Islamic world and Europe. Well acquainted with the literature of his predecessors, he based his book (completed c. 977) as much on his own observations as on those of other writers.

Edwards, Amelia B. (1831–92)
Amelia Edwards wrote for journals and published novels and travel books. In Egypt in 1873, she became so absorbed that her resulting book retains its authority on the spirit of the ancient civilization of Egypt. Shocked by wanton destruction of the monuments, she funded scientific excavations and founded the Egypt Exploration Fund in 1882 (now the Egypt Exploration Society), which still finances archaeology in Egypt.

Egeria (the Blessed) fl. 380
Probably abbess of a Spanish convent, Egeria went on a three-year pilgrimage in 381–84, with the Bible as her only guide. She traveled twice to Egypt, and ascended Mount Sinai.

Elwood, Anne Katherine (fl. 1840)
Wife of an East India Company officer, Mrs. Elwood traveled through Egypt with her husband to India in the winter of 1825–26 and wrote observantly and entertainingly of her experiences.

Fabri, Friar Felix (1441–1502)
A Dominican monk from Germany, Friar Felix twice left his quiet priory (1480 and 1483) to visit the Holy Land. The scholar H.F.M. Prescott chronicled his two journeys in *Jerusalem Journey* and *Once in Sinai,* bringing his views and humor to a wide audience.

Farman, Elbert (1831–1911)
Farman was American Consul at Cairo 1868–75. He traveled up the Nile, and to Sinai and the Red Sea. His account of his Egyptian experience, published in 1908, is a descriptive narrative of the country, particularly focusing on its political situation and Anglo-American relations.

Fay, Eliza (1756–1816)
Mrs. Fay, barely educated but adventurous, set out for India with her lawyer husband in 1779, through Egypt and the Red Sea. They separated, but she returned to India to try various business ventures. Her story comes to us through letters to her family, published in India after her death.

Fernea, Elizabeth Warnock (b. 1927)
Elizabeth Fernea lived in Cairo from 1959 to 1965 while her husband taught at the American University in Cairo, and her three children were born in Cairo. She is the author of a number of books and the maker of several films on Egypt and the Middle East.

Finati, Giovanni (1787– c. 1829)
Finati, an Italian recruited to the French army, deserted to the Turks and served in Muhammad 'Ali's army. He acted as dragoman/janissary to the British Consulate, accompanying W.J. Bankes, who edited his memoirs, and other British travelers around Egypt and the Near East. He eventually visited Britain, and later established a hotel in Cairo.

Fitzmaurice, William (fl. 1830s)
The son of an aristocratic family, the Honourable William Fitzmaurice traveled in Egypt and on to Palestine and Greece.

Fuller, John (fl. 1820)
An Englishman, John Fuller traveled through the East in 1818–19 and displayed a quiet, accurate sense of the places he sensitively observed.

Gadsby, John (c. 1809–93)
A British printer and publisher who visited Egypt frequently for his health between 1847 and 1860. He travelled to the Second Cataract twice.

Ghosh, Amitav (1956–)
Ghosh was born in Calcutta and studied in Delhi, Oxford, and Alexandria. He traveled extensively and is widely acclaimed as a novelist. *In an Antique Land* is a narrative of his experience as a post-graduate student in Egypt.

Golding, William (1911–92)
One of Britain's more renowned literary figures, Golding won the Nobel prize for literature in 1983. He visited Egypt twice and wrote three texts about his travels. Egypt also informed many of his fictional writings.

Hahn-Hahn, Countess Ida (1805–80)
The German aristocrat and novelist, Countess Hahn-Hahn, after her divorce, traveled in the Near East with a male partner in the mid-1840s. She converted to Catholicism in 1850, established a convent in Germany, and lived there for the rest of her days.

Haight, Sarah (fl. 1836)
Mrs. Haight, 'a lady from New York,' toured the Middle East with her businessman husband in 1836 and wrote, thoughtfully, from a conventional, well-to-do, middle-class background, of her travels.

Hassanein, Ahmad (1889–1946)
Born to a middle-class Egyptian family, Hassanein was educated in Cairo and Oxford. He worked in the Ministry of the Interior in Cairo before joining the diplomatic service. A gifted linguist and clever negotiator, in 1923 he embarked on a journey across the Western Desert of Egypt and rediscovered some of its lost oases.

Hay, Robert (1799–1863)
First visiting Egypt while in the navy, Hay lived there in 1823–24, studying and recording both ancient and Islamic monuments. He published *Illustrations of Cairo* in 1840. He also made plaster casts of the monuments, now in the British Museum. His vast records are preserved in the British Library.

Hennicker, Sir Frederick (1793–1825)
A young British aristocrat who traveled with great enjoyment in Egypt in 1820. He was the first foreigner known to have climbed to the apex of Khafre's pyramid.

Lady Herbert of Lea (fl. 1840–60)
Elizabeth ('Lizzie') Herbert was the beautiful and talented wife of Sidney Herbert, British Minister of State for War. They both worked closely with Florence Nightingale on questions of nursing in the Crimea and the British army. After her husband's death, 'Lizzie' traveled in the Near East in 1865 and wrote and illustrated her experience in her book *The Cradle Lands*.

Herodotus (c. 484–424 B.C.)
Born in a Greek colony in Asia Minor, Herodotus visited Mediterranean countries, including Egypt, Babylon, Scythia, and Greece, observing the physical and social make-up of each region. He was in Egypt at about 460–455 B.C. He went as a colonist to Italy and was given land and citizenship there.

Holthaus, P.D. (fl. 1840s)
Holthaus was a journeyman tailor, a member of a historic group of apprentices from central Europe who traveled the world to learn their craft in other lands. For sixteen years (1824–40) "the qualification of his passion for travel depended solely on his needle." His resulting book was translated into English by William Howitt.

Hopley, Howard (fl. 1880)
Author of a Nilotic version of *Three Men in a Boat*, his volume *Under Desert Palms* (1869) was also about a journey with two friends. Hopley was ordained in the Church of England in 1871 and sank into quiet obscurity.

Hoskins, George Alexander (1802–63)
Hoskins, both a traveler and an antiquary, was in Egypt twice, 1832–33 and 1860–61. He published accounts of his travels, including *Travels in Ethiopia* (1835), *Visit to the Great Oases of the Egyptian Desert* (1837), and three volumes of drawings.

Ibn Battuta (1304–77)

Son of a Tangier family, Ibn Battuta set out on pilgrimage in 1325, hoping to meet famous scholars. His passion for travel grew and he determined to travel through the Earth. Beginning his travels in 1325, he twice went to Mecca, and visited Egypt, East Africa, Asia Minor, the Crimea, Constantinople, India, and China. He returned to Mecca in 1348, visited Spain and traveled in West Africa, and finally settled in Morocco.

Ibn Jubayr (1145–1217)

Son of an Arab family from Valencia, Ibn Jubayr worked as secretary to the governor of Granada. In 1183 he went to Mecca, keeping a daily record of two years' travel. He traveled the Nile and crossed the desert to the Red Sea. On his return journey, in Damascus he witnessed the triumph of Saladin over the Crusaders. In 1204, he set off on his last journey, to Mecca, Medina, Cairo, and Alexandria, where he worked as a catechist and teacher.

Ibn Umar, Mohammed al-Tunisi (1789–1857)

Brought up in Egypt, Ibn Umar of Tunis traveled from his youth through northern Africa and later, after settling in Tunisia in about 1820, wrote of his travels from memory, noting the customs and cultures of the people he had met. The traveler and writer Bayle St. John translated his writings from the French and published them as *Travels of an Arab Merchant* in 1854.

Irby, Captain Charles Leonard (1789–1845)

Resigning his naval commission in 1816, Irby set off with James Mangles to tour Europe. The journey developed far beyond their original design and they ended up assisting Belzoni in opening the temple at Abu Simbel.

Jarvie, William (1841–1921)

Jarvie, a dentist from New York from 1872 to 1916, accompanied his brother and sister on a long holiday in the Middle East in 1903. The letters he wrote home were printed for family members.

Khosraw, Naser-e (1003–88)

A Persian man of learning, Khosraw worked as a civil servant, but at forty, tiring of his luxurious life, he set out on a seventeen-year journey in the Islamic regions. He visited Egypt twice: first for eight months and later for two years. He was closely acquainted with the Fatimid caliph, al-Mustansir.

Kinglake, Alexander (1809–91)

Kinglake's *Eothen*—Greek for 'the East'—is one of the most popular accounts of Eastern travel. It is a book of the 'frankness and wonderment' of a young man interested in life rather than monuments. He later wrote the history of the British campaign to the Crimea.

Kingsford, W.E. (fl. 1900)
Mr. Kingsford's book *Assuan as a Health Resort* (1900) coincided with the opening of the Cataract Hotel and was, undoubtedly, a public relations exercise.

Kipling, Rudyard (1865–1936)
Born in India and educated in England, Kipling returned to India as a young man to work as a journalist. His stories and poems brought him fame, and in 1889 he settled in England, continuing to write and to travel. He was awarded the Nobel prize for literature in 1907.

Lane, Edward (1801–76)
Lane learned classical and vernacular Arabic before moving to Egypt in 1825, where he chose to live as an Egyptian, apart from other foreigners. He traveled widely and studied ancient, modern, and Islamic Egypt. His *Arabic-English Lexicon* (1877) is still a great authority and his *Description of Egypt* was finally published in 2000 in Cairo.

Lepsius, Dr. Richard (1810–84)
German Egyptologist who was chosen to lead the well-equipped Prussian Expedition to Egypt and Nubia in 1842–45. He traveled to Khartoum and also visited Sinai. In 1865 he was appointed Keeper of the Egyptian collections in the Berlin Museum and the Royal Library.

Light, Henry (1782–1870)
While serving with his regiment in Malta, Light traveled in Egypt in 1830–31, to the Second Cataract. He returned to England to recruit for Egypt's navy, and served on the paddle-steamer *Nile* until 1835.

Lord Lindsay (Alexander William Crawford) (1812–80)
Lord Lindsay inherited the title twenty-fifth Earl of Crawford. He traveled in Egypt and Palestine in 1836–37 with William Ramsay, and published an account of their travels in 1838.

Lorimer, Norma (fl. 1907–15)
Traveling on her own to Tunisia and Turkey, Norma Lorimer went to Egypt in 1907. Her account of that journey is based on her diary. She traveled up the Nile and to the Kharga oasis.

Loti, Pierre (1850–1923)
Loti traveled widely as a French naval officer, and later became a novelist and travel writer, memorializing the places to which he had journeyed. He created an extraordinary house (now a museum) in his birth place of Rochefort in northern France.

Madden, Dr. Richard R. (1798–1886)
An Irish doctor, Madden traveled in Egypt in 1825 and 1840. In 1825 he became physician to Consul General Henry Salt, and attended him when he died. He went on to various appointments concerned with bringing slaves and other peoples, including the Irish, to independence.

Mangles, Captain James (1786–1867)
A naval officer who, with his friend Charles Irby, traveled in the East in 1817–18.

Manning, Samuel (1822–81)
A Baptist minister, Manning's lively prose and extensive illustrations of his Egyptian travels are a pleasant surprise.

Martineau, Harriet (1802–76)
Although Harriet Martineau suffered from 'feeble health and deafness,' neither stopped her from publishing political and feminist articles, consulting cabinet ministers, traveling in America (1834–36), and publishing three books about that journey. In 1848 she set off to explore Egypt and Palestine, a journey she recorded in three volumes.

Maspero, Sir Gaston (1846–1916)
Born in Paris, Maspero became Professor of Egyptology at the Ecole des Hautes Etudes in 1869 and Director of the Egyptian Museum in Cairo in 1881. He was Director of the Egyptian Antiquities service from 1881 to 1914. He wrote extensively on archaeology, the collection of the Egyptian Museum, and in 1910, wrote a book of reminiscences.

Melly, George (fl. 1850)
Son of a Liverpool merchant, Melly traveled as far as Khartoum with his family in 1850–51. They returned across the desert via Korosko, but sadly his father died on the journey and is buried in the village cemetery at Gagee.

Merrick, E.W. (fl. 1900)
Miss Merrick, a portrait painter, met American journalist-explorer H.M. Stanley in Egypt and was commissioned to paint his portrait, and that of the Khedivah. Realizing the opportunities for a female artist in India, she went there with success.

Meryon, Dr. Charles (1783–1877)
The biographer of Lady Hester Stanhope, with whom he traveled for several years in the Middle East, Meryon wrote her memoirs and about his own travels. He was twice in Egypt: with Lady Hester in 1810, and again, on his own, in 1812.

Morton, H.V. (c. 1890–1975)
H.V. Morton was a journalist. His *In Search of* . . . books appeared from 1927 to

within a few years of his death, and have seldom been out of print. His *In the Steps of the Master* appeared first in 1939, and his *Middle East* in 1941.

al-Muqaddasi, Shams al-Din Abu Abdalla Mohammed Ibn Abu Bakr (c. 946–1000)

Born in Jerusalem, al-Muqaddasi was educated in Iraq. He traveled extensively in the Arab regions, recording observations and experiences in *Ahsan al-taqasim fi ma'rifat al-aqalim* ('Best Divisions of Regions')—the most original of the writings of Arab travelers and geographers. He led the life of the people he traveled among, his extensive family giving access to many social circles.

Nightingale, Florence (1820–1910)

Before visiting Egypt, Florence Nightingale, founder of modern nursing, had little experience of nursing. Soon after, she visited Kaiserwerth Institute in Germany and later trained there. In the Crimean War she was invited to take nurses to Scutari, accompanied by the Bracebridges with whom she traveled in Egypt. She worked for the next fifty years to improve health in the British Army and in Britain.

Norden, Captain Frederick (1708–42)

Captain Norden of the Danish navy was sent by his king to Egypt in 1757 to obtain a full account of the country. His *Travels* (1751) went into several editions.

Palmer, Edward Henry (1840–82)

An expert in Oriental languages, Palmer compiled a dictionary of Persian and a grammar of Arabic, and translated the Qur'an. The full title of his book explains his presence in Egypt: *The Desert of the Exodus: journeys on foot in the wilderness of forty years' wanderings, undertaken in connection to the Ordnance Survey of Sinai* (1871). Visiting Egypt again in 1882, he was murdered by robbers near Suez.

Pliny the Elder (A.D. 23–79)

A Roman scholar, Pliny practiced as an advocate and underook military service in Spain, Africa, and elsewhere. Of his many literary works only the *Natural History*, in thirty-seven volumes, survives. He died during the eruption of Mt. Vesuvius.

Pococke, Richard (1704–65)

Pococke reached Alexandria in 1737 and went up the Nile to Philae, traveling at the same time as Captain Frederick Norden. In fact, he and Norden passed each other on the river in the night. Pococke went on to Jerusalem, Asia Minor, and Greece, and later became Bishop of Meath in Ireland—where he planted seeds of a cedar of Lebanon.

Poole, Sophia (1804–91)

Sophia, sister of the Arabist Edward Lane, lived with her two sons in Egypt for seven years. In 1844–46, she published a study of the life of Egyptian women, *The*

Englishwoman in Egypt (republished in 2003). In England, she collaborated with her younger son on photographic books of the Middle East.

Pratt, Fanny (fl. 1840–60)

Mrs. Pratt accompanied her husband to India and later Australia on his army appointments. For twenty years she wrote to her children in England from these postings. On her first journey east she passed through Egypt in 1843 and wrote from Alexandria and from the Red Sea.

Prime, William Cooper (1824–1905)

Prime, a lawyer with links to the world of American journalism, became president of Associated Press in the 1860s. His visit to Egypt and the Middle East in 1855 led to *Boat Life in Egypt* (1857) and *Tent Life in the Holy Land* (1857). He was a principal promoter of the Metropolitan Museum of Modern Art in New York.

Puckler-Muskau, Prince Hermann Ludwig Heinrich (1785–1871)

An aristocrat with estates in eastern Germany, Puckler-Muskau traveled in Egypt and Sudan in 1837. His account was translated into English in 1845.

Quibell, Annie (1862–1927)

Annie Quibell, excavator and draughtswoman, worked with Flinders Petrie and married archaeologist James Quibell, who was Keeper of the Egyptian Museum 1913–23 and Secretary-General of the Egyptian Antiquities Department 1923–25.

Ramsay, William (fl. 1830s)

A Scotsman, William Ramsay traveled with Lord Lindsay in the Middle East. He died shortly after their trip and entries from his diary were added to Lindsay's account.

Richardson, Dr. Robert (1779–1847)

Richardson was physician to Lord Belmore for his two-year tour of the Eastern Mediterranean. His *Travels* (1822) are observant and thoughtful, and Byron, having read it, remarked in a letter to Lady Blessington, "The author is just the sort of man I should like to have with me in Greece—clever both as a man and a physician."

Roberts, David (1796–1864)

Roberts, a theatrical scene painter, spent five months painting in Egypt in 1838–39. Were he alive today and receiving royalties, he would be a rich man, for his books and postcards of his paintings are everywhere for sale. In 1851 he was one of the Commissioners of Britain's *Great Exhibition*.

Romer, Isabella (c. 1805–52)

Isabella Romer married an army officer, but soon separated from him and returned to her own name. She traveled to the eastern Mediterranean and Egypt and wrote a successful account of her travels.

Russell, Reverend Michael (fl. 1830)
This Scottish clergyman and lawyer set himself the task of "presenting, in condensed form, all that is known of Egypt," contrasting the ancient with the modern culture and life.

St John, Bayle (1822–59)
Bayle St John traveled first with his father and worked with him on a book about the people of ancient Greece. In 1846 he went to Egypt to study Arabic and journeyed to the oasis of Siwa in the steps of Alexander the Great. He returned to Egypt in 1851 to collect material for a book on village life. He translated the travels of Ibn Umar from the French (1854).

Sandys, George (1578–1644)
Son of the Archbishop of York, Sandys toured the eastern Mediterranean extensively in 1610, publishing an account in 1615. From 1621 to 1631 he went to America as treasurer of the Virginia Company, and later became a Gentleman of the Privy Chamber to King Charles I.

Savary, Claude Etienne (1750–88)
French traveler who visited Lower Egypt 1776–79, to study the manners and monuments, and later wrote about the country using previous travelers' records as sources. He translated the Qur'an (1781), wrote a life of Muhammad (1783), and an Arabic grammar, published posthumously in 1789.

Scott, Charles Rochfort (d. 1872)
Scott was co-author of a biography of the Duke of Wellington and wrote about travels in Egypt and Crete (1837) and Spain (1838).

Sherer, Moyle (1789–1869)
A British army officer, Sherer served in India and, returning overland through Egypt, published accounts of his impressions of both India and Egypt.

Sitwell, Constance (1888–1974)
Daughter of a tea planter, Constance lived the life of the Edwardian gentry: London 'seasons,' summers in Scotland, and travels with her parents. She went to Egypt twice, evoking the country beautifully in two books.

Sladen, Douglas (1856–1947)
A traveler and writer, Sladen made good use of his varied life, becoming Professor of History at Sydney University and Editor of *Who's Who* (1897–99). He wrote a number of books on Egypt between 1909 and 1913.

Smith, Agnes (Mrs. Lewis) (1843–1926)
Agnes and her twin sister traveled in the Middle East before discovering the

earliest known manuscript of the Gospels in the library of the convent at Mount Sinai. They returned to transcribe it in the convent library in 1892.

Smith, Reverend Alfred Charles (fl. 1860s)
An Anglican clergyman, Smith traveled in Egypt with his father and a friend (both clergymen) in the 1860s, publishing his *Attractions of the Nile and its Banks* in 1868.

Stanley, Dean Arthur Penrhyn (1815–81)
Stanley became Regius Professor of Ecclesiastical History at Oxford in 1856, the year he visited Egypt. He was Dean of Westminster from 1864 until his death.

Stephens, John Lloyd (1805–52)
An American lawyer, Stephens went to Europe for his health. His tour extended to Greece, Turkey, Russia, and in 1836, Egypt. He met others with an interest in archaeology, and traveled to Sinai, Petra, and the Holy Land, returning home to write *Incidents of Travel* (1837). From 1839, he explored Central America and the Yucatan, with which his name is most linked.

Strabo (c. 63 B.C.–c. A.D. 23)
Of a distinguished Greek family, Strabo, geographer and historian, studied in Rome and elsewhere, traveling widely around the Mediterranean and to Ethiopia. It is only of his Nile journey that there is a detailed record.

Stuart, Villiers (1827–95)
An ordained minister, Stuart gave up holy orders to enter politics. He was attached to the mission of reconstruction of Egypt in 1883, and commissioned to investigate the condition of the country.

Taylor, Bayard (1825–78)
Taylor was commissioned to travel and write for American magazines: about Europe in 1846, the California Gold Rush in 1849, and then the Middle and Far East. He returned to Egypt in 1875. He was appointed American ambassador to Berlin not long before he died there.

Thompson, Charles (fl. 1750)
Thompson's full book title explains his travels: *Travels through Turkey in Asia, the Holy Land, Arabia, Egypt and other parts of the world: accounts of what is most remarkable in manners, religion, polity, antiquities, and natural history of these countries.* He hoped in publishing his book to encourage overland travel between Europe and India.

Twain, Mark (Samuel Langhorne Clemens) (1835–1908)
Twain was apprenticed to a printer at twelve, became a river pilot on the Mississippi, and later city editor of a newspaper. *The Innocents Abroad* (1869) tells of his travels to Europe and the Mediterranean on one of the first American cruise ships.

Warburton, Eliot (1810–52)

A lifelong friend of Kinglake, Warburton gave up a law career to travel and write. In 1843 he toured Syria, Palestine, and Egypt, and wrote *The Crescent and the Cross* (1844), which went into seventeen editions. In 1852, traveling to South America, his steamer caught fire and he perished.

Wilkinson, Sir John Gardner (1797–1875)

Wilkinson went to Egypt in 1821 to discover the meaning of the hieroglyphs, not returning to England until 1833. He wrote *Manners and Customs of the Ancient Egyptians* (1837), and *Murray's Travelers' Handbook* (1847), encouraging others to follow him to Egypt, where he returned in 1842 and 1855.

Young, Cuthbert (fl. 1850)

From North Shields, near Newcastle, Young wrote his *Wayfarer's Notes* following his journey in 1846–47 with two purposes in mind: to sketch the religious features of some countries and to add to the descriptions of the Egyptian monuments.

Bibliography

Baghdadi, 'Abd al-Latif. *The Eastern Key: Kitab al-Ifada wa'l-l'tibar.* Translated by Kamal Hafuth Zand and John A. and Ivy E. Videan. London: George Allen & Unwin Ltd., 1965.

Bartlett, W.H. *The Nile Boat or Glimpses of the Land of Egypt.* London: Arthur Hall, 1849.

Belzoni, Giovanni. *Narrative of the Operations and Recent Discoveries in Egypt and Nubia.* London: John Murray, 1820.

Bevan, Samuel. *Sand and Canvas: a Narrative of Adventures in Egypt.* London: C. Gilpin, 1849.

Bird, Isabella. "A Pilgrimage to Sinai." *The Leisure Hour,* February–April, 1886.

Browne, W.G. *Travels in Africa, Egypt and Syria from the Year 1792 to 1798.* London: T. Cadell and W. Davies, 1799.

Buckingham, James Silk. *Autobiography of James Silk Buckingham, including his voyages, travels, adventures, speculations, successes and failures, faithfully and frankly related.* London: Longman, Brown, Green, 1855.

Burckhardt, John Lewis. *Travels in Nubia.* London: John Murray, 1819.

Burns, Jabez and Thomas Cook. *Help-book for the Traveller to the East.* London: London Cook's Tourist Office, 1870.

Burton, Isabel. *(see Wilkins)*

Burton, Richard. *A Pilgrimage to Mecca and Medina.* Edited by Isabel Burton. London: George Bell, 1855; reissued New York: Dover, 1964.

Cailliaud, Frederic. *Voyage a l'oasis de Thebes et dans les deserts 1815–1818.* London: R. Phillips, 1822.

Capper, James. *Observations on the passage to India through Egypt, and across the great desert, with occasional remarks on the adjacent countries, and also sketches of different routes.* London: W. Faden, 1783.

Carey, M.L.M. *Four months in a dahabeeh, or narrative of a winter's cruise on the Nile.* London: Booth, 1863.

Carne, John. *Letters from the East.* London: Henry Colburn, 1826.

Castlereagh, Lord Frederick William Stewart. *A Journey to Damascus through Egypt, Nubia, Arabia Petraea, Palestine and Syria.* London: Henry Colburn, 1847.

Champollion, Jean François. *Letters Written during His Voyage to Egypt in 1828–9.* Paris, 1829.

Charmes, Gabriel. *Five Months in Cairo and in Lower Egypt.* London: Bentley, 1883.

Chateaubriand, Vicomte de F.R. *Travels in Greece, Palestine, Egypt and Barbary 1806–7.* Translated by Frederic Soberl. London: Henry Colburn, 1811.

Clarke, Edward Daniel. *Travels in Various Countries of Europe, Asia and Africa.* London: T. Cadell and W. Davies, 1810–23.

Conan Doyle, Sir Arthur. *The Tragedy of the Korosko.* London, 1897; republished London: Hesperus Press, 2003.

Cook, John Mason. *Handbook.* Peterborough: Thomas Cook Archive, c. 1870.

Cooper, Elizabeth. *The Women of Egypt.* London: Hurst and Blackett, Ltd., 1914.

Cottrell, Leonard. *The Mountains of Pharaoh.* London: Robert Hale Ltd., 1956.

Cox, Samuel S. *Orient Sunbeams or from the Porte to the Pyramids by Way of Palestine.* New York: Arno Press, 1977.

Curzon, Robert. *Visits to Monasteries in the Levant.* London: Arthur Barker, 1855.

Denon, Vivant. *Travels in Upper and Lower Egypt during the Campaign of General Bonaparte.* Translated by E.A. Kendal. London, 1802; reissued London: Darf Publishers Ltd., 1986.

Duff Gordon, Lucie. *Letters from Egypt.* London: Macmillan, 1875.

Ebn Haukal. *The Oriental Geography of Ebn Haukal, an Arabian Traveller of the Tenth Century.* Translated by Sir William Ousely. London: Knt. Ltd., 1800.

Edwards, Amelia. *One Thousand Miles up the Nile.* London: Longmans Green, 1877.

Egeria's Travels. Translated by John Wilkinson. Warminster: Aris and Phillips, 1971.

Elwood, Anne Katherine. *Narrative of a Journey Overland to India, and a Voyage Home 1825–8.* London: Colborne and Bentley, 1830.

Fabri, Brother Felix. *The Wanderings of Felix Fabri.* Translated by A. Stewart. London: Palestine Pilgrims Text Society, 1892–7.

Farman, Elbert E. *Egypt and its Betrayal: an account of the country during the period of Ismail and Tewfik Pashas, and of how England acquired a new Empire*. New York: Grafton Press, 1908.

Fay, Eliza. *Letters from India*. Calcutta: privately published, 1821.

Fernea, Elizabeth Warnock. *A View of the Nile*. New York: Doubleday & Co., 1970.

Finati, Giovanni. *Narrative of the life and adventures of Giovanni Finati*. London: John Murray, 1830.

Fitzmaurice, William Edward. *A Cruise to Egypt, Palestine and Greece, during a five months leave of absence*. London, 1834.

Fuller, John. *Narrative of a Tour through some Parts of the Turkish empire*. London: John Murray, 1829.

Gadsby, John. *My wanderings: being travels in the East*. London: privately published, 1860.

Ghosh, Amitav. *In an Antique Land*. New York: Alfred Knopf, 1993.

Gohary, Jocelyn. *Guide to the Nubian Monuments on Lake Nasser*. Cairo and New York: The American University in Cairo Press, 1998.

Golding, William. *An Egyptian Journal*. London: Faber & Faber, 1985.

Goulburn, Edward Meyrick. *John William Burgon, late Dean of Chichester. A Biography*. London: J. Murray, 1892.

Hahn-Hahn, Ida Marie. *Letters from the Orient or Travels in Turkey, Egypt and the Holy Land*. London: Colburn, 1845.

Haight, Sarah. *Letters from the Old World by a Lady of New York*. 2 vols. New York: Harper and Brothers, 1840.

Hassanein, Ahmad M. *The Lost Oases*. London: Thornton Butterworth Ltd., 1925.

Hay, Robert. Unpublished diaries 1825–34. British Library: Add. MSS 29,857.

Henniker, Frederick. *Notes, during a Visit to Egypt, Nubia, the Oasis, Mount Sinai and Jerusalem*. London: John Murray, 1823.

Lady Herbert. *Cradle Lands*. New York: Catholic Publication Society, 1869.

Herodotus. *The Histories*. Translated by Aubrey de Selincourt. London: Penguin Books, 1972.

Holthaus, P.D. *Wanderings of a journeyman tailor through Europe and the East 1824–40*. Translated by William Howitt. London: Longman, Brown, Green, and Longmans, 1844.

Hopley, Howard. *Under Egyptian Palms or Three Bachelors' Journeyings on the Nile*. London: Chapman and Hall, 1869.

Hoskins, George Alexander. *A Winter in Upper and Lower Egypt*. London: Hurst and Blackett, 1863.

Ibn Battuta. *Travels in Asia and Africa 1325–54*. Translated by Sir H. Gibb. London: Routledge and Kegan Paul Ltd., 1958.

Ibn Jubayr. *The Travels of Ibn Jubayr*. Translated by R.J.C. Broadhurst. London: Jonathan Cape, 1952.

Ibn Umar [Muhammad ibn Umar al-Tunsi]. *Travels of an Arab Merchant in Soudan*. Translated by Bayle St John. London: Chapman and Hall, 1854.

Irby, Charles Leonard and James Mangles. *Travels in Egypt and Nubia, Syria and Asia Minor; during the years 1817 & 1818.* London: privately published, 1823.

Jarvie, William. *Letters Home from Egypt and Palestine.* New York: privately printed, 1904.

Khosraw, Naser-e. *Naser-e Khosraw's Book of Travels.* Translated by W.M. Thackston Jr. New York: Bibliotheca Persica, The Persian Heritage Fund, 1986.

Kinglake, Alexander. *Eothen.* London: J. Ollivier, 1844.

Kingsford, W.E. *Assouan as a Health Resort.* London: Simpkin Marshall, 1900.

Kipling, Rudyard. *Letters of Travel 1892–1913.* London: Macmillan, 1913.

Lane, Edward. *Description of Egypt.* Cairo and New York: The American University in Cairo Press, 2000.

————. *Manners and Customs of the Modern Egyptians.* London: Charles Knight, 1837; Cairo and New York: The American University in Cairo Press, 2003.

Legh, Thomas. *Narrative of a Journey in Egypt and the Country beyond the Cataracts.* London: John Murray, 1816.

Lepsius, Dr. Richard. *Letters from Egypt, Ethiopia, and the Peninsula of Sinai.* Translated by Leonora and Joanna B. Horner. London: Henry G. Bohn, 1852.

Light, Captain Henry. *Travels in Egypt, Nubia, Holy Land, etc in 1814.* London: Rodwell and Martin, 1818.

Lindsay, Lord. *Letters from Egypt, Edom and the Holy Land, (including notes of William Ramsay).* London: Henry Colburn, 1838.

Lorimer, Norma. *By the Waters of Egypt.* London: Methuen, 1909.

Loti, Pierre. *Egypt.* London: T. Werner Laurie, 1910.

Madden, Dr. R.R. *Travels in Turkey, Egypt, Nubia and Palestine.* London: Whittaker, Treacher and Co., 1829.

Manning, Samuel. *The Land of the Pharaohs. Egypt and Sinai: illustrated by pen and pencil.* London: The Religious Tract Society, 1875.

Martineau, Harriet. *Eastern Life, Past and Present.* Philadelphia: Lea and Blanchard, 1848.

Maspero, Sir Gaston. *Egypt: ancient sites and modern scenes.* Translated by Elizabeth Lee. London: T. Fisher Unwin, 1910.

Melly, George. *Khartoum and the Blue and White Niles.* London: Colburn and Co., 1851.

Merrick, E.M. *With a Palette in Eastern Palaces.* London: Sampson Low, 1899.

Meryon, Dr. Charles. *Travels of Lady Hester Stanhope.* London: Henry Colburn, 1846.

Modern Traveller II: Egypt, Nubia and Abyssinia. Edinburgh: Oliver and Boyd, 1827.

Morton, H.V. *Through Lands of the Bible.* London: Methuen, 1938.

al-Muqaddasi, Shams al-Din Mohammad Ibn Ahmad. *The Best Divisions for Knowledge of the Regions.* Translated by Basil Anthony Collins. Reading: Centre for Muslim Contribution to Civilization, Garnet Publishing Ltd., 1994.

Nightingale, Florence. *Letters from Egypt: A Journey on the Nile.* Ed. Anthony Sattin. New York: Weidenfeld and Nicolson, 1987.

Norden, Frederick. *A Compendium of the Travels of Norden through Egypt and Nubia.* Dublin: J. Smith, 1757.

Palmer, E.H. *The Desert of the Exodus.* Cambridge: Deighton, Bell, and Co., 1871.

Pococke, Richard. *A description of the East and some other countries.* London: privately published, 1743–45.

Poole, Sophia. *The Englishwoman in Egypt.* London: Charles Knight, 1844 and Cairo and New York: The American University in Cairo Press, 2003.

Pratt, Fanny. *Exiles of Empire.* Edited by Mona Macmillan and Catriona Miller. Edinburgh: Pentland Press, 1997.

Prime, William C. *Boat Life in Egypt and Nubia.* New York: Harper and Brothers, 1874.

Puckler-Muskau, Prince Hermann. *Egypt and Mehemet Ali.* London: Henry Colburn, 1845.

Quibell, Annie. *A Wayfarer in Egypt.* London: Methuen, 1925.

Ramsay, William. *(see Lindsay)*

Richardson, Dr. Robert. *Travels along the Mediterranean and parts adjacent in company with the Earl of Belmore.* London: T. Cadell, 1822.

Roberts, David. *Egypt and Nubia.* London: F.G. Moon, 1836.

Romer, Isabella. *A Pilgrimage to the Temples and Tombs of Egypt, Nubia, and Palestine.* London: Richard Bentley, 1846.

Russell, Rev. Michael. *View of Egypt.* Edinburgh: Oliver and Boyd, 1831.

Sandys, George. *A Relation of a Journey begun An. Dom. 1610: The Turkish Empire and Egypt, the Holy Land, etc.* London: privately published, 1615.

Savary, Claude Etienne. *Letters on Egypt.* Dublin: P. Byrne, 1787.

Scott, Charles Ronchfort. *Rambles in Egypt and Candia.* London: H. Colburn, 1837.

Sherer, Moyle. *Scenes and Impressions in Egypt and Italy.* London: Longman,1824.

Sitwell, Constance. *Lotus and Pyramid.* London: Jonathan Cape, 1927.

Sladen, Douglas. *Queer things about Egypt.* London: Hurst and Blackett, 1910.

Smith, Rev. A.C. *Attractions of the Nile and its Banks.* London: John Murray, 1868.

Smith, Agnes Lewis. *In the Shadow of Sinai: travel and research 1895–1897.* London: Macmillan and Bowes, 1898.

Stanley, Dean Arthur Penrhyn. *Sinai and Palestine.* London: John Murray, 1856.

Stephens, John Lloyd. *Incidents of Travel in Egypt, Arabia Petraea and the Holy Land.* London: Ward, 1876.

Strabo. *The Geography of Strabo*, Book 17. Translated by H.C. Hamilton. London: Bohn's Classical Library, 1857.

Stuart, Villiers. *Nile Gleanings.* London: John Murray, 1879.

Taylor, Bayard. *Egypt and Iceland in the year 1874.* London: Low, 1875.

Thompson, Charles. *Travels through Turkey in Asia, the Holy Land, Arabia, Egypt and other parts of the World.* London: J. Newberry, 1767.

Twain, Mark. *Innocents Abroad*. London, 1879; reprinted London: Century, 1988.

Warburton, Eliot. *The Cross and the Crescent*. London: Hurst and Blackett, 1845.

Wilkins, W.H. *The Romance of Isabel Lady Burton*. London: Hutchinson and Co., 1898.

Wilkinson, John Gardner. *Murray's Handbook to Egypt*. London: John Murray, 1847.

Young, Cuthbert. *A Wayfarer's notes on the shores of the Levant, and the Valley of the Nile* . . . Edinburgh: W.P. Kennedy, 1848.

Index of Travelers